RETURN TO THE HIGH VALLEY

RETURN *To*
The HIGH VALLEY

UNIVERSITY OF CALIFORNIA PRESS   *Berkeley Los Angeles London*

Coming Full Circle

KENNETH E. READ

University of California Press
Berkeley and Los Angeles, California

University of California Press, Ltd.
London, England

Library of Congress Cataloging-in-Publication Data

Read, Kenneth E.
    Return to the high valley.

    Includes index.
    1. Gahuku (Papua New Guinea people) 2. Ethnology—
Papua New Guinea—Field work. 3. Read, Kenneth E.
4. Papua New Guinea—Social conditions. I. Title.
DU740.42.R43   1986   306'.0899912   85-16385
ISBN 0-520-05664-7 (alk. paper)

Printed in the United States of America

1 2 3 4 5 6 7 8 9

Here is a glimpse of the High Valley thirty-one years after I saw it

for the first time—a token of my friendship and admiration.

I hope you enjoy it.

CONTENTS

on pain of death or excommunication, to bear the stamp of your own image. And since human material is malleable, such efforts may be successful for a time; but human material also has a peculiar propensity to escape from the bonds of social engineers, political ideologues, and moral savants. Perhaps it never "knows" precisely where it is going. The ultimate horizon is always veiled. There is always one behind another, and the journey forward is a labor of Sisyphus.

We never see more than a small part of what is possible, but our frequent mistake is thinking that the small part is all there is.

By the same token, cultural and ethical relativism is not the answer, for if it is applied without question it represents a denial of the very faculties for criticism and imagination with which man, apparently alone among all animals, is endowed. Perhaps all one can do, and it is not a very satisfactory solution, is to try not to make egregious evaluations, to make clear the bases for your own dissent, to allow criticism from others, and to trust that they will accord you the same right with respect to theirs. It is not by fiat but only through dialogue that the Sisyphian journey progresses step by faltering step.

Gahuku are our companions on this journey. They, no less than others of our common kind, do not know precisely where they are headed. But it is also clear that they have sloughed off the case of their traditional chrysallis and have begun to unfurl the incipient wings formerly restrained by ideas as limiting in their own way as any other monolithic attempt to produce generation after generation of individuals from the same mold. There are still threads that link them to the shell of their past. It has not been an abrupt emergence into free air, a total metamorphosis to a new form, and the markings on the wings carry the imprint of an earlier stage in development. Perhaps this is discernible only to someone who saw and knew them long ago, who was present (to return to an earlier image) at a phase that will never be repeated in its entirety. Certainly Gahuku who were younger than my own age (thirty-two) when I went to live with them have interests and have had experiences vastly different from those of their fathers and grandfathers; and now there is yet another generation, born after I left in 1952, for whom even that period has little relevance, being little more than the talk of old men reminiscing around a fire (though Gahuku old men seldom do much reminiscing). The great climactic rituals, the gathering points for both pride and fear, have gone, and apparently without much regret. Life tends to flow more softly now, though of course, it was never one of completely separated areas of black and white, without any intermediate shading. And despite the appearance of quite radical change, there is much that is comfortably familiar.

Both my 1981 and 1982 visits to the Gahuku-Gama were too brief to undertake anything that might reasonably be called systematic or intensive research, if you understand this to include formal interviews, questionnaires and the collection of statistical data; indeed, I had no intention of attempting to collect such material on either of these visits, and I found there was no need to do so for the limited goals I had. I was familiar with the structure and plot of the previous acts of the "play," and was known personally to many of the players in the current act, or by reputation to many more who had come on stage since my departure. In fact, I found that a "role" had been written for me and was waiting for me to assume. Basically this role is that of an accepted member of the clan and the extended family of Makis, who was my companion, friend, elder brother, and mentor from 1950 to 1952. Formally at least, I have been placed in a position appropriate for my generation in a network of kinship ties and other group identifications, so that numerous people are my brothers, agemates, children, grandchildren and relatives by marriage. Thus, the biological children of Makis are my real sons and daughters, particularly Lokilo and Lucy Makis, and I have no hesitation in saying that the affective and reciprocal relationship I have with them is little different from my relationship with my own biological son. Sometimes I think that my concern for Lokilo and Lucy may be even greater, in the sense that since they are so far away, and because I cannot keep in close touch with them, I cannot hope to know or share the myriad details of their lives that are so important in our relationships with those for whom we have a great personal caring: I worry for them. And, incidentally, my own son has been given a "role" that is waiting for him should he ever be able or wish to assume it. He was with me for a short while in 1950, when he was only six months old, and large numbers of people not only remember this (and chastise me because I have not brought him back) but have also placed him, *in absentia*, in the appropriate niche in my own clan and extended family. And, being realistic people, they point out that since I cannot expect to live many more years I should think about his future and return him to his kinsmen, among whom he will have both land and assured support. Alas, they do not fully comprehend that the immigration laws of national states override anything that might be permitted, accepted and desired under their own customary rules and procedures.

I mention these things simply to point out that the "work" on which this book is based consisted principally in being "brought up-to-date" by relatives at a family reunion for a member separated from them for a long time. Many of my kinsmen shared my house with me, and almost anywhere I went in the valley (including even the crowded streets of Goroka, the provincial capital), there were people who greeted me as Goroha Gipo, not knowing any other name for me. In addition to this recognition based on past associations, it was far easier to communicate with almost everyone; and it was natural now, because they recognized that I had a great deal of catching up to do and may have forgotten some things, to ask questions and receive answers. Many aspects and details of the private lives of individuals (which I may have been reluctant to inquire about thirty years ago, because of my own reticence and dislike for those who consider they have a right to know everything about another person) were revealed or referred to as something with which I ought to be familiar, as though if I didn't know them, I *should* know them. This is a dividend of a trust forged and remembered, and I have no intention of betraying it in this book, which, for the most part, is a descriptive account of changes (that is, the more obvious of them) in the broader dimensions of Gahuku life, as well as a compilation of some material from the past I have not published previously.

My recognized position as a member of a particular family and larger group means that some parochial issues were presented to me from what may be considered a prejudiced point of view; being aware of this, I did not necessarily accept such inside accounts at face value. And having a relationship that extended far beyond familial boundaries, I received volunteered information from many different perspectives. In this sense, my work was little different than it had been when I first went as a complete outsider to live with the Gahuku, consisting of assimilating and checking various accounts against one another with the ultimate goal of producing generalizations concerning the principles and processes of social life.

If returning after a long absence in 1981 proved to be easier and more fruitful than I had expected, so returning a year later for a second time was, in a way, even more of a revelation. Even though the lives of individuals and groups are orchestrated by principles and rules that mostly persist from one generation to another, these rules and principles are expressed differently in events that occur subsequently to the point at which an outside observer must, perforce, conclude his study. Time, as I said, is frozen in such studies; and to some extent, it would have been frozen, too, if I had made but one return to the Gahuku in 1981. For by the time I left in 1982, some significant breaches in relationships had been healed, giving rise to the promise of some reorganization and the burying of animosities going back to the death of Makis.

It is possible that my mere presence may have contributed a little to this healing process, although I did not intervene in any way—keeping a distance between myself and the cross-currents of purely local and internal politics. Yet I do not think I am far wrong (or guilty of hubris) in feeling that my presence acted—at least for some people—as a kind of catalyst, providing them with the necessary excuse to express regret and to admit some part of the blame for the events that divided a population Makis had consolidated and held together.

Why do I feel this, and what evidence do I have to warrant it? The first reason stems from the recognized fact that I was brought in by Makis. My formal position derives from him, and he is still widely remembered, not only in his tribe but also in quite distant places. Thus, in some ways I may well appear to many as a representative of some aspects of a past subsequently shattered by competing ambitions. His own biological children are too young to stand for these nostalgic elements of memory and some accompanying regret for mistakes. But the very fact that I had no part in the events (yet have a universally accepted position as the younger brother of the pivotal figure) may remind some of those who are my own age or a little older of some of the things they may have lost through using the death of Makis to exploit some traditional weaknesses in the edifice he had constructed.

As to other evidence to support this feeling, I can vouch for the fact that while I was there on both my recent visits, the conversation returned again and again to Makis whenever people gathered in my house and even when I went to visit more distantly connected relatives; and those who were blamed for the course of events following his death were customarily members of the group exchanging anecdotes. Perhaps I may have encouraged these constant references to him, but it was largely unintentional. Some emphasis must be placed on largely, however, for long ago I had espoused his cause and had been captured by his gifts and his personality, and I regretted and felt some anger at the shortsightedness of those who had dissipated their heritage from him and at their shabby and grasping treatment of his young and relatively defenseless descendants. In other words, I felt it was incumbent on me to preserve and restate the lifetime accomplishments of someone whom I loved, since these are all-too-frequently forgotten, particularly in a rapidly changing world. Yet it was also inevitable that his name would recur, for all my recollections of the past included him. And whenever people recounted or referred to events in which I had been involved, his name had to be voiced and his shadow, at least, was there.

There is other more specific evidence as well; but I shall leave it until the conclusion of my book, for it was expressed openly in the heart-wrenching context of the farewell meal given for me on the evening before my departure near the end of September, 1982. Gahuku are emotional people (perhaps this is why I feel a close affinity with them!), and on this occasion I was almost devastated for a while by the soaring release of pent-up frustrations and feelings of injustice, not from anger but from reconciliation with others who admitted blame and performed what amounts to a moving act of contrition. But this must wait.

I suppose I was the first professional anthropologist to work for an extended period in the Highlands of Papua New Guinea. This part of the country had been discovered by Europeans only in the 1930s. The life of the people with whom I lived had not changed radically even though it was not precisely the same as it had been less than twenty years earlier. That past was still a vital component of the present, and some of the events I witnessed have not occurred again since then. Changes have been extraordinarily rapid.

It is impossible to mention by name all those who helped to ease me back into the life of the Gahuku, but among those who are not Gahuku I am particularly indebted to Dr. Kerry Pataki-Schweitzer, Dr. Paul Crouch, and Mr. Winston Jacob. Among the new generation of Gahuku I have great pleasure in acknowledging my new friendship with Mr. Kopi Manove, a member of the Meniharove clan of Nagamidzuha, who had been only a child of about three years old when I had known his father. He and his wife Claire (and their small children

Konrad and Philomina) helped to make my return memorable. By no means least of all, there is Hunehune Opomari, a companion of my youth; my daughter Lucy Makis; my son Lokilo Makis; and each and every member of the extended family of my former elder brother, his widows Mohoasaro, Gotome, Guma'e, his other daughters Toho and Lava, their spouses, and their children. But there are too many more to name. I thank all of those who had known me and had not forgotten, and those who had only heard of me but who were prepared to act kindly on what they had heard. There is nothing more I could ask.

Finally, I offer this book to Lewis L. Langness and Gilbert H. Herdt, representatives of a brilliant younger generation of anthropologists who have studied the people of Papua New Guinea. I feel privileged to have contributed a little to the formation of their interests, but most of all, I am deeply grateful for their friendship and understanding, which go far beyond the conventional respect due to elders.

BACKGROUND TO THE BOOK AND ITS PEOPLE

Since there are sure to be some readers of *Return to the High Valley* who have not met the Gahuku before, it seems advisable to say something about its relationship to its predecessor, *The High Valley*, in which they also appear. At its publication some reviewers referred to that book as "an experiment in ethnography," probably because of two things I attempted to do in it. First, I tried to convey to its lay readers something of the personal experience of doing field research, how an investigator feels and reacts to the heat of the human crucible in which he is placed—a crucible far more intense than any others associated with the social sciences. And second, I adopted the rather unorthodox course of trying to delineate a culture by focusing on the movements and persons of a small but representative cast as they entered and passed through some of the personal and institutionalized events and crises of their lives. The resulting work was episodic, though I trust the cumulative direction of the episodes positioned some of the principal landmarks on the continent of Gahuku traditional culture.

The first of these goals has a conspicuous place in the present book. For virtually the whole of this century, field-work has been considered the crowning jewel of anthropological methods, but this term for an instrument to knowledge does not begin to convey what is involved in using it. Ultimately, every anthropologist must learn how to use and profit from fieldwork. And unlike other experimental procedures in dealing with human material, the subject of the experiment is the observer, not those from whom he or she hopes to learn.

A leitmotiv of this book is my reaction to the crucible of Gahuku culture today. The quality of its heat has changed during the thirty years that have passed since I first experienced it, and now I feel it more intensely on areas of sensibility untouched by it then. The book is still a personal record like its predecessor, even, perhaps, a little more personal, and I hope it may convey to those who are attracted to anthropology some of the complexities of the instrument they will be required to use.

It has not been possible to follow my prior route through the human geography of contemporary Gahuku life, however. This is because the boundaries of traditional life have been extended to include a far larger and more diverse territory of relationships, motives, goals and institutions than existed in 1950. Some of the landmarks I identified previously exist only as experienced presences to me and a diminishing number of the older generations of Gahuku; urban encroachments, with their attendant diversification of employment, have made it virtually impossible to watch so closely the daily lives of most individuals. It is only a slight exaggeration to say it is not possible nowadays for the observer to be everywhere and see everything; for the statement is relatively true as a contrast to former conditions when village life was more or less self-contained, when you held it in your hand, so to speak, being able to find the same individuals whenever you wanted them and when, with some exceptions, you could move in and out of their various activities. In addition, the demographic shifts mentioned in chapter two meant that I was not able to renew former relationships with some people. For example, I had only one fleeting encounter with Goluwaizo, a man to whom I devoted the greater part of a chapter in *The High Valley* (chapter six). He saw me from a sidewalk in Goroka when I was shopping for supplies before moving to the village of Susuroka in 1981 and, rushing inside, almost knocked me down in an outburst of voluble effusiveness which astonished the other customers and which even I thought was rather eccentric behavior. And I may not have been far wrong, for when I inquired about him later, it seemed to be the general opinion others had of him. Though I would have liked to see more of him—to find out what had happened to him in the three decades since I had had the temerity to assess his character and motives in my book—I found that he lived in a relatively isolated homestead with the members of his nuclear family and was regarded tolerantly, but humorously, as a recluse. It did not seem to be an unlikely progression for the man of thwarted ambitions I described so long ago but, of course, I shall never know.

This also applies to the group of age-mates (*The High Valley*, chapter four) who were with me almost constantly from 1950 to 1952. Of those who are living, I saw only Hunehune frequently. Hasu brought his children to visit me several times, but I did not meet Hutorno. None of them are domiciled in Susuroka now, and though I knew they were part of the human landscape, they—like some institutional landmarks—had faded so far into the background that they were like a childhood memory that is difficult to place in current surroundings. As to the new people around me, I had insufficient time with all but a few to reach the kind of intimacy which is a cherished part of my relationship with some of their parents and grandparents.

But other considerations also inhibit me from treating specific individuals with the immediacy that brought them forward in *The High Valley*. I never anticipated that my prior work would be printed on three continents in two languages or that in their own country it would project my friends into a limelight somewhat more public than that experienced by the subjects of many other more specialized anthropological reports. They had not chosen this personal exposure and, after the event, I felt some guilt and embarrassment on meeting them again.

The problem is not so much that all those who are old acquaintances have read how they are frozen in my printed words, but that some of the younger generation can read the narrative and locate living individuals in situations which may sometimes show them to disadvantage. It is because of this that, with minor exceptions, there are no attempts at such detailed portraiture in this book. Furthermore, I have not identified some individuals who have a conspicuous place in *The High Valley*, even when they were the catalysts in events which occurred after my departure in 1952. This is so in the case of the Ozahadzuha man who appears in chapter two, "In Memoriam Makis," and reappears briefly at the end of the book. I gave him some prominence in *The High Valley* and it may have served the purposes of dramatic continuity to identify him explicitly, but I think the reader will see why I did not do so here.

The few exceptions to these self-imposed restrictions include personages whom I knew, recorded and remember from the past and who are dead and thus, presumably, beyond the reach of embarrassment (and beyond the reach of dissent), and a few members of my own Gahuku family. I suppose you could say I have used a certain family license in giving a personal presence to the latter, but I have done little more than paint the kind of picture commonly provided when others ask us about relatives in whom they may be interested.

For some of the reasons already indicated, it has not been possible to repeat the institutional focus used to develop some Gahuku themes in the previous book. These themes have not been forgotten, however. Like its predecessor, the present work tends to be episodic. Indeed, it is obvious that *I* am the principal connecting link throughout it. It is my memory of past events and people—even of some things in which I participated that took place outside the Gahuku dominion but which replicate events there before I knew them—that weaves these more recent observations and impressions. But a few of the past themes are present again, slightly altered by time yet having almost as much prominence as before. One of them is the relationships between men and women. Another is the structuring of relationships between and within the different generations.

As Herdt and Poole said in a recent essay presented at a symposium on male/female relationships in Papua New Guinea, the problem of such relationships has held a significant interest for ethnographers at least since Mead published

Sex and Temperament in Three New Guinea Societies in 1935.*
Since then there has been a vast increase in the number and
the quality of such studies, particularly in recent years; but it
is probably true to say that Mead's work is the only one to
have gained a considerable readership beyond the ranks of
professionals, as it is not too far from the truth to say that a
lot of the more recent work is not well known beyond the
ranks of specialists in Melanesia. Herdt and Poole's essay is
recommended to readers of both categories who may wish to
learn more about the contours of male/female relationships
in a part of the world which has long had a fascination for
Westerners because of the exotic character of many of its cultural configurations. Sociologists (and psychologists) studying the same question in our own society may also profit from
extending their perspective a little, and from giving some
consideration to the various theoretical issues and directions
in anthropological works on the region. Herdt and Poole's
essay will serve them well. Among other things, it provides
a concise comparative account of findings in four regions of
Papua New Guinea, it scrutinizes (and finds wanting) some
of the conceptual tools that have been used historically both
to explore and to contain "certain characteristics of many
types of relationships," and it offers a theoretical appraisal
and some suggestions for a future orientation.

I do not think it would further the intentions of this book
to burden it with a discussion of these matters. Melanesianists
will be well aware of the background in which my work

---

*Gilbert H. Herdt and Fitz John P. Poole, "Sexual Antagonism: The Intellec-
tual History of a Concept in New Guinea Anthropology" in *Sexual Antagonism,
Gender and Social Change in Papua New Guinea*, Fitz John P. Poole and Gilbert
H. Herdt, editors, Social Analysis, Special Issue Series No. 12 (University of
Adelaide, 1982).

should be placed (and able to judge its shortcomings against that background), and those who are unaware of it may turn to Herdt and Poole's essay first of all and then, perhaps, to some of the other ethnographies and theoretically oriented analyses they mention.

The sections on men and women in chapter four are neither addressed to the areal specialist alone nor designed to critique or to add appreciably to past and present theoretical orientations. I do not seriously dissent from some rather mildly stated views that the way in which I treated the subject in much earlier work was oversimplified or, let us say, less sophisticated than the more recent work of many others. Anthropology does not stand still, and as I have said elsewhere, there are some ways in which the anthropologist I was in 1950 resembles the glaciated bones of a woolly mammoth compared to my younger colleagues today.* I have not attempted to rectify such shortcomings in the relevant section of this book, however, either by refining the concepts I used formerly or by "fitting" the new material into some of the conceptual frameworks currently employed and debated. For all its shortcomings, oversights, and omissions, I think the earlier work gave an accurate account of some important components of the configuration of relationships between Gahuku men and women. This configuration has undoubtedly changed over the three decades since I lived with them. But using it as a baseline, the material presented here tries to show the points at which it has changed and some of the factors contributing to it. A few of these are the suppression

---

*Kenneth E. Read, "The Nama Cult Recalled," in *Ritualized Homosexuality in Melanesia,* Gilbert H. Herdt, editor (Berkeley, Los Angeles, London: University of California Press, 1984).

of traditional warfare, the demise of the ritual male cult, increased spatial mobility, the diversification of employment and forms of association following a degree of urbanization, changes toward a cash economy, Western education, Christianity, and changes in cosmologies and ideologies about the nature of things. Interacting with one another, all these factors have wrought some alterations in the configuration of inter-sex relations described in the earlier work, and since the importance of studying such changes has received increased recognition in recent years, the material I present may assist this particular enterprise.*

The structuring of relations between and within the generations (principally the generations of men) was treated and displayed with reasonable fullness in my earlier work.** Indeed, it was impossible not to *see* it in 1950, for it was a matter of day-to-day observation of such ordinary things as customary dress, the associations between members of the same age group, and the manner in which the different generations separated on all occasions concerned with public affairs—not to mention what took place in the undoubtedly violent transition rites for boys.† The configuration of the traditional "generational" structures is not as sharply focused in contemporary Gahuku life. Those who were born after or who have reached adulthood since 1950 have had far more intense and varied experiences than their parents and grandparents in a twentieth-century world which was barely beginning to unfold at that time. They are not only more familiar with and involved in its opportunities, demands and directions, but

*See the essays in Poole and Herdt, *Sexual Antagonism*.
**Kenneth E. Read, *The High Valley*, chapters three and four.
†*The High Valley*, chapter three particularly.

these have also altered to some extent the character of their former dependence and subordination to their elders, as they have also removed some of the ideological justifications upholding that formal subordination. Some of the concerns which vigorously exercised the elders in 1950 have lost significance for today's younger generation and in a few instances have no pertinence at all to the contemporary pattern of their lives. Chapter four of this book, "The New Generation," addresses some of these alterations, placing them against a backcloth of things as they were.

This book therefore, is concerned with social change, but it is more a memoir than an analysis of social change. It suggests no theoretical perspectives for analyzing social change in general and, indeed, I do not claim—given the duration of the observations on which it is based—that it is an exhaustive or fully articulated account of Gahuku society at present. I do not know the whole cloth of the contemporary life of these people. All I have done is to show some of the ways in which that life has altered since my prior and more intense experience of it.

But the reader who is unfamiliar with my previous account of that experience may have two questions: he may want to know who the Gahuku-Gama are and how I am connected to them as a people and to the persons whom I mention by name. Apart from saying that they are a small group living in the Eastern Highlands in the interior of the country of Papua New Guinea, it does not seem profitable to say much about the "deep structures" of their society. I have said more about these in earlier specialized papers and in *The High Valley*, which is still available to the general reading public. As an adequate orientation it may be enough to say that in 1950 they numbered about five thousand people and that this population was divided into named groups which I called and will continue to call tribes. Each tribe contained a number of smaller groups of varying size, which were named or unnamed and in which membership was ideologically and quite largely determined through male ancestry (patrilineal descent). Before the imposition of alien authority and institutions beginning in the colonial period (about the mid-1930s) none of these groups possessed centralized forms of government and administration: each was a relatively autonomous social entity. They were a warrior society. Tribe fought against tribe, though the pattern of warfare was contained both by temporary alliances and more permanent ties of traditional friendship. Gahuku did not fight for the reasons we have gone to war for century upon century: to impose our own ideologies and sovereignty on others and for aggrandizement of territory. They had no hereditary authority. Their positions of leadership were based on personal achievement, reputation and influence. The conduct of public affairs was founded on the ideal of a consensus reached between the responsible members of the social groups involved.

These people lived in villages (traditionally fortified) in the grasslands of the Asaro Valley. They had a subsistence economy based on horticulture (hunting was not of much significance) and pig husbandry. There were no markets, but there were elaborate systems of ceremonial exchange. They had a rich ritual life, but their conception of nonhuman powers and agents did not include personalized deities, and they did not assume that their own formulations represented an absolute truth which should or had to be embraced by everyone lest they somehow show themselves to be less worthy, less elect.

I lived primarily with the Nagamidzuha tribe of the Gahuku-Gama, being domiciled in one of its villages, Susuroka. It was a man named Makis who may be said to have invited me there.* He was then the most influential man in the tribe, and he was seldom far from me throughout the following two years. In a way, he is as much a presence in this book as I am, for I can think of few things from a former time in which he was not involved, and my observations and experiences of things as they are now inevitably raises the ghost of what they were when he figured so prominently in them. His complex character, as I perceived it, is depicted fully in *The High Valley*, but it may be of service to provide a brief summary for readers who have not met him in those pages.

He was no taller than five feet seven inches—slightly shorter than I am but a little above the average height for Gahuku men—but his commanding presence and beautifully proportioned body made him seem much taller. The sheer force of his personality, his sense of self, and his assertive pride projected him to the forefront of all public occasions, so that he seemed to have a physical stature at least equal to that of Namuri, who was several inches taller and was the man on whom Makis seemed to place the greatest reliance. Makis had been a distinguished warrior and conformed to the type of personality Gahuku called "strong" or "hard"— aggressive, dominating, prideful, and quick to counter behavior that seemed to slight his group or to threaten the prerogatives and position of men. Indeed, many women— including his own daughters—recall that he treated them harshly. I saw some examples of this, and it was not behavior I either admired or failed to protest in some personal ways. But, in all fairness, his treatment of women was not as extreme as that of some other men.

The High Valley, "Introduction" and chapter two.

Makis was not all pride and bluster, however. The extremes of intransigence associated with undiluted strength or hardness were a handicap to leadership in a society where public decisions were based ideally on consensus reached between equals. The type of man who rose to influence required great managerial skills—not only the kind of skills that helped him to accumulate wealth but also the astuteness to gauge the direction of public opinion. He commanded no instruments by which he could force others to follow him. He required a sensitivity which was lacking in the hardest Gahuku men: the acuity to know when to yield, the willingness to listen and to embrace compromise when it was necessary. Makis had all these qualities. His pride, his aggressiveness, and his harshness were layered over a deeper vein of inwardness and gentleness. Chapter two of this book is my memorial to him. It is an inadequate memorial to someone to whom I owe so much, but my propriety restrains me from revealing the full depth of my affective bond to him.

All the other Gahuku who are named in this book are connected to me through him, not only those to whom my ties are closest—his wives, his children, and their spouses and their children—but also a far wider circle of acquaintances within and beyond his tribe. Even though he has been dead for fifteen years, my place still tends to be fixed by reference to him. A large number of today's young people did not know of this particular link—indeed, there were many who knew little or nothing about Makis—and in the cosmopolitan urban bustle of Goroka and in the countryside beyond the ridge of Susuroka, I often saw them casting puzzled glances when they saw me in the company of village people. If their curiosity did not abate, the quality of their watchfulness altered and they seemed to relax some of the reservations they have—

not always unjustly held, I may add—for people of my kind when my companions identified my connection to them, a connection which often went back to their parents and grand-parents by way of Makis. It was reminiscent of a time more than thirty years ago when white men were still something of a novelty in the valley and strangers, almost everywhere I went, appeared to be satisfied when they were told I lived with the "line" of Makis and belonged to him.

For reasons already mentioned, I do not think it would be right to complete the individual portraits of many people who appear in *The High Valley*, even though failing to do so detracts from the continuity between the present book and its predecessor. In several cases, this has meant omitting some intrinsically interesting biographical material in the subse-quent lives of people who are mentioned once again. For example, the course of the life of the young girl whose first marriage moved me so deeply in a different time (*The High Valley*, chapter five) surely deserves more attention than I have given to it. Some of her experiences since that event are an astonishing illustration of how far the social horizons have been extended, for when I knew and described her it would have been impossible to imagine what her future might be. I did surmise that her first marriage would be brief, and the fact that she has had several husbands since then is not at all unusual for Gahuku, but no one could have foretold that one of them would be a member of the national parliament sitting in Port Moresby.

I do not know of any way in which I might put more flesh on these bare biographical facts without risking offense, and this also applies to other people. There are passages in this book which are cross-referenced to its predecessor, however. Where personal names are mentioned, readers may wish to turn to it to identify particular individuals as they were when they were young, for if any damage was done to them there I cannot undo it now. And if this is not entirely satisfactory, I can only say it would be redundant to reproduce extended passages from the former work in this one.

ONE

COMING HOME

1 I returned to the Asaro Valley by air, as I had arrived and departed over thirty years ago, but now it was a scheduled flight by jet from Port Moresby rather than the light single-engine plane I had chartered in Lae to carry myself and my gear to the beginning of a new segment of my life; and this time the point of departure was not Australia but America, differences that say a great deal of what had happened to me in the intervening years.

It is a short flight from Port Moresby, and the jet flies high above the clouds. Though I was exhausted from earlier stages of the journey, I looked out from my window seat hoping, unsuccessfully, that as we came nearer I would recognize some terrain over which I may have walked with Makis when there had been no other way of traveling. The first glimpse of the valley had been a revelation then, an experience like penetrating the outer surface of a crystal and breaking into a fountain of prismatic light where colors were refracted from one another and the world seemed almost as young and innocent as it may have been on the miraculous day of creation when the firmaments were divided. This flight was unlike that relatively slow approach resembling the course of a summer butterfly: dipping low to skim a ridge—almost, it had seemed—wondering whether to alight on a brown stone rising from the pewter colored water of a stream or the bare earth of a street lined with round thatched beehive houses—then, like an afterthought—lifting up again to seek a more rewarding place to land. But on this occasion, there was no time to become at home with the landscape or even to think about the possibility of turning back. With hardly any transition we had landed on the paved runways of the Goroka airstrip and had stopped in front of the terminal building.

Perhaps my feet touched the very piece of ground on which I had stood to say good-bye to Makis. The airstrip is in the same place, though its runway had been only cropped grass then, and there had been no terminal building, no bustle of vehicles going and coming in the direction of the town and its suburbs. No curious crowds of people had gathered then behind chain link fences to watch the arrivals and departures, much as the inhabitants of small country towns gravitated to the railway station each evening to observe the arrival of the Northwest Mail in the years of my Australian childhood. The people who clambered into carriages and sleeping cars would be carried off beyond the perimeters of a world which was the only one many of those remaining had seen. Perhaps the same vicarious attraction brings these scores of different people to the only substitute for a railroad station.

I had not lost all contact with the villagers of Susuroka during the intervening years, though the contacts had been both infrequent and indirect. When I had left in 1952 there had been no one I knew who could write, but now and then a few tourists familiar with my book had visited Susuroka, and on their return to the United States had sent me verbal messages and, occasionally, a taped cassette on which the villagers spoke to me in their own language. In 1969 a member of the then-colonial government also sent me the news that Makis had been killed. But gradually even these lines of communication withered and I heard almost nothing more until 1979, when I received a letter in English from Kopi Manove. He introduced himself, told me he belonged to the Meniharove clan and asked if I had any photographs I would care to give to the museum in Goroka. I could not find my negatives but told him I would send some prints when they had been returned to me by the publisher who was preparing a new edition of *The High Valley*.

I had not thought seriously of going back to the Gahuku-Gama. I had not forgotten them. In many ways the valley and its people were as close to me as when I had lived there. It was no effort to dissolve the walls of my house in a flash and place myself once more in the street of Susuroka, in its swimming light, among the sea-colors of the mountains and the slow progression of shadows cast by monumental clouds. I often felt a sudden tug of loss, an emptiness that grew deeper as it seemed less and less likely I would be able to fill it; for I was very much aware of increasing age and the limitations it imposed on traveling to a place where the living conditions are far better suited to those who are young and resilient. I began to think I would never experience the valley again except in these vivid memories.

Then in 1979 I had completed another book and had seen the manuscript go to press. In the subsequent hiatus I began to wonder what I might do next. I was not about to turn into a vegetable or have nothing to do but cultivate my garden, and the routine of teaching (though I enjoy it) had lost a little of its former gloss, and that, too, would soon be unavailable when I retired. I began to think of the Gahuku-Gama again, not seriously (and with considerable misgivings) but more like a possible (and remote) hedge against a dull future.

In this frame of mind I applied to the Wenner-Gren Foundation for assistance, having little hope it would be granted because my age might be considered a risk, and perhaps even wanting a rejection that would absolve me from having to make a decision and begin an enterprise I was by no means certain I was capable of finishing. The grant came through and I accepted it; but up to the day of my departure from Seattle (indeed, until a day or so after my arrival in Goroka) I was uncertain whether I would be able to manage.

I have never had an obsessive concern for my health, but no one would characterize me as being particularly robust, and it seems to have surprised my family that I not only survived but also surmounted several experiences that might be thought physically and emotionally taxing for those endowed with stronger constitutions. I was helped by a determination that others should not judge me by appearances, and that a degree of inwardness, a love for words, for the rhythm of sentences juxtaposed within a paragraph, and a delight in visual properties are not things to hide or be ashamed of, any more than one should be ashamed of the feelings that those responsible for my schooling in Australia distrusted and sought to suppress, trying to channel them into the more conventional activities of team and contact sports (which I hated). But eventually it is useless to deny the passage of time and the limitations of increasing age, and I began to feel that if I did go I might never come back.

In this divided state of mind I wrote to Kopi Manove, telling him I was returning, and asking him to give the message to any villagers who remembered me and were still living. I did not know anyone in Goroka and had absolutely no conception of what the town was like after thirty years. Surely it had changed from the time when it had consisted of only four newly built frame houses, but no one could have prepared me for what it is.

I was shaking as I walked from the plane toward the terminal, a combination of tiredness and uncertainty. It might have been different if I had stepped out into anything resembling the images in my mind, but this was an entirely different world, and as a defense against the shattering of everything I had preserved so carefully I tried not to record anything I saw. I closed off, in an act of rejection, the senses on which I had learned to rely, and encased myself in a contrived cocoon of indifference and an unwillingness to give the slightest recognition to the changes around me.

Having had no response to my letter from Kopi Manove, I did not know if any villagers would be there or, if they were, how we could recognize one another. Though we had never met, Paul Crouch (who had been advised that I was coming by a mutual friend) found me almost at once, and I offer him a belated apology because I probably seemed less than enthusiastic and unable to say more than a few customary and inconsequential pleasantries. I scanned the faces of the crowd while waiting for my luggage. There was nothing there. Everyone was dressed in Western style clothes, much of it tattered and soiled, and I was distressed by a strong acrid sweet-sour smell as heavy as the lingering aroma of garlic on the breath of someone sitting next to you on a crowded bus. I could not recall anything of the same kind before, and with something like panic I felt a rising nausea in which my tongue seemed to cleave to the roof of my mouth.

During this brief scrutiny I had noticed a woman nearby who was looking at me uncertainly, her face and eyes puzzled and a little anxious. My glance passed over her cursorily and returned a moment or two later because I felt somehow that she wanted to speak. She still seemed shy and uncertain; her lips moved tentatively and almost inaudibly, eventually producing the word: "Kenneth?"

None of the Gahuku had ever used my English personal name, preferring the one Makis had given me (Goroha Gipo), but Kopi and I had used it in our correspondence, so I thought she must have some connection with him. She was his wife Claire and, though shy, was greatly pleased that she, who had never seen me, was the first to find me. In the next moment Kopi was there, and soon he told me to turn and look behind me.

At a distance of a yard or so I saw a thin man possibly about forty-eight years old. He was shorter than my own height of 5 feet 7 inches, dressed in a shirt, green trousers, and thongs and wearing a crumpled denim hat. He did not come forward but stood there looking at me with an expression of disbelief, which I returned without a trace of recognition. Perhaps we may have parted and never come any closer, but Kopi said in English, "This is Hunehune." The gap between us closed and we were holding one another in the Gahuku's customary embrace of welcome, unconcerned by the curious stares of the crowd and, on my part, the possibility that this comforting form of greeting may well have been discarded with the donning of western dress and all the other changes that had taken place. Hunehune, as a handsome and gentle youth of about eighteen, had looked after me throughout my previous stay in Susuroka, and of his own accord had come to care for me when the illness that terminated my fieldwork confined me to bed in Goroka in 1952. I had a great fondness for him. He had been more than someone (a "boy") whom I paid to take care of some necessary chores. His endearing, humorous attitude of *laissez-faire* had provided me with a greater refuge than he ever realized, had buoyed my spirit and made me laugh and relax; and though he occasionally tried my patience, I could never be angry with him, and had found myself making the excuses he never offered himself. And now he was here again, the first person out of that past, the first of whom I could say that we had shared some of the same experiences. At that moment this flood of memories held at bay the ebb of sadness that would come when I realized how greatly both of us had changed.

Then there were others, most of whom had been too young to awake any recollections. I think I repeated their names when I heard them, but I made no effort to file them away for future reference. As I parted from Hunehune, my uncertainties returned with a rush and I felt too tense to cope with strangers. The short ride through the town to the Bird of Paradise Hotel seemed like a hallucination. The disagreeable smell returned with greater strength. My glimpses of the streets, buildings and crowded sidewalks were corrupted by it, and I felt for them the same unreasoning dislike and rejection.

After I had registered at the hotel, the villagers came to my room, sat on the bed and looked as though they might never leave. Eventually, I told them that I had to rest, promising I would see Kopi the following day to buy some household things I would need when I went to the village. As I went to bed that night I had virtually convinced myself I had been foolish to imagine I could return. Excepting only Hunehune I had seen nothing and no one having any connection with an old but important period of my life; if I stayed would I be compelled thereafter to qualify everything I had written with interminable footnotes, revising it until there was nothing left but a faint trace of an ambience? Far better, perhaps, to leave the crystal on a shelf gathering the dust of whatever years remained to me. Against this, I thought it would be difficult to justify my running away to those helping to support me; and behind it all I felt the chronicle of the Gahuku-Gama from 1950 to 1981 would not be complete unless I, the original recorder, ventured into the stream of their life again.

The debate was not resolved the following day. Walking from store to store with Kopi, buying the barest of necessities, my disaffection with the town increased. In 1950, Goroka had been little more than a promising outpost of the Australian administration. Land for the town (including the airstrip constructed by American forces in the last years of the war) had been acquired only recently from seven tribal groups (the Nagamidzuha were not one of them); only two of the first four frame houses had been completed and the handful of government officers were divided between them and older thatched houses situated to the north on a hilltop called Humeleveka, where there was an older, completely inadequate airstrip. The Highland Highway, which runs between the coastal town of Lae to Mount Hagen in the far northwest, was only an infrequently traveled track not yet completed even as far as the Daulo Pass, separating the Asaro and Chimbu valleys to the west, or as far as Kainantu, the earliest government station in the Highlands, to the east. There was one small trade store in the town, owned by James Leahy and selling a limited range of inexpensive goods to the few members of the native population who could afford them. Excepting only locally grown vegetables, all supplies for whites came in by air from Lae or Port Moresby. The sale of liquor to the local people was prohibited. Patrol officers were still engaged in mapping the land and contacting new people at a distance of only about three days' walk from the settlement. There was a native hospital of a kind (staffed at my arrival by a relatively untrained European medical assistant) situated on a ridge between Humeleveka and the new town site. The compound and barracks of the native constabulary were in a small valley below it near the Zokozoi River. Kerosene lamps provided the only kind of lighting; and though a system of irrigation channels tapped into nearby mountain streams, household water was mainly rain caught in galvanized iron tanks. Farther out in the valley two early settlers had leasehold property for coffee, which was not yet sufficiently mature to produce crops. By the time I left, these European holdings had increased by two. There were a few other government personnel: a postmaster, an agricultural officer and some other foremen employed by the Public Works Department.

In the introduction to *The High Valley* I described my feeling of exhilaration and personal discovery on being driven by jeep from the airstrip to Humeleveka where I stayed for a time in the thatched house of Dudley Young-Whitforde, the Assistant District Officer; and I described how from this elevation the exhilaration seemed to build day by day until it had the impossible pain of a revelation. Standing at the edge of the old disused airstrip or sitting beside the water in the irrigation ditch under the filigreed shadows of casuarinas, I felt I could cup every detail of the landscape in my two hands, looking at it with the suspended wonder I used to feel as a child at the seaside, when I would sit above a tidal pool in the rocks listening to the surf breaking at a distance, watching the surface of the pool rise and fall gently like the pulse of the ocean, and marveling at the miniature forests of kelp and the moving patterns of refracted light on the golden sand— almost afraid to move lest it might all be taken from me.

The country landscape of my childhood had been beautiful but strange, hardly comfortable or close, never giving all it had but holding back and keeping an essential privacy from which it watched with an independent will born of timelessness and possible indifference to anything as new and transitory as man. It showed in the low eroded hills and the vast brown sweeps of plain that disappeared behind a mirage in the noonday heat, and in the patient and persevering forms of gum trees that, contrary to most natural expectations, shed their bark rather than their leaves to emerge reborn like snakes each year. Sometimes I felt it cared for no one but the Aborigines who had wandered its reaches without fixed abode, who respected it and had left no trace of their passage except some sacred paintings on the walls of caves. It had not been kind to me, but I don't think there was anything personal in this. Having almost no pigmentation, I should never have been in this land. My eyes stabbed with pain in its fierce and unrelenting light, and on one occasion when I was about ten it sent me to bed with second-degree burns on my hands, face and back.

But this valley had been completely different. Though I still had to protect myself from sun and light, I found I could look into distances I had not seen before. In the mountains, every hanging valley seemed close enough to touch if I stretched out my hand. I could almost count each tree on the crests of distant ridges, and the foliage was softly hued. Water, bearing the coldness of its mountain source, broke around stones in cascades of iridescent foam, and the sound of voices seemed to have been distilled and captured from another dimension. These feelings had never left me, but now I began to wonder if they had been nothing more than tricks of my imagination.

The tiny settlement had developed into a town of over ten thousand people. The streets and sidewalks (some of which may have been indicated on a blueprint in the district office in 1950) were paved and crowded with people and vehicles—trucks, vans, pickups, and cars, including an occasional Mercedes Benz. The hill Humeleveka and the ridge where the native hospital had been were a part of North Goroka. Only a small section of the old airstrip at Humeleveka remained, a playing field for the Goroka Teachers College. A second suburban development, West Goroka, enclosed the airport and reached almost to the outskirts of the nearest village of the Gama tribe. The town was bursting the seams of the original land purchase. There is almost no space for future development, and owing to the reluctance of the tribes to relinquish more, there is talk of starting a "satellite" farther away in the direction of Bena Bena.

The commercial section of the town offers most urban amenities: department stores, supermarkets, a pharmacy, banks, bookstores and speciality shops, a movie theater and discotheque. A large, vivid and flourishing public market abuts the highway, its stalls overflowing with fresh local produce. The public sale of liquor was partially legalized in the early sixties, before Papua New Guinea received independence from Australia, and alcohol has penetrated deeply into the social fabric of Gahuku life. The town has a tavern near the public market, bars and lounges in the hotel, and liquor departments in the larger stores. Suburban streets are paved, lined with trees and two-story residences served by public water and electric systems. Almost lost in this crowded modernity, the four original frame houses have been preserved in their gardens (one is now the residence of the premier of the provincal government). Long ago, seeing them as harbingers of the Goroka existing now, I expressed my dislike for them, contrasting their materials and style with the unobtrusive native houses; but now I approve the efforts to protect them as historical buildings. Set well back from the street under fully grown trees and showers of bright bougainvillea, they are a nostalgic echo of a more simple time that has slipped away so quickly.

There are almost no reminders of that time in the appearance of the people plying the sidewalks and dodging traffic on the streets. Even outside the town, "traditional" dress is worn only infrequently by some of the principal participants at ceremonial events. The qualification implied by placing the word within quotation marks is necessary. Some items of ceremonial apparel are the same—shells and the tossing plumes of the bird of paradise—but assaulting my own taste, tawdry Christmas tree tinsel festoons arms and necks, and there are always some women who wear white bras outside a colored blouse. They are not for the sake of modesty but are eclectic additions to the panoply of feminine body decoration, and my qualified cultural relativism does not embrace the vulgarism, a harmless prejudice there is no reason to conceal.

In the town the dress is Western: shirts and trousers, different kinds of footwear and a sprinkling of hats for men; brightly colored blouses, long skirts or dresses for women, very few of whom appear to have adopted high heels. The clothing is often soiled, and laceless boots sometimes gape over bare feet. It is rare to see a man in traditional clothing. In all my visits to the town (which were admittedly few) I saw only one. I do not know his tribe or for what purpose or how far he may have traveled; but his costume bore the stamp of the valley people. Naked except for bark cloth loincloth, a necklace of large cowrie shells and a halo of lacy plumes on his head, he seemed inches taller than members of the Westernized sidewalk crowds, an illusion probably due to his unique appearance in their company. He was magnificently alone, walking with a slow and dignified stride, the soles of his bare feet striking the pavement deliberately with each step. The shape of his nose and lips could have been lifted from a stone relief decorating an ancient Mayan temple. Not stopping or speaking to anyone, he looked straight ahead, self-contained and indifferent if not disdainful. No one seemed to remark him, but my eyes were riveted on him, his pride and assurance bringing back to me all the occasions when I had marveled at the presence, the arrogance and dramatic flair of the Gahuku's hard men. For a moment I felt the shadow of Makis beside him, seeing him again when he played his role on the brave occasions of village life—standing at the center of a circle of seated men (the women relegated to a distant muffled chorus), light shaking his colored plumes and flashing from his shells as his long hair tossed in response to the outflung gestures of his arms.

As the first day ended I told Kopi I would spend one more day resting at the hotel. I knew I could not turn away; but the decision to remain was half-hearted, prompted by duty rather than enthusiastic choice, and though I needed the additional rest I was also trying to delay the inevitable.

Kopi and Hunehune joined me for dinner in the hotel restaurant. As I was about to go to my room to sleep, Hunehune announced he wanted to spend the night there with me. I hesitated only a moment, for looking into his lined face I saw a reflection of the concern that had prompted him to leave the village and to care for me during my illness. Throughout my visit he showed the same unflagging attentions. He relinquished all his other duties to share the house the family of Makis loaned to me, and was hardly ever far from my side. These were not inconsiderable sacrifices, for he was married, had both fully grown and young children, was an elected officer of the Village Court and a member of the board of directors of a sizeable coffee plantation.

After I retired that night I watched him silently for a while as he lay in his bed a few feet from me. Suddenly he sat up and began to chant softly in Gahuku. Then he lay down and slept easily, and I slept more easily too, feeling for the first time that I may not have mistaken the quality of some of my former relationships.

I spent the following day alone, Hunehune having returned to the village. There was no one in Goroka whom I knew or needed to contact—no one I wanted to talk to.

In the afternoon in the hotel bar, a rawboned Australian about my own age tried to start a conversation, asking who

I was and where I was going. When I replied I was merely having a vacation, that I had lived here more than thirty years ago and intended to return to the same village, his face lit with interest and he said he must have been here at about the same time, when he had been a foreman with the Public Works Department of the colonial government.

"What's the tribe?" he asked.

"Nagamidzuha," I said.

He looked puzzled for a moment, then corrected me. "You mean *Namoi*ufa. I used to know a coupla those blokes."

Since *Namoi* had been the name of the river running through part of my father's property in New South Wales, I thought that if we continued conversing we might, unfortunately, discover a few more things in common, and I had no stomach for the prospect. I was also rather childishly irritated by the correction and mispronouncing of the tribal name. It is no secret (and there is no reason it should be) that anthropologists tend to develop proprietary attitudes toward the people they study, and his simple mistake seemed like an unnecessary slight to "my" people.

I dined alone with a book in the hotel restaurant and went to bed early.

Kopi and Hunehune called for me after noon the following day. After a stop at Kopi's suburban house to collect a bed and mattress, sheets and blankets, plates and a few other utensils he was lending me, we left for Susuroka in his Mazda truck.

I remember when we were children and coming home from vacations by car with my parents, we (myself, my sister, and two orphaned cousins who lived with us) always played a game, a competition to be the first to see a familiar landmark by which we could tell we were almost there. There were not many in that almost featureless landscape of plains and gum trees, but three were notable because they alone were elevated slightly above the horizon. One, the Nandewar Range, was higher than the others but more difficult to find because it was far more distant, close to fifty miles from our property. Four miles beyond the town nearest to our house, a grey stone monolith rose about one hundred feet from the earth, the only bone remaining of what may once have been a sizeable hill. Said to have been used as a lookout by a nineteenth-century bushranger, from which he watched for the telltale clouds of dust raised by the horses of pursuing troopers, it bore his romantic outlaw name: Thunderbolt's Lookout. The most personal sentinel of our private domain was a solitary flat-topped hill, however. Only some dull green scrubby gums and silvery cootamundra wattles persevered in its shallow inhospitable soil. It was the home of scurrying dragons (goannas and frill-necked lizards), and very rarely at night pinpoints of light, ruby eyes in the darkness, flickered from its lower slopes—the camp fires of itinerant swagmen or a small band of Aborigines, who may have had their own legends about the hill. But since Binnalong (the hill) was only half a mile from one of the boundaries of our property it was almost our own possession. We used to ride there to picnic in the thin shade of its gum trees and to scramble to its summit over the crackling aromatic debris of dead bark and leaves, feeling, when we reached the top, like conquistadors surveying the untraveled reaches of the Pacific Ocean. And the game of coming home was won by the first of us to see the familiar hill and call out, "There's Binnalong!"

Leaving Goroka for the four mile ride to Susuroka, I was again looking for landmarks to reassure me I was coming home. There were none. This section of the Highland Highway had passed through open grassland when I had known it, but now the whole valley has been reforested; no one seeing it for the first time now could recognize it as the place I described in 1950, when the few trees had been mainly native casuarinas hand-planted in gardens surrounding the scattered settlements. Now it is densely foliaged with imported varieties of pine and eucalyptus as well as native species. Gahuku who are my chronological contemporaries are usually quiet about the past and the newer generation have little interest in trying to unlock their memories, but time and time again the older people liked to remind their children and grandchildren (and turned to me to corroborate them) that once upon a time it had been possible to see almost the entire ridge from Susuroka and to look over the whole valley in all directions, marking every small stream and settlement and surmising what events were taking place in them from the columns of blue smoke lifting into the still air. The village of Asarodzuha, through which I sometimes took a shortcut on my walks to and from Goroka, is now almost enclosed by urban sprawl. I could not find the windy little hilltop in the compound of the old native hospital where I had spent the restful, magic weeks of my convalescence in a deteriorating thatched house belonging to a European medical assistant (*The High Valley*, pp. 247–253). The grass airstrip on Humeleveka has also disappeared, the approaches to it recognizable only from a highway sign directing traffic to the hill. There is still a single-lane wooden bridge across the Zokozoi River, but it lacks the thatched roof that protected its more rickety predecessor from the weather.

Passing this bridge, where the highway widens and begins to rise slightly, the Zokozoi Hotel is on the right-hand side. More tavern than hotel, it had not been there before. A large unsightly building of galvanized iron walls and concrete floors, it is heavily patronized and has an unsavory reputation as a gathering place for rascals, the Papua New Guinea equivalent of hoodlums and urban gangs. While rascals are a greater problem in Port Moresby, Goroka has its share of them, enough to prompt the villagers of Susuroka to warn me against strangers and to see I did not go on walks alone. They were probably overanxious. Wherever I went in the tribes adjacent to the Nagamidzuha, there were people who recognized me or knew of me (word of my return having spread quite rapidly), and the canopy of kinship and past relationships (still remembered in lively detail) was a sure protection, though nowadays the roads and other public places are shared with large numbers of strangers.

The Zokozoi Hotel is remarkable only because Makis was killed there in 1969. The letter I received at the time (news that stunned me as much as the loss of any other person I have known) did not tell me how he had died, only that he had been hit by a truck on the Highland Highway, and because of his importance his death had caused a potentially dangerous commotion. The basic facts, as I learned on returning, are these. He had been drinking late into the night at the Zokozoi and was "sparking" (that is, drunk). A youth (now a young man) tried to persuade him to leave and walk back to Susuroka, but he says his concern provoked only an angry "kick in the ass." Much later Makis staggered out and was hit by a truck as he crossed the highway. He died a few days later in the Goroka Base Hospital, and I have always thought the manner of his death is an ironic comment on the changes that have overtaken his people.

Only a short distance beyond the Zokozoi there used to be a path branching to the left and running southwest along the crest of the ridge to Susuroka. It was really no more than a dirt lane the villagers had cut with bush knives through the tall kunai grasses, and I doubt it was used more than about eight times by any vehicle during the two years I lived there.

The present road branches from the highway at approximately the same place, but now it cuts through the side of the ridge below the crest. Unsealed, it resembles any number of minor country roads but carries far more traffic than those that went past my father's property in Australia. It lurches on and on beyond Susuroka, passes Ekuhakuka at the southern extremity of the ridge, descends to the floor of the valley, crosses a bridge over the Asaro River and continues into the blue folds of the distant mountains—to Lapigu, Siane and other places that used to lie outside the boundaries of the Gahuku's circumscribed and parochial world.

Kopi parked the truck at an unmarked place beside the road. I could not see any houses. Trees screened the crest of the ridge, which lay about thirty feet above us to the right, but a score of people, children and young and elderly adults, were gathered at the bottom of the path that led toward it. I climbed down from the truck and crossed the few yards toward them with misgiving. I did not expect to recognize any of the children or those who had been children thirty years ago, but time had also erased anything familiar from the faces of the elderly, as I am sure it had in the face they were trying to recall as they looked at me. But there was a difference: they at least knew who I was, for they were expecting me and were able to say my name without hesitation, whereas I had no clue to help me match a face with any one among the long litany of their own remembered names.

Momentarily I recalled the first time I had set foot in the village of Susuroka, after a bumpy ride by jeep along the dirt lane between the kunai grass. Stepping out into the exposed street of the new settlement, the sky and distant mountains had appeared to swing around my head and "the ground seemed to lift to meet my feet, as though I had stepped on some insubstantial construction of vine and cane bridging empty space" (*The High Valley*, pp. 16 ff.). The villagers had been taking their evening meal outside the line of round thatched houses and had risen in startled confusion to surround us. Then Makis had emerged from the crowd and without a moment's hesitation had clasped me to his naked chest in the Gahuku's traditional welcome. Only a little later, I had watched him as he took a stick and inscribed a circle on the bare earth, the blueprint for the house that became my home.

Now these strange people crowded around me. Recognizing my difficulty, Hunehune and Kopi prompted me with their names. Men and women my own age did not hesitate to fold me in their arms, crying my Gahuku name and touching parts of my body in the more intimate gestures that used to evoke a sniggering amusement from Europeans. My "children" (those whom I had known only as toddlers or had not known at all) were content with the embrace, and others of the newer generation mostly offered their hands. Old women accompanied their already emotional handling with the ritual tears and wails appropriate for the dead or for those meeting again after a long separation, a recognition of the changes that interrupt the continuity of every life. Almost no events, great or small, were left unmarked by Gahuku. All were part of the drama of life worthy of their respective weight, not to be concealed, kept from the sight of children or thrust to the very edge of adult consciousness; and in these ways if not in some others I think their customs gave a greater dignity and worth to each individual life. I found myself responding to my welcome with genuine tears and, surprisingly, with the formal phrases in Gahuku I thought I had forgotten.

I cannot remember any details of the walk from the road-side to the house prepared for me. It was only a short walk up the slope, through the trees, and into the village street, but the progress was slow for at intervals along the way other people were waiting, and each of them required the customary emotional recognition. But even while occupied with these formalities, I noticed the village still occupied its old site. The houses were still round and thatched, and, except for the enclosing trees, the bare street in front of them was very much the same as the one I used to enter from my house. But our destination was different from anything present in that other time.

At the southern end of the village street, facing the line of ground-hugging round houses, a fence of crude posts strung with four strands of barbed wire enclosed a yard of bare earth, which had been swept clean of leaves in preparation for my arrival. Inside the yard, set back against the perimeter of the trees separating the village from the road below, was the frame house Makis had been building but had not completed when he was killed. I had received a few photographs of it from people who had visited the village and had viewed his grave, which is only a few feet from the veranda of the house, so it was not completely unfamiliar. Architecturally, it was similar to scores of houses belonging to small farmers in the countryside of my Australian childhood: a simple rectangle of milled board siding elevated several feet above the ground and roofed with galvanized iron and gutters. A single door opened from the veranda to the interior, which contained four small rooms lit by louvered glass windows. Neither walls nor roof had been painted, and steps from yard to veranda had not been built. At one end there was an iron tank to hold the rain flowing from the gutters; but since its base was rusted and leaked, it was unusable and was mainly a breeding place for mosquitos in the rainy season. The house had no furnishings. There was no plumbing, stove or fireplace; its floors were bare, its interior walls unpainted composition board. The village had no electricity; the pressure lamp I bought in Goroka was the only source of light at night.

Makis had never lived in his house, and after his death it had been closed, the front door locked (its key kept by his daughter Lucy) and used by no one. But people said that while he was building it he had often expressed the hope that someday I might return and share it with him. Since I am also his younger brother, no one questioned my right to use it, and others (particularly Hunehune and my daughter Lucy Makis) shared it with me, though two of his widows (Gotome and Guma'e) would not enter it or even come inside the yard.

As I entered the yard, people pointed out the grave next to the house. While Makis has a special place in my memory as my closest Gahuku friend and my mentor (always there to help, guide, and instruct me) during my two years with him, I think it is reasonably clear that the liking, even the affection, was not one-sided. Our relationship was formed even before I had begun my work, when I went with him on a first contact patrol (under the leadership of Dudley Young-Whitforde) through a large area of country to the south and southwest of Mt. Michael. For three arduous weeks we had walked together through places quite as unfamiliar to him as to me, worlds far beyond any of his known horizons, and these shared experiences began the bonds that strengthened during the subsequent two years. I doubt there was much difference in our ages; but of course I was immeasurably younger, and inexperienced (even ignorant) insofar as I had none of his knowledge of Gahuku life and of the values and ideologies that moved his people. In this sense, the younger and older character of our relationship (also implied by the name he gave me) was entirely appropriate, and at times he did not hesitate to correct me with some acerbity, or to show both impatience and even boredom with my importuning questions and obtuseness. This is simply as it should have been, and after such outbursts he always returned to explain patiently anything I had failed to understand or he had been too busy to discuss. His relatives knew and did not question the closeness and special quality of our relationship, and far from having been forgotten, it had endured for more than thirty years and formed the basis of the special kinds of bonds I have with his survivors.

All this (and much more) was in my mind as I stopped briefly beside his grave, not really knowing what those who were with me might be expecting me to do in way of recognition. There would be time later, I thought, to show that I remembered in more private and personal ways, so I turned away to enter his house.

The next half hour was complete confusion as people crowded inside, carrying my few stores and possessions, setting up my bed in one of the rooms and even bringing a few things from their own homes to make me more comfortable. In the crush, someone thrust a small key into my hand, which I thought, erroneously, must be a key to the lock on the front door. I hung it on a nail in the bedroom wall where Lucy had placed a colored *bilum* (string bag) both as decoration and as a welcoming gift. Others also began to press gifts on me: a papaya here and there, a pineapple, a bunch of bananas, some sugarcane and other vegetables. Hunehune, who had taken charge of the kitchen, stowed them on top of the cardboard boxes containing my own tinned food. I sat down on the floor, letting them do as they liked and hardly bothering to remember the names of those who came to me to take my hands—the old ladies who squatted in front of me to weep and caress my thighs or the small shy children who were thrust forward to be introduced to their "grandfather." There was no resting yet, however. Kopi informed me he must take me down the ridge to other settlements where people were waiting. We returned to the truck and continued down the road, making several more wayside stops where the welcome was the same.

Only two of these need mentioning at this stage of my narrative. The first of them brought us to the enclave occupied by Namuri, who used to live in Susuroka and next to Makis had been its most important man. In *The High Valley* there is a photograph of him as he had been then, in traditional dress and hairstyle and posed in a fighting stance with drawn bow and arrow. His commanding height and presence are described there, as well as his close attachment to his wife Mukito and their small son Giza. Though he was often in my house I had never been particularly close to him. He spoke no pidgin (and still has not learned it), but he had also been less forthcoming than Makis, always holding back a little, maintaining a reserve and distance between himself and others, excepting only his wife and child. Something of this same quality informed the way he embraced me now, but he brought a wooden bench from his house (which is a completed version of the one Makis had been building, painted white with bright blue shutters) and sat on a stool facing me. I felt awkward, not only because I had to speak to Namuri through Kopi but also because I was suddenly aware that excepting Hunehune and Asemo none of the villagers of Susuroka had come with us. I tried to remind him of a few incidents in the past. He nodded, smiled slightly and said a few assenting words, but I felt he had something else he wanted to say. When Kopi translated his words, I found I had received an invitation to live with him in his house. I had not expected this, particularly since he must have known that my kinsmen had loaned me the house in which I was to live. There were some undercurrents here that had no meaning for me yet. I replied it was already decided where I would live, but I would surely see him many times before I had to go back to my own home, and after a few more minutes I suggested to Kopi we should continue with our round of visits.

Our next stop brought us to where Gihigute lives, a place on the ridge still called Gohajaka that thirty years ago had contained an older and much larger settlement than Susuroka. It alone of the villages on the ridge had been surrounded by casuarinas and was the home of most of the Ozahadzuha clan of Nagamidzuha. It had also been the place where the final dramatic events in the marriage of the young girl Tarova had been enacted, where late one moonlit night I had sat among a crush of people inside her father's house almost overcome by the singing and the poignancy of the farewell to her, and where, in the gathering dusk of the following day, I had watched her being carried away and had followed her procession, stumbling through the long grasses, through the darkening valley to Gama, where we left her among her husband's people. Both in 1981 and 1982, older men who had been present on this occasion delighted in regaling younger people with accounts of my own part in the event of Tarova's marriage. The fact that I, too, had been threatened and attacked during the women's ritual of rebellion described in *The High Valley* (pp. 194–198) was a matter that provoked warm and approving laughter. This had become, I thought, part of the folklore concerning my own position in the community—something that illustrated both the place they had granted me and their perception of differences between myself and others of my kind with whom their few personal contacts had been more impersonal, constrained and distant. But Gohajaka was not the same now. Indeed, the large village I remembered had disappeared, its place having been taken by a series of small, separate (fenced) but interconnected hamlets, in one of which Gihigute lives.

Gihigute is Tarova's father. Probably he had not been as old as I thought when I knew him before, but he is grizzled now, thin as a matchstick, almost toothless but still able to walk considerable distances even though he must often lie down to rest. Indeed, few people whom I knew in 1950 have died, and I remember that there had been no deaths in Nagamidzuha from 1950 to 1952. I do not know what this says for the general health and longevity of the people. Most of the deaths I recorded as occurring before I arrived in 1950 were attributed to warfare ("killed by Uheto," "killed by Notohana," and so on), which included not only pitched confrontations but also stealthy assassinations of men, women and children.

Gihigute had developed a joking relationship with me. He delighted in teasing and testing me, picking me up with his arms clasped round my upper thighs and carrying me about that way to the great amusement of others. In other ways as well he'd push me to see how far he could go with his antics before I protested. He remembered me now, and his filmy old eyes lit momentarily with a glimmer of his former mischief; but he seems unable to concentrate on anything for very long, and on many later occasions he looked at me without a sign of recognition.

That night I cooked my first meal in Makis' home and, sitting on the floor, shared it with the members of my extended family. Others came in later, filling the kitchen room outside the one in which I slept. The renewal of acquaintances continued. After a while I even found a few words and phrases of Gahuku were coming back to me, but almost everyone knew pidgin now, and I could talk to Lucy and her sister Lava (and Lava's husband Henderson Mokoru) in English.

I collected my flashlight and went to bed early, closing the door to the kitchen room where the others remained until a late hour, where Hunehune slept on the floor each night, often with his wife Komini and almost always with his small daughter. Lucy's room (with a door opening to the front veranda) was the last at the opposite end of the house from mine.

Lying in bed I did not mind the voices that kept me from sleeping. While sitting in the crowded kitchen earlier I had been moved in unexpected ways by some small things indicating I was well remembered. The key thrust into my hand on my arrival turned out to belong to a suitcase I had used thirty years ago. Lucy slept on the mattress I had given her father when I left the village, and in her room she had one of my suitcases containing six white shirts I had sent to him from Australia. Another man owned the folding camp stool I had used when writing up my notes at night, and near the grave of Makis, six lilies (that did not flower) poked through the bare earth, undisturbed through all the years since I had imported the bulbs and planted them in my garden.

At last, people in the kitchen began to leave. I heard Hunehune, his wife and small daughter talking softly as they settled down to sleep beneath their blankets on the floor. There was silence for a while; then suddenly the house itself seemed to become alive. It did this every night while I was there, having a peculiar propensity to "fire up," its walls resounding with loud creaks and thumps as though someone was pounding on them from outside. I did not mention the phenomenon to anyone until the morning of the day on which I left in 1981. It had been particularly noisy during the preceding night and others were complaining they had been unable to sleep. I agreed it had been a restless night, and when I remarked I did not know what caused it, they looked at me with disbelief. "It was your brother who sleeps down there," they said. "He knows you are going and wants to fasten you to your land and family." I accepted their explanation without question. It was far more satisfying than any naturalistic one I might have found.

Despite the house, I slept comfortably that night, waking to sounds familiar to me from all the other early mornings in the village. By the time I had dressed and carried an enamel basin of water to the front veranda to shave and wash, I felt a confidence (that grew throughout the subsequent weeks) that, contrary to the pessimistic dictum of Thomas Wolfe, you can go home again.

I mean several things by this. First, there is the immense pleasure and sense of gratitude from renewing personal ties to people who, in my youth, I knew almost as well as anyone I have known; second, there is the realization that I shared with them a base of understanding and experiences that was virtually unquestionable, and that no one from my background meeting them for the first time could share. Despite changes, despite the disappearance of traditional institutions that had been critical, and despite many new customs that seemed like bowdlerized adaptations of mores I do not find particularly admirable in my own culture, there was a continuity perceptible only to someone who had been there in another time. There were things I could take for granted, that I would never have to learn again; and it was enormously gratifying that people granted me this backlog of knowledge. But ultimately, I suppose, "coming home" is a state of mind in which you are reassured that you have not made egregious misjudgments, and that there is an agreed upon baseline from which, without too much difficulty, you can begin to appreciate the present as an extension to the past.

TWO

IN MEMORIAM MAKIS

1   Makis' house stands only several yards from where my own house had stood. Nothing, except the alien but persevering lilies, remains of that insubstantial dwelling; its site is occupied by a grove of fully grown coffee trees. The main village has also moved a little to the north, and the old houses of Guma'e, Gotome, Namuri, Bihore and Helekohe no longer stand across the street from my own garden. Next to it there is a *haus lotu* (church) belonging to the Swiss Evangelical Mission. This is also new. Services are held in it on some evenings and twice on Sundays. I never went inside it, but from my veranda I could hear the sermons and the singing, which always included a popular hymn (in Gahuku) set to the tune of "My Darling Clementine." Makis had not been converted and most of his

direct living descendants are not Christian—Lokilo, his son, explaining with a humorous twinkle that almost all of them are "satan." And as far as I can tell, this does not disadvantage them in any way; Gahuku do not seem to have been exposed to religious bigotry yet.

Looking west from my veranda, trees hide the ranging view toward the mountains and the Daulo Pass, but near the place where Helekohe's house had been there is a clump of bamboo under which I had sat often with the boy Asemo (the last of Nagamidzuha's youths to have been initiated into the male secret *nama* cult), the two of us silently contemplating the gathering dusk and the last glimmers of light on the surface of streams where mists were beginning to throw a veil across the gardens. The bamboo stood at the top of a path leading down to a stream separating Susuroka from Gorohadzuha, the nearest Gehamo settlement. It is overgrown and unused now, people taking a different route to the stream when they wish to bathe or wash their Western style clothes.

Though I could no longer watch over the entire village from the veranda of Makis' house, it came to life each morning in much the same way as I remembered. People rose early and pigs were the first creatures to leave and break the silence of the street. There are fewer of them now, however. Though still an important part of ceremonial exchanges, they do not have the pride of place they occupied among traditional forms of wealth. The younger generation shows only moderate interest in them, nothing comparable to their elders' obsession and the ceaseless planning and discussions concerning the ends to which their husbandry was directed. Money is more important now.

At first sight, there is little except their Western clothes to distinguish the people leaving the houses from their predecessors. Not yet fully awake, and barely speaking, they sit on the ground in family groups outside their dwellings. Women remove their breasts from their blouses and nurse small children; a man may start a small fire with a smoldering brand he has brought from the hearth inside the house. As the sun begins to penetrate the trees and the mountain chill of night dissipates in the opening day, voices become more audible and movement increases. A nursing mother passes a baby to its young father, who cradles it in his arms while he and his wife discuss their plans for the day. Older children become more noisy and active, and, like their counterparts almost anywhere, those who are pupils at the government school—a short walk's distance across the highway at Kabidzuha—procrastinate until the last minute, disregarding their parents' increasingly forceful and impatient reminders that they must be on their way.

This is an entirely new element of experience. There were no schools in 1950, and the girls who are now wearing their school uniforms would have been setting out at the same hour for the gardens with their mothers and other women, already caught up in the round of daily tasks custom assigned to their sex, while their brothers, prior to their initiation into the *nama* cult, would have had little more to do than to roam the grass-covered countryside of their clan territory in bands of their peers, filling the hours by hunting for bush rats or by spying on adults, splashing in the streams or planning some foray in a secluded clearing.

The schoolchildren leave eventually, not to return until the afternoon, and the adults rise to begin their day. For many of them their work is the same as it had been. Most women set out for the gardens, which still provide almost everything necessary for subsistence, but the proximity of the town, and some new primary industries not far from Susuroka, provide some part-time alternatives for those who want them. A very few who are well educated are employed full-time in nontraditional jobs, and some commute daily to the township. Men's work was always more varied, splashed with brilliant highlights. This work was glimmering with secrets; punctuated with bravura colors and the violence of warfare; bonded by the maneuverings of power and the intricacies of politics; and enriched by male guardianship of ritual. It is still more varied, not only because political control and authority have not passed from their hands but also because the urban environment presents them with more alternatives. In settlements along the ridge a number of men own trucks which they use for contract work in and around the town. Others have permanent jobs there (some living in its suburbs rather than commuting daily from the villages), and yet others have sizeable coffee groves or interests in holdings large enough to be called "plantations." These do not need continual attention throughout the year, however, and many men earn little from the town. But the presence of Goroka is always there, unseen from the ridge but sending its vibrations to introduce a new theme even into the composition of sounds beginning every day.

Even as I woke, before the pigs had been released, vehicles were traveling along the road below the house, reminding me of the morning sound of traffic on the boulevard skirting the lake where I live in Seattle. It was totally unexpected, and I was surprised that only I seemed to find it worthy of comment. In 1950, the few occasions when someone had come to visit me by jeep had caused commotion. People heard the engine long before I did, lifting their heads alertly and identifying it even before the vehicle had turned from the main road into the dirt lane. They were on their feet, children swarming toward it, before it appeared at the entrance to the village. They had shouted the news of its arrival with clamorous excitement, and had vied with one another, to the accompaniment of imprecations, cuffs, and kicks, for the few available places should its owner decide to give them a short ride on his return along the dirt lane. Now they are blasé. The younger do not know a time when trucks and cars were rarities. If they do not want to walk to the town, they simply wait at roadside below the village for a passing vehicle, many of which will take them there for less than one *kina* (a unit of the national currency for which the exchange rate is approximately U.S. $1.50), and the more sophisticated youths and young men are as interested in identifying various makes and models as some of my Australian contemporaries had been when I was young, a competitive pastime that never had an appeal for me.

It is impossible to escape the presence of the town for long. Minor roads traverse the valley in all directions, radiating from the Highland Highway. Places that took the better part of a day to visit from Susuroka are only short jaunts now; even the Daulo Pass, once the entrance to a different cultural world, is less than an hour away. It is here I had stood with Makis at the end of the three-week patrol we had shared. Both of us had looked eastward over the great sweep of grasslands, marking the myriad villages by their groves of casuarinas and the frail blue smoke rising from them in columns to meet and merge with the opalescent light on the underside of the immense Constable clouds. Each of us had searched for the grove that Makis called home and which I had thought of as my home, too. Perhaps like any place we knew in childhood and return to at a later stage of life, the distance of maturity compresses features that seemed much larger once. Gardens that seemed as wide as a universe, and hedges that were once unscalable ramparts protecting imaginary castles, are nothing more than a square of lawn and some regimented shrubs separating formal beds of roses. The valley still has the same dimensions, but now it has also contracted and come closer, having a slightly prosaic quality it did not possess when just a few miles away the next stretch of land had been enemy territory, to be given a wide and wary berth when journeying to friends or allies on the other side of it.

The presence of the town even intruded on my walks. I did not go as far or as frequently as I had been accustomed (old Gihigute seemed to have more stamina for walking than I did) and I was never allowed to go alone, either Hunehune or Lokilo (and sometimes both of them) always accompanying me; for Hunehune took seriously the possible threat of "rascals," even if I did not give any thought to them. He even suggested it was risky to leave the grass louvres of my windows open at night, for rascals surely knew I was there and had been known to come into villages. I disregarded this advice, saying they could hardly climb inside without waking me, and I could hit them over the head with my flashlight before they could squeeze through such narrow openings, a piece of bravado he did not find amusing though he did not go so far as to prohibit me from acting foolishly.

The difficulty of going anywhere alone had been something I resented on my previous visit. Then it had been the bands of roaming youths and children who always dropped whatever they were doing to materialize suddenly from the grasses when I least wanted them. Eventually, I learned to be "alone" even in their company, shutting my ears to the sound of their voices and closing my mind to their presence, seeing and hearing only what *I* wanted. Often on those occasions I felt as though I was isolated on the highest pinnacle of the universe. Audible only to some more finely tuned interior ear, I could hear the whole life of the valley welling round me, its multitude of interweaving sounds distilled from the sun and the honeyed scent of grass and crotolaria; and a sense of confidence and care rushed in to lift and fill my chest as my eyes held and cherished even the minutest details of the landscape. I could not quite recapture those moments, though the valley remains one of the most beautiful I may ever hope to see, and its life still strikes a responsive chord. Now it is not possible to feel the same exalted isolation—cut off from the rest of the world—when the sprawling town is just beyond the next ridge, when its life intrudes on all the roads, in the passing noise of scheduled jets and the rackety sound of helicopters making slower journeys from one Highland valley to another.

These walks also offered poignant evidence of things that have happened in Nagamidzuha since the death of Makis. It is still possible to walk without hindrance from settlement to settlement along the ridge, but whereas the population (excluding members of the Meniharove clan, who always lived on the floor of the valley) had been concentrated in only two principal villages (Susuroka and Gohajaka) it is now strung out from north to south along the crest in smaller and more numerous enclaves separated from one another by post and barbed wire fences. This new pattern responds to events in recent years, and to understand it, it is necessary to rewind the film of Gahuku life to a past that in many ways still colors the act in progress at the present time.

2 Gahuku social groups are organized by the ideology of patrilineal descent. Men and women who are related to one another by descent through males from a common (sometimes putative) male ancestor form social units such as named clans and subclans (which are not named), and these are further interrelated with one another at higher levels into the named groups I have referred to as tribes. Tribes are connected in one of two ways: by traditional friendship or traditional enmity. Those who are friends intermarry, participate in ceremonial exchanges of wealth and assist one another in warfare. Enemy tribes do not intermarry, do not cooperate in exchanges, and warfare (in the past) was the constant, expected and virtually irrevocable state of their relationships. Unlike conditions in a few other parts of the Highlands, the aim of warfare was not to impose political sovereignty over enemies or to acquire their land. The villages of enemies were often destroyed and their inhabitants forced to flee and seek refuge with friends and allies elsewhere, but the victors did not attempt to occupy their vacated territory, and the defeated always planned to return to it when they had regained their strength. Characteristically, some enemy tribes occupied adjacent territories, sometimes separated from one another by less than a mile and by strips of unused "no-man's-land" (*game mikasi*).

Several important elements of traditional life were related to this pattern of ceaseless hostility. One was the prime importance (for men) of producing warriors from the younger generations of males, and most of their efforts were directed to this end. The ideal male was one who was *amuza* "strong" or "hard": aggressive, prideful and self-assertive, disciplined, superior and touchy with respect to his reputation—the epitome of the warrior. At the opposite pole there were those males who were characterized as *hoipa* "weak" or "soft." These were no less masculine than the others. They were not feminized men; but they lacked a reputation and had no chance of rising to leadership or positions of generalized influence in their groups. Men had, in effect, no choice in careers. There was only one: being a warrior.

Against this background, almost every group suffered many vicissitudes and changes of fortune during the course of its existence. The members of clans and subclans became scattered here and there among friends and allies and often lived in exile for more than a decade. At any point in time, the composition of groups on the ground was fluid, in a state of potential flux or change, though beneath this flow of population the ideology of patrilineal descent and the patrimony of territory remained, to be reasserted and reclaimed when fortunes improved or swung in another direction. The processes were not random, but rather (as my colleague James B. Watson has characterized them in another part of the Eastern Highlands) those of "organized flow" as groups and leaders, seizing the main chance, attempted to augment and consolidate their "strength."

In these processes, a crucial concern was the strength of groups in numbers and, of course, the number of males who were strong rather than soft. The birth rate was low, owing primarily, I think, to postpartum taboos on sexual intercourse between husband and wife from the birth of a child until weaning at about age three, and also because young men were not permitted to have sex with their wives until about age twenty-three. The children in a family were mostly spaced from one another by two to three years in 1950. But adult male mortality through warfare also appears to have been relatively high.

The aim of strength through numbers could be assisted in two principal ways: first, by infant or child adoption.* This was (and remains) a common practice, but since no Gahuku man or woman is immune to gossip that they are childless, the true parentage is always concealed. It is close to being "screaming secrets," however. Though never openly referred to, the biological parentage of adopted children is always known, and by the time they are adult they, too, know it. They could, moreover, always reclaim their patrimony and membership in the social group of their male biological parent, and frequently did so, often with embarrassing and even tragic consequences to those who had nurtured them.

A second method of augmenting group strength was to bring in adults who were not members of the patrilineal core but connected to it by what anthropologists refer to as cognatic ties of kinship. This is one of the reasons why refugees generally found semipermanent acceptance in groups where they sought sanctuary. But such people also did not lose their patrimony and latent membership in their natal groups. They could reclaim it when it suited them or, alternatively, they could be forced to do so by the exigencies of internal politics in the groups accepting them. Part of the strategy of leaders was both to "bring in" cognatic kinsmen and to "bring back" to the agnatic (patrilineal) core those members who were scattered. In summary, it may be said that the "permanent" patrilineal core of social groups tended to be encased in a softer

---

*Co-wives often give children to one another, and such adoptions are also common between sisters and people who are members of the same clan.

pulp of potentially divided loyalties, and the consequence of flux and change was a characteristic Gahuku experience and entered into the long-range plans of men who were ambitious, who aspired to "making a name" and exercising a generalized influence not resting on the sanction of hereditary criteria of fitness.

The Nagamidzuha in 1950 were at one stage in this process, a stage which apparently continued on its course until 1969 and thereafter changed direction again as a consequence of internal maneuverings following the death of Makis, who had been largely responsible for the rehabilitation of the tribe.

Though I mention only two clans of Nagamidzuha (Meniharove and Ozahadzuha) in most of my reports dating from 1950 onward, there are actually five, two I did not know existed and one other I knew but found no reason to mention. This, as well as the fact that the clan of Makis and his agnates is wrongly identified as Ozahadzuha, does not necessarily indicate sloppy fieldwork or deliberate misrepresentation by those on whom I relied for information. To the outsider, finding one's way through the subtle shading of internal politics is frequently more hazardous (and tiresome) than investigating the areas of culture that are never-to-be-revealed institutionalized secrets, of which there were many in Gahuku life, including basic masculine ideologies and the major rituals concerned with manhood. In the very delicate climate of relationships outlined above, there were cogent reasons for giving a simplified picture of some personal and group relationships, as well as reasons for someone as close to me and as trusting as Makis to give misleading information on a matter as fundamental as group membership. It is for this reason that when I arrive at the part of my narrative concerned with current politics I shall not be able to mention any names or give an unequivocal account of relationships important to events that happened when I was there or may happen in the not-too-distant future. The past may take care of itself, however.

The principal enemies of Nagamidzuha (but not the only ones) were Uheto and Notohana. Closer than either of them, Gehamo was also an enemy, but not exclusively; for there was some intermarriage and periods of rather uneasy peace between the two. Nagamidzuha's nearest friends were Asarodzuha and Gama, but there were others much farther afield to the north, east and southwest. It was a relatively small tribe, much smaller, for example, than the Gahuku whose name (due partly to my usage) became the label generally attached to all the central valley tribes belonging to a more inclusive cultural-linguistic unit. The people themselves did not recognize any kind of inclusive label, however.

Nagamidzuha had suffered many vicissitudes at the hands of its enemies. Its people excused this dismal but rather characteristic record by pointing out they were not only in the middle but also small (lacking numerical strength) and therefore, it could be said, fair game for enemies. Many members of its clans were scattered, and had been for a considerable time; I do not know how long, but in some cases it was almost certainly more than two decades. The most recent of these routs occurred sometime before whites arrived in the valley in the 1930s. Under the combined attacks of Uheto, Notohana, and Gehamo, members of the ridge clans had fled to sanctuary elsewhere and the greater part of their territory was unoccupied. Much later some of them began to return, as was customary, no matter how long a period of exile lasted.

Makis was born in exile in Gama, the son of Urugusie, apparently a noted warrior who had been dead for some time before I arrived in 1950. Urugusie, during a period of peace, had married a Gehamo woman. Her son, Makis, was thus the *kantri* (a pidgin term) or maternal kinsman of members of her natal Gehamo group (Gahuku: *gimive* or "given child"). These relatives eventually "called back" Makis and some of Urugusie's other kinsmen. These people included not only members of Urugusie's patrilineal clan (which was very small) but also members of the far more numerous clan Ozahadzuha. They settled on the ridge at Gohajaka, which was the oldest and largest settlement in 1950. Makis also lived there for a time, but not more than two years before my arrival he had moved out to establish a settlement at Susuroka closer to Gehamo and on land that was part of the patrimony of Urugusie's clan. He was joined in this enterprise by men belonging to both Ozahadzuha and Meniharove.

Prior to founding Susuroka, Makis was already an *agulizagive* ("man with a name"), a noted warrior (his war name was Urugusie, the same as his father's) and the possessor of qualities required by leaders and influential men. He combined strength tempered by a judicious recognition of the motives and rights of others and the ability to persuade followers to a middle course of action, ultimately encouraging and forming consensus on important issues. The truly hard men (though the qualities subsumed by the term were the masculine ideal) were unlikely to achieve these positions, for their desire to dominate and their sometimes overweening sense of self-esteem brooked no equals. They tended to be pigheaded rather than subtle in dealing with others or in pursuit of their own interests, and they were often an uncomfortable thorn in the side of the body politic. Men of generalized influence sufficient to attract and to hold supporters had to be hard in some sense, that is, they had to have demonstrated a successful commitment to the activities exemplifying hardness, but it is not going too far to say that within the Gahuku scheme of things they also had to be experts in human relations, managers who saw more sides to an issue than one and who employed this talent not only to the ends of group unity but also to amass over time the forms of traditional wealth whose disbursement in ceremonial exchanges placed others in their debt and helped to generate and support the influence they achieved.

This involved foresight, not to say an appreciation of where the main chance lay, and in this respect the career of Makis may have been assisted by some of his relationships with some of the earliest representatives of the colonial government in the valley. It is not that he was a sycophant. He neither kowtowed to whites nor accepted enthusiastically all their demands, but because of his already known reputation he was useful to them in their effort to extend both the presence and knowledge of the government among all the groups they were bringing within the mantle of a pax Australiana. It was a two-way process. The early representatives of government sometimes took him along on their exploratory and "first contact" patrols, as, for example, the one on which I was his companion. His presence in their company could be interpreted as a harbinger of their future by those who were confronted with an apocalyptic event in their lives, but his own horizons were also extended and, assuredly, he was expected to contribute to broadening those of his people when he returned and recounted his experiences. As a consequence of this role, he had become probably the best-known man in the valley west of Goroka when I arrived there. Time and time again people in distant groups involved in disputes and other litigation passed through and stopped at Susuroka on their way to the district office at Goroka, seeking his counsel on possible issues and on procedures with which they were unfamiliar.

There is no question that he was the most important person in Nagamidzuha by 1952. His influence was paramount in the tribe as a whole, but particularly among the clans on the ridge, which he held together in a unity they do not now possess.

His influence and the consolidation of his people continued after I left. For example (a common step in the careers of such men), by the late fifties he had begun to recall or bring back the scattered exiles as well as attaching some cognatically related individuals. Many of these people are now part of the population of Susuroka (which is much larger despite the departure of others who used to live there), and there is an entire new settlement below the ridge near the stream separating it from Gehamo. Perhaps the influence of Makis could have preserved the unity of the ridge clans beyond 1969, but at any time, internal rivalries and oppositions are a factor in the fluctuations of group identifications and cooperation. What may seem expedient or even necessary at one stage of the process may be supplanted by other considerations and ambitions as circumstances change, and in their advanced years big men, though retaining respect as elders, may find themselves less persuasive than others coming up. Should they die, their death may release their rivals from the expediency of submerging their differences.

All these factors have contributed to changes in the composition and relationships of the ridge clans from 1950 to the present day.

3 The death of Makis precipitated the major swing in social relationships observable today, though some of the underlying strains that came to a head with that event may have been present in 1952. From all accounts it was a sudden and dramatic eruption, however.

On my first tour of the ridge I could not help wondering what, if anything, lay behind the new and more scattered residential pattern of small hamlet clusters divided from one another by barbed wire fences. Only Susuroka remained as a village in any obvious meaning of the word. After a day or so I also learned that a number of men (and their families) had moved away, either to one or another of the small hamlets or even farther afield. A few other men who had been young and close to me had also left to live with their wives in their natal groups, but this had no necessary connection to other events. Normatively, residence after marriage was with a husband's group, but there had always been some men who did not follow the rule. Expediency was most frequently the reason, particularly if the wife was the child of or closely related to an influential man. Makis, for example, adamantly refused to allow his favorite daughter to move away after she married. Influential men could also assert their personal will in the matter of conjugal residence in order to add to the number of their followers.

Gradually, largely from listening to and talking with members of my extended family, a pattern of events began to emerge, revealing the soft underside to the unity promoted and held together by Makis. I am sure that everyone knew what I learned, though undoubtedly some may have provided slightly different accounts from the perspective of their own interests, but no one referred to the situation in public. On the surface it simply did not exist. The direct descendants of

Makis were open with me, since I belonged to their family—quite astonishingly so—considering the vehemence of the hostility in many of their comments. Their openness applied only to situations when we were alone, however. They stopped abruptly when anyone else approached and warned me not to drop a hint that I was privy to some of the more personal pieces of information. I shall try not to betray this confidence and will omit some information, yet the general course of events is so well known that recounting them is no disservice to me or my kinsmen. Admittedly, the latter had a personal axe to grind, since they were the people most closely affected; but the consequences spread far more widely through the population, and other accounts verify their information on most points.

I did not personally observe any of these events, but I had an opportunity to witness their ramifications during the course of a dispute over land boundaries. Indeed, this brought forward additional information confirming what had been largely hearsay.

The death of Makis a day or so after he was struck by the truck outside the Zokozoi Hotel caused a considerable commotion. Hunehune says that when he saw Makis in the hospital he, Makis, said that no one must think he was about to die. His internal injuries, however, were so severe that there was no possibility of his living. The wrath of Nagamidzuha focused on those who had been in the truck; and possibly because none of them were Gahuku, the emotional climate was intense. The letter I received from the patrol officer indicates that their anger reached the flash point of violence, and the apparatus of government was marshaled to deal with the litigation concerning the amount of the indemnity they were bound to demand. Officially, they held the driver and occupants of the truck to blame. The fact that Makis may have been responsible for his own death because of his drunkenness carried no weight at all. Gahuku do not recognize the finer shades of culpability commonly applied to certain felonies in Western law. But apart from this the truck and its driver were only the instrument, not the *cause* of his death, in the view of many. This, in the firm opinion of his close kinsmen and others who resent the subsequent course of events, was sorcery.

Belief in sorcery (*poisin* in pidgin) has not diminished. It is the most frequent explanation for serious or persistent illnesses and death, cited by even the relatively sophisticated and by Christian and non-Christian alike. Even the educated who have one foot firmly planted in the urban environment of Goroka and the other foot in the villages will say with a faint hint of apology that their country kinsmen diagnosed sorcery as the cause of one of their recent illnesses, clearly not disassociating themselves from the diagnosis but, rather, offering it tentatively because they assume it will be received skeptically by their Western audience. Excepting possibly only the truly old, sorcery was said to have caused the deaths of every person whom I had known and who had died prior to 1981, including Piripiri (*The High Valley,* p. 95) and his two small children who were drowned while crossing the Asaro River.

It was said that the eminence and success of Makis provoked resentment in those who had received no comparable recognition. "Only he has a name," they are said to have thought enviously. "It's 'Makis, Makis' all the time. 'Makis this' and 'Makis that,' and no one knows us." So they decided to kill him, causing him to weave and stumble into the path of the truck when he left the Zokozoi Hotel. They did this either by tampering with his beer or causing him to become disoriented at the crucial moment. Even the assistance of a deliberate push by someone may be suggested without subtracting from the allegation of sorcery, for he had to be *made* vulnerable to it.*

From this point of view, one might say perhaps that those who were in the truck that killed Makis were not really culpable—that is, unless they were in collusion with those wanting him dead, and the latter was not suggested. But as I shall point out in another context later, the issues in Gahuku disputes, whether factual or based mainly on suspicion, are seldom as clear-cut as they appear to be in their official presentation. The view that sorcery killed Makis is held unshak-

---

*Automobiles may be characterized as potentially lethal weapons in our culture, but this potentiality often has an added dimension in Gahuku attitudes toward automobile accidents and deaths. As in the case of Makis, the automobile may be the immediate instrument of death but not necessarily the sufficient cause, or automobiles may be perceived as a more obvious kind of weapon in accidents involving people from groups who are traditional enemies. Only a day before my arrival in Goroka in 1982, during the Eastern Highlands Show (which is the largest, most eagerly awaited and nationally publicized local and contemporary event, drawing scores of tourists and crowds of people from every tribal group within the province), an accident on the Highland Highway not far from Susuroka resulted in the deaths of eight people. The victims were members of the Asarodzuha group, and their "killers" were members of a tribe who were their traditional enemies. There was immediate violence in the town. Opposing factions had to be separated and dispersed by police using tear gas; and the public market was closed for the following ten days. During this time, even up to the day I left to return to the United States, large numbers of people from the opposing sides (those of the victims and the "aggressors") did not leave their villages without their arms—bows, arrows, and knives—and some even patrolled their local territories at night. Traditional friends (that is, allies) joined to give support to those with whom they were affiliated, the Nagamidzuha coming out to help the Asarodzuha. Members of these patrols, going on their rounds, dropped in occasionally to chat with me shortly after dark.

ably by many people, and disgruntled members of his own tribe are not excluded from suspicion.

The amount of the indemnity was arranged in the courts at Goroka. Apparently it was large, commensurate with the importance of Makis. The patrol officer who broke the news to me is also said to have arranged for a government contribution of money to his followers. I did not check this with any official records in Goroka, but if it is true it was an unusual gesture, possibly arranged in recognition of his past services. I am inclined to accept the villagers' word for this, since in some cases they are able to give an account of where and to whom portions of the government money went. The amounts they mention are by no means precise, but at a rough guess the government contribution could have been in excess of one thousand pounds Australian.

Events move on to the distribution of the indemnity and of Makis' personal valuables and movable property. This is customary procedure, governed by rules concerning who is entitled to share and the degrees of their entitlement based on kinship ties to the deceased. On this occasion, however, the rules seem to have been thrown to the wind, and the distribution became a somewhat unseemly scramble in which the greatest part of everything was "misappropriated" by people who had no right to keep as much as they did.

Makis left few direct descendants who were adults. His only acknowledged son was perhaps about ten. One of his daughters was nineteen (I know her precise age because I named her at her birth in 1950), two others were older and one younger, but in any case they were women, and should not have had any say in the distribution of his property. There were other young adult male members of his clan about the same age as Hunehune, which would have been somewhere near their mid-thirties in 1969, but their opinions carried no weight against the seniority of the man who managed the disbursements.

He belongs to the Ozahadzuha clan, which I had believed was also the clan of Makis. His behavior on this occasion, foreshadowing more direct action later, is cited as causing the split evident in the separate hamlet enclaves on the ridge today and the resurfacing of clans formerly submerged beneath the facade of unity. It was he and other members of Ozahadzuha (some younger than Hunehune) who shared almost everything. Guma'e, third and youngest of Makis' wives and the mother of both his son and the daughter I named, is said to have received two hundred Australian pounds, and a smaller portion of the government's contribution was held in trust (at the government's insistence) for his son; otherwise almost nothing went to members of his clan (which, I know now, is Guminakudzuha). Hunehune says he was offered a share but refused it, not only because of his personal distress at Makis' death but also because he wanted no part in the injustices of the unseemly scramble. The daughter whom I named in 1950 did protest, however. Showing an independence of spirit and action that has grown since then, she spoke out when the mattress on which she sleeps was being given away. "You cannot have it," she said. "It was my father's; my other father, Goroha Gipo, gave it to him. It belongs to me." She also managed to keep the suitcase that had been mine and the six white shirts I had sent her father from Australia. Apart from these, none of his personal property or valuables appears to have passed into the hands of any of his clan kinsmen. Alone from among all his plumes and shells, there is a necklace of large white cowries hanging from a nail on the wall of the kitchen room in his unfinished house, brought there for me during my stay.

The money disbursed was not put to any constructive use, but squandered. One young man of Ozahadzuha used his portion to make the down payment on a truck; but he and others used the vehicle almost solely for ostentatious joyriding and it was quickly repossessed for their failure to pay the installments on the loan.

Makis' relatives place the entire blame on the senior member of the Ozahadzuha clan conducting the distribution, but they also include other members of that clan who willingly acceded to his avariciousness. And they hold him and those who followed him responsible for everything that has occurred among the ridge clans since that date.

I know the man quite well, our acquaintance going back to the very beginning of my relationship with the Nagamidzuha. He was one of the Ozahadzuha who had followed Makis when he founded Susuroka, and his house had been just across the street from mine. Proud, as all Gahuku warriors were proud, he was not outgoing but reserved and superior. He was not a prime example of the "hard" man, but he possessed some of their qualities in greater measure than Makis, and lacked the latter's sensitivity and lightness, smiling or laughing rarely, and never joking. But Makis had consulted with him, and he always played a conspicuous role on public occasions. He is still a dour, unsmiling person. He often visited me in Makis' house, either alone or with his wife, who is an old lady of great personality with a bawdy and engaging sense of humor, which is completely uninhibited when she has had a little too much beer. Since she speaks fluent pidgin, it was comfortable and relaxing to be with her, and sometimes after I had gone to bed I listened to people in the kitchen responding to her stories with sidesplitting laughter. Her husband seldom laughed at her jokes, however, and I was uncomfortable when alone with him. He simply sat on the floor and mostly observed me silently, occasionally breaking into Gahuku, almost all of which I had forgotten. But I did not dislike him and did not share the glee with which my relatives recounted a personal tragedy that had recently befallen him.

With the new information (and possibly a little prejudiced against him because of the quality of my personal ties to the kinsmen of Makis), I reviewed what I had known of him in the past, trying to see if there had been anything in his attitudes and behavior hinting at this abrupt rejection of the man with whom he had been closely affiliated. I have no doubt he had a strong sense of self-importance and, being about the same age of Makis, may have chafed against the constraints of his subordinate position. They were age-mates, that is, they had been initiated into the male cult at the same time, and their careers had run along parallel courses. Traditionally, the bond between age-mates had been very close, virtually the only kinship tie not carrying some elements of superiority and subordination. Age-mates moved through the status structure of society on a basis of ideal equality. They not only passed together through the traumatic events of incorporation into the company of adult men but were also betrothed and began conjugal relationships with their wives at the same time; ideally they were companions and confidants throughout their lives. But such commitments to equality were not easily achieved against countervailing pressures toward demonstrating superiority. The actual relationship between age-mates often included competitiveness, veiled dislike, and antagonism; and the admired qualities of hardness did not, in their extreme manifestation, foster a comfortable acceptance of equality—one reason why the truly hard tended to be unsuited to the delicate maneuverings of guiding people toward the formation of consensus, which was the ultimate legitimizing sanction for public decisions.

I do not think the Ozahadzuha man possessed these essential qualities for leadership, being more inclined to dictate than guide. There was also the matter of clan membership.

Ozahadzuha was the largest of the ridge clans, while Guminakudzuha was and remains a small group. Thus it was mostly Ozahadzuha who began to return to the ridge from exile when the Gehamo, recognizing their maternal ties to him, recalled Makis; it was again mostly Ozahadzuha men who followed Makis when he founded Susuroka. Indeed, I had the impression that virtually all the male members of Susuroka belonged to Ozahadzuha. This is the clan to which they are assigned in my genealogies, the clan with which almost everyone, including Makis and his patrilineal kinsmen, were identified by my informants. I never once in any context, including all my conversations with Makis, heard the name Guminakudzuha mentioned, and I think I know the reasons for this subterfuge.

I do not think that leaders characteristically arose in small clans, but in groups where they had a sufficient number of patrilineal kinsmen to provide a potential core of supporters. Given also the importance of strength in numbers, small groups necessarily sought close ties with those that were larger, these political considerations sometimes leading to virtual if temporary merging of the smaller with the larger, even to the extent of blurring of their separate clan identities. This applies to a third ridge clan (Guminadzuha) whose name I knew but saw no reason to mention in earlier reports for it was even smaller than Guminakudzuha. All its members lived with Ozahadzuha and to all intents and purposes were thoroughly merged with it.

In the pursuit of political advantage, it had been advantageous to Makis to identify with Ozahadzuha, just as it was advantageous to that group to support him during his rise to ascendancy. Gahuku recognized that power, prestige, and the achievement of important group and personal values rested on a base of numerical strength, and the bringing-in of cognatically related people, the acceptance of refugees as well as infant and child adoption, and the shift in group identifications contributed to these ends. All of these strategies might be said to represent expediencies suited to a particular situation at a given point in time, but the catch was this: situations change and relationships based on expediency can be dissolved, often with quite astonishing abruptness.

The death of Makis provided the Ozahadzuha man with such an opportunity. Makis had been the most important member of that group and, with his death, the newcomer apparently tried to reassert his group's dominance by a public repudiation of the figments of group identification that had served their purpose, no doubt also anticipating that the mantle of accepted leadership would pass to him.

I do not know the precise date when this took place, nor do I know all the details, but it was apparently a sudden decision announced not long after Makis died. At a meeting of the ridge clans he reportedly proclaimed the separation of the three other ridge clans (Guminadzuha, Guminakudzuha and Lavakadzuha) from Ozahadzuha, pointing out that Makis and his agnates belonged to Guminakudzuha and similarly assigning clan identities to other people. This was news to at least some members of the younger generation, and it was generally interpreted (as it was no doubt intended) to put others in their place under the changed conditions. Coupled with resentment for the high-handed manner in which he allegedly handled the distribution of wealth on the death of Makis, it created rifts along clan lines resulting in the residential separation observable on the ridge today. Though concealed, resentment and animosity for him and other members of Ozahadzuha is strong and not confined only to Guminakudzuha, who were those most closely and personally affected. And the game continues, with new twists evidencing the inherent softness of some Gahuku relationships characteristically concealed by a facade of unity. These twists surfaced in a dispute concerning land boundaries that began during the summer of 1981 and had not been concluded when I left.

The dispute began in a familiar way. Men from Gehamo accused the Ozahadzuha man and another younger member of that clan of breaking ground for gardens on land belonging to Gehamo. The Ozahadzuha refused to recognize Gehamo's claims to ownership and decided to refer the matter to the Village Court, the lowest level of the judicial processes. Members of the Village Court are elected by popular ballot and its members are drawn from several different social groups. In this case, one of them was a member of Guminakudzuha, but others had no connections with either the principal Gehamo protagonists or the ridge clans of Nagamidzuha. The dispute was presented as one between the ridge clans and Gehamo, but the interests involved were far more complicated.

Prior to the first hearing by the Village Court at the disputed boundary, the ridge held several meetings in the hamlet of the Ozahadzuha man, who was the person named as principal litigant by the Gehamo. During all of them, the descendants of Makis remained silent, their abdication of any close concern lending support to the official picture that it was a dispute between the tribes Nagamidzuha and Gehamo and therefore reflected traditional enmities. Following a familiar pattern, the case supporting the Ozahadzuha man rested largely on oral histories, going back several decades, of who had used the land and when the boundary had been "marked" (that is, the circumstances under which it had been established).

Outside these public discussions, however, the heirs of Makis interpreted the actions of the Ozahadzuha in starting gardens on the land as another example of designs on their patrimony. They also said privately that the land belonged to Makis and that its use by Ozahadzuha was a basic usurpation of their overriding rights. It also transpired that the Gehamo litigants were secretly supporting them in protesting the trespass. The secret facts are as follows.

Two very close agnates of Makis had been adopted in infancy and reared in Gehamo. Their biological parentage was one of the "screaming secrets" typical of all adoptions, known to those with whom they lived and to their true patrilineal kin though not necessarily to every person to whom they were connected. It would not be referred to openly unless they revealed it for personal reasons of advantage or, far less likely, because members of their adoptive group wished to force them out. Their submerged rights to the patrimony of Guminadzuha were threatened by the trespass, as well as those of their secret clansmen in Susuroka, and they could count on the support of the Gehamo because they had been nurtured there and because of that tribe's traditional enmity with Nagamidzuha. The heirs of Makis living in Susuroka could not muster the support necessary to protest the trespass forcibly or even openly on their own behalf and it did not serve their present ends to widen the existing rift with Ozahadzuha and place themselves in greater isolation. Moreover, the secret clansmen had let them know of their intention to return and publicly reclaim their membership, and the patrimonial rights associated with it, when the death of their adoptive parents released them from obligations based on nurturance.

These were the principal undercurrents in the dispute, though the privacy of information therein does not permit me to deal with them in greater and more personal detail. It turned out that I could have verified one portion of the oral history if I had been asked to do so. Unable to reach any kind of decision when they heard the case at the boundary, the Village Court officials referred it to the higher judicial level of the District Court in Goroka, performing a Pilate-like washing of their hands. At the first hearing in the District Court, the magistrates produced and read from old documents stating I had been present and had walked along the boundary when it had been marked in favor of Makis by the then-assistant district officer. This had been in 1950. The villagers had forgotten it and were astonished at hearing my name in court, calling out: "That *lapun* (old man or elder) is back with us now. Ask him about it." I had also forgotten it, not even recognizing it as the same piece of land when I attended the hearing held at the site by the Village Court. I was not called as a witness, however. The District Court continued the case and it had not been resolved by the time I left.

There was so much that was secret that the proceedings I observed seemed to belong to the genre of the absurd with the various participants apparently bending their efforts to bring a decision in one direction while also hoping and working for its opposite; and although he did not disqualify himself, the Guminakudzuha member of the Village Court (whose rights and group interests were being served by the Gehamo) could not speak on behalf of his fellow clansmen but had to behave as though the Ozahadzuha litigants' presentation represented the position of all the ridge clans. The easiest way out for him and his fellow Court officers was to pass the matter on to a higher and more authoritative level.

People forecast there would be violence when the Village Court held its hearing at the disputed boundary, and they went to it armed with an arsenal of weapons (axes, tomahawks, bush knives, and bows and arrows) which they concealed close at hand in the long grasses. This was fairly typical Gahuku behavior as I remembered it, for they always went to disputes with a maximum show of potential force, but it is possible that recourse to self-help (though always an ultimate threat) is a little more common now than it was in the days when the judicial institutions were the instruments of an imposed colonial administration. If this is so, I offer the speculation that in those times court decisions, though by no means always well informed, emanated from an external authority buttressed by the mystique of virtually unassailable power. Though I think they often tried to do so, these authorities could not be aware of the manifold strands of loyalties, oppositions, and resulting competition that reflected the current state of affairs. Western justice assumes the existence of absolutes. Though it considers extenuating circumstances in assessing degrees of guilt and penalties, it operates with an ideology of fixed rules. Gahuku generally did not, despite my remark that they made no real distinction between manslaughter and homicide. Almost all deaths were homicide from the perspective of the groups sustaining them but not from the perspective of those to which the alleged perpetrators belonged, for there were no *absolute* rules, and in the colonial experience the imposition of Western ideology (often with the best of intentions) resulted in an artificial rigidity that obscured fluctuating, though not random, processes.

It seems to me that the difficulty reaches major proportions at the local level of the Village Courts, where the legitimacy of the authority of the Court's officers is not taken too seriously, particularly since Gahuku traditionally gave no individual the right to impose binding decisions, or the instruments for enforcing them, on any group. The difficulties of the Village Court officers are also exacerbated because they are elected by popular vote. To preserve their position they must often walk a tightrope between divided loyalties which inhibit decisions. The net result is that they must frequently disqualify themselves by passing a case to a higher and more authoritarian level, and this amounts to doing nothing.

This was the action taken by the Village Court in the land dispute. It was inevitable and therefore hardly remarkable. Similarly, the threatened force, being customary, is less interesting than the unstated question: "Who will support whom?"

In private situations (in my yard or kitchen), I heard women upbraiding and urging men of Guminakudzuha to carry their weapons to the hearing and to use them. This was *not* usual behavior, but I did not know at first who they were urging the men to fight, assuming that since they belonged to one of the ridge clans their fierceness was directed against Gehamo. Not so. Their anger focused on the Ozahadzuha man and his supporters, and they were urging the Guminakudzuha to back up their "secret" supporters in Gehamo. I think it was extremely unlikely that the men would have come out into the open as the women urged. They could not act until the Guminakudzuha who had been adopted were ready to reassert their patrilineal membership in the group of Makis, but this time was eagerly anticipated because of the extra "strength" it would provide in opposing the clan they held responsible for most of their misfortunes.

The Ozahadzuha man has not been able to take the place of Makis. There is no one within the ridge clans or the whole of Nagamidzuha who has the influence he had, no big man. The failure of the Ozahadzuha man to fill the vacuum, and the animosities generated by his attempt to do so, surely reflect the flaws in his character I mentioned earlier, and these flaws are probably partly responsible for two personal tragedies. In 1950 he had a small son to whom he was extravagantly attached, and it was a screaming secret that neither he nor his wife were the boy's biological parents. Some time after the death of Makis, this boy (grown to young manhood and with children of his own) publicly repudiated his adoptive parents and left, never to return. This was a severe blow to the Ozahadzuha man's self-esteem. It is said he was so ashamed that he refused food for two weeks and was sent to the Goroka Base Hospital, where his physical condition was diagnosed as an ulcer. About the same time his own brother, who was the son's real father, quarreled with him and left. He has a house in Susuroka (not far from Makis' house), but lives mostly at Gama and does not interest himself in any of the affairs of Ozahadzuha or the other ridge clans. The minimal connections he keeps alive are with the clan of Makis rather than Ozahadzuha.

4 Makis was never far from my mind during my return visits, but he was particularly close during the final days of both of them. The only visible reminders of him were his ceremonial necklace of white cowries hanging on the kitchen wall, and his grave, which was no more than ten yards from where I slept each night and only several feet from the veranda of the house where I sat in the mornings and the afternoons. His children and his wives were there in the village. One of his daughters shared the house, and his son spent part of every day with me; yet I had never set eyes on the son before, and the daughter had been only a little over a year old in 1952, beginning to talk but still a naked little child. I had known his wives as well as I knew any other adult women, and this does not mean I knew them very well; it was not possible for men (particularly outsiders) to interact freely with women, and even Gahuku men had only a partial view of them. There were also many other people who had been there in the past, who could recall with me almost innumerable episodes in which I had been involved with Makis. Sharing these recollections quickened my memory of him until I sometimes expected him to appear silently in my room, emerging with a marvelous physical solidity into the circle of light cast by my lamp, all the planes of his chest, his face, his abdomen and thighs chiseled from black and shining marble, his lips lifted upward with the natural pride of an aristocracy owing nothing to the accidents of birth, and his eyes holding mine with the implications of at least a partial understanding neither of us could express in words.

I am not exaggerating this dimension of our relationship. I suppose that all anthropologists have found and feel a particular indebtedness to someone among the populations they have studied and lived with, but my relationship to Makis went far beyond the simple recognition of indebtedness to those who have helped you and that authors usually mention in the final paragraph of prefaces to books.

I don't think this was ever expressed unequivocally by either of us, and I don't think his survivors remember him in the same way that I do. Perhaps they cannot do so, for the relationship I refer to transcends mere acceptance into groups other than your own. It involves a mutual concern to give recognition to the *person* of the other, and though discovering the person of others is always a hazardous endeavor, it is far more difficult to do so across the boundaries of culture. "Understanding," in the broadest glossing of the word, has no necessary connection to it. This is so in the sense that my training (and that of all professions concerned with human subjects) should have led me both to seek and to acquire an understanding of the diversity of cultures and of the values and ends that propel people forward in any one of them, of the institutions through which they gain them, and of the beliefs that color all their effort.

I do not say the special understanding I had with Makis is a prerequisite of the search for understanding on which all anthropologists are engaged. It is probably rather rare, and therefore the more vividly cherished when it occurs; and unfortunately there is no simple word for it. How can I convey without degenerating into sentimentality that the mutual quality in my relationship to Makis is more like a vibration than a firmly stated theme? It was there whenever I was with him but I cannot say precisely when it began, for it seemed to grow from nowhere, rising only gradually to the level of recognition. Perhaps this happened one evening about six months after our first meeting in Susuroka, an occasion described in *The High Valley* which I will reproduce here because it was written at a time when the experience was closer to me.

It was the perfect time of day when the sky assumed the color of a milky emerald and the thatched houses, rising from a bar of shadows, were a boy's dream of some barbaric encampment. All along the village street families were gathered near the steaming ovens, and strident voices screamed imprecations at pigs whose greed drove them to anticipate their share of the evening meal. Sitting near the door of his house, I was watching Makis distributing the food from his ovens, taking out the bundles of grubby sweet potatoes and yams, and the corn wrapped in its tender green husks. When all had been removed, he placed a portion of each variety on the sections of banana leaf that served as plates, naming the completed piles for individual members of his household. This duty done, he did not follow his usual practice of joining the rest of his family, but picking up his bow and arrows he turned abruptly and walked down the path leading away from the settlement. Something in his manner held my attention, and I rose to follow him.

Catching up with him at a point where the path seemed to turn in the air above the valley, I called his name and asked him where he was going. Though I was no more than a pace or two behind him, he gave no sign of recognition. I was vaguely disturbed, wondering if I had offended him, and I kept the short distance between us as he turned aside from the path and stood among the tall grasses. His profile was silhouetted against the green question of the sky as he fitted an arrow to his bow, drew the string with slow deliberation, and released it into the gathering dusk. Then his body relaxed, and when he turned to me his eyes held a quietness I had not seen before.

Walking back with him, I was aware of the sudden freedom, the effortless release that arrives so unexpectedly at certain turning points on the path to understanding others. There was no need for an explanation, and it would have been difficult for him to try. But he seemed to want to talk, and somehow he made me know that there are times when a man is so oppressed by a heaviness of spirit that it is good for him to be alone and to shoot his arrows at the air. He, too, was familiar with the disenchantment that settles on us unawares in a crowded existence, with the untutored pause the mind seems to take while it lets the world recede and shows us to ourselves poised on the edge of the abyss.

The vibration that made its presence known on that occasion did not subside or go away; rather, it became omnipresent, whether I was alone with and learning from him or watching him from a distance as he performed his public roles. I did not like some of the things in which he was involved. On one occasion I was angered by his seemingly harsh if not brutal treatment of one of his wives and would not speak to him for several days, and I was upset by his eager participation in the shattering rites of initiation, which included vindictive assaults on the persons of boys and youths who were being transformed into men. Indeed, almost everything fostered and subsumed by the Gahuku concept of strength was alien to my own temperament, being in many ways an approximation of the very ideologies that caused me considerable suffering when I was young, and which I had rejected and refused to internalize. But in the long run, the manner in which the Gahuku values were tempered by his sensitivity provided ground on which we could meet. He had the rather rare ability to place himself at a distance from the stream of the life in which he was immersed. This may happen on occasion with other people, when, instead of becoming bored by repeated questioning, something said seems momentarily to release a shutter that has hidden a dimension of customary behavior they had not known existed. But they seldom pursue the unwanted vision, whereas with Makis it was a faculty that was almost always present. In some ways it is an uneasy gift, for it opens new perspectives on the social and cultural forces shaping the life of every individual and the life to which they must perforce return. This, I think, was what Makis communicated to me on that evening so long ago when he stood among the grasses above the valley and released his arrow at the watching sky, pausing there for a brief moment before turning to reenter the crowded life of the village with its peaks illuminated by the bright and violent colors of ambition, and whose dominant hues were so contrastive and assertive that the more gentle passages often seemed to be obscured by a lurid glare.

I am sure it was this quality that had sustained his career from its beginning, a quality, too, that had enabled him to ride through the eye of the storm generated by the entry of my own people on to the stage of Gahuku life in the 1930s. He had maintained his position until his death; his unfinished house and his grave are testimonies to this. The latter is surely the only one of its kind in the entire valley, not excluding the manicured cemeteries within the boundaries of Goroka. A concrete vault set in the ground, its top a rectangular slab rising several inches above the earth, it lies inside a hedge of dracaena and is shaded by immense gum trees whose trunks and upper branches are festooned with bougainvillea. Outside the hedge, my ancient lilies poke through the soil, and against the trunks of the gum trees a simple slab of wood carries in crude white lettering the legend: "Makis, Feb 11, 1969." Two more simple graves, merely mounds of earth outlined with empty bottles and marked by wooden Christian crosses flank it; but the kinsmen of Makis dispute their right to be there. When tourists come to see his village and to view his burial place they invariably ask who lies in these two graves, and his kinsmen shrug and say, "We don't know." They do know, of course. They are the graves of a child of the adopted son of the Ozahadzuha man (the son who eventually repudiated his adoptive parents) and a wife of the brother who quarreled with him and left to live at Gama. The kinsmen of Makis regard their presence and their Christian crosses as one more attempt by the Ozahadzuha to trample on their rights, but they did not protest, and feigning ignorance is their only way of expressing disaffection. When justifying their passive acquiescence in everything that has befallen them, they say, "We are a small group. We keep to ourselves in Susuroka; we listen, that is all." But their hostility (veiled by public politeness) is expressed privately almost every day, and they look forward to something that may change their situation: the return of their lost kinsmen from Gehamo, or the death of the Ozahadzuha man. When he was reported to be refusing food again, a daughter of Makis remarked, "That's good! I hope he dies, then we may all come together again. He's responsible for everything."

During my last days in Susuroka, I often sat alone on the veranda of Makis' house looking at the spent flowers of bougainvillea drifting round his grave. A breeze ruffled them, piled them together, then scattered them in shifting patterns—a metaphor for what has happened to the people who are almost an intrinsic part of me. I felt most deeply for the changes that touched Makis, but these were only the most personally significant. There were many others, some worse and some better from my point of view, and many of these, too, will divide and reassemble like the magenta blooms on the bare earth of his memorial.

THREE

SCENES FROM A CHANGING WORLD

<table>
<tr><td>1</td></tr>
</table>

The back-and-forth swing of personal and group relationships was experienced by every generation of Gahuku. Colleagues whose work is chronologically later than my own have reported similar fluctuations in other cultures of the Highlands of Papua New Guinea. These people, it seems (and it is certainly true of the Gahuku-Gama), were not locked into a timeless frame of reference. Theirs was not some mythic "dream-time," in which the features of the landscape, as well as social groups and the institutions by which people live were established once and for all, the present being simply the drumbeat of the past, the future a mere repetition of the same invariant rhythm. It is not that the Gahuku lacked any moorings. Patrilineal descent and patrimony were fundamental ideological lines of attachment, yet they were not taut. They slackened or tightened in counterpoint to changing tides, and in some instances were severed by the pull of competing forces.

Because some of the most important works in anthropology focus on the symbolism and function of myths, we are probably disposed to assign myth a central place in all cultures. Consistent with my own training in the functional schools of Malinowski and Radcliffe-Brown, I searched, almost desperately, for the mythic charters that justified the forms of Gahuku relationships; when I was frustrated, I felt it must be because of my own inadequacies in fieldwork. I tried every ruse I could think of to press the magic button to release the flood of information that *must* be there; for example, translating and recounting for the benefit of captive listeners myths from the Trobriand Islands and other parts of Melanesia, exercises that generally produced polite comments on the order of: "Well, that's interesting, but we have nothing like that." Sometimes, someone would say, "Oh, yes, there's a man 'over there' who talks about that sort of thing. Perhaps you ought to go and see him." And I would go, spending most of a day getting there, only to be met with blank looks and polite tolerance for my peculiar interests. Gradually, I began to feel that sending me so far afield was simply a way of dealing with someone whose peculiar obsession had become a bore.

I abandoned the attempt to find dogmatic charters for all critical institutions and relationships, allowing them (where they existed) to emerge gradually. Gahuku had no systematic cosmological beliefs. They had some stories about how things began, about some mythic heroes (unnamed) who discovered the techniques of gardening and pig husbandry and passed them on to benefit mankind. And there were some mythic supports for the forms of some relationships, particularly those between male and female. But these characteristically included a recognition of dynamic oppositions where the facade of ascendancy and the ideal of stability were erected on unstable sands.

I do not think the Gahuku had a closed perspective of their social universe. It was a parochial universe, in the sense that it was isolated from centuries of recorded change that are part of the historical experience of some other people, but within its own parochial boundaries it was a world of flux and movement in which individuals and groups sought the main chance to advance their personal ambitions and group interests. Even the supernatural power on which the accomplishments of men depended was not subsumed by codified and dogmatic charters of belief and faith. This power (or force of life) did indeed inform everything and, to a far greater degree than with us, was palpably manifest in the vines growing in a garden and the trees and grasses of the landscape, as it was also manifest in the differential accomplishments of individuals and groups. This is what I meant when I said so long ago that I would not be able to see precisely what another man saw as I sat beside him in the sunlight in his garden, looking at the rows of sweet potatoes, corn, and other produce. For he could see in them, in the entire processes of growth, a mystery that was present to his senses every day, a vibration we feel and reach for but which may escape us, for there is no sure way of knowing it or tuning in to it such that you can be certain it is under your control. Ultimately unknowable, there are thus many possibilities in approaching it, and success measures the efficacy of possible alternatives.

Gahuku were pragmatists, looking for the best advantage within the boundaries of their own sociocultural universe, qualities that should recommend them to other cultures in which individual perceptions of the main chance and achievements reflecting the "right" (and sometimes opportunistic) choice are admired. And these are qualities that influenced their reaction to the sudden breaching of their universe by the arrival of my own people.

A long while ago, even before matters had progressed to their present point, I suggested they would have little difficulty in accepting and incorporating into their perspective the changes being brought to them. I suggested that those who succeeded under the changed social and economic circumstances would not be a new breed but, rather, men (and women) who would have succeeded under the old conditions: those who saw where the best advantage lay, and set out to use it to achieve and support positions characteristically based on such foresight and a talent for manipulation. I did not see any inherent clash in the confrontation of one culture with another, such that those whose lives had been invaded felt they had to protect and maintain something that was pure from contamination. They may have had (and still retain) some resentment for the superior and subordinate aspects of relationships within the imposed colonial order, but they did not perceive it as threatening inviolate traditions that had to be preserved at all cost. They were (as I shall try to show at a later stage of my narrative) prepared to abandon, without significant pressure, ideas and institutions that may have been designated critical by anyone observing them at some previous point in the chronicle of their lives.

The changes introduced by Europeans were of a different order than anything experienced by the Gahuku over a long period of their unrecorded history, different both in kind and in magnitude from the internal alterations and fluctuations in relationships referred to above (though James Watson for one has suggested that the introduction of the sweet potato into the Kainantu region about four hundred years ago had radical effects on the preexisting patterns of subsistence and forms of social organization). But Gahuku accepted and began to incorporate them very rapidly (as did other Highland people), giving the lie to the popular tendency to view such lost tribal groups as particularly vulnerable to the rude shattering of the chrysallis of tradition and inevitably thrown into disarray by it.

Gahuku were *not* thrown into disarray, nor did they resist. Very early in the process they set their sights on acquiring the material elements of the alien culture, but they also showed a willingness to try out or experiment with new garden produce, sometimes collecting seeds from the kitchen refuse of government households and planting them to see what would happen. They tried passion fruit at a time (1951) when some whites believed it might have a commercial future. And when coffee was only in the testing and experimental stage, numbers of Nagamidzuha men had a few small trees in their gardens, which they always took me to see, not really knowing their possible value or their uses. Similarly, they found decorative uses (that often amused Europeans) for such mundane things as labels from jam and soup cans and cigarette packages. They were also able, more or less deliberately, to abandon altogether or make changes in some basic institutions.

This kind of openness or receptivity does not represent anything like a revolutionary about-face, or anything as dramatic as a shattering conversion, but reflects their native pragmatism and a degree of openness characteristic of their traditional societies, which were closed only because their total universe had limited boundaries of knowledge and experience. But even within these boundaries, Gahuku recognized there were other ways of doing things, other ideas and other beliefs concerning the same phenomena. They did not necessarily dismiss these as error as, for example, Christians—convinced of their monopolistic hold on truth—regarded Gahuku beliefs and many of their institutions.

Gahuku, like all people, were ethnocentric up to a point. Those outside the range of their sociocultural system were "not the same as us"; and the farther one moved away from the center, the more outlandish the characterizations of other people, until zones were reached that resembled the blank areas on maps that early cartographers filled with humanoid, animal, and vegetable monsters.

This zone began not more than twenty miles from the ridge of Susuroka, just beyond the mountains to the south, west and north; in the east, it commenced before reaching Kainantu. Closer to home, the Nagamidzuha, who were almost in the center of the Gahuku-Gama, had some direct contacts with people in the foothills of the mountains across the Asaro River and in the nearer areas of Bena Bena. Though these people spoke different languages, their cultures were similar to that of the Gahuku with, however, a few variations in detail sufficient to make them "different," elements that could endanger Gahuku who came in contact with them. For example, in Heuve—in the foothills to the west—the *gerua* boards (ceremonial objects worn on the heads of men) could cause illness to Gahuku. When I went to a ceremony at Heuve with a party of Nagamidzuha, I was warned I must not allow any man wearing a *gerua* to stand or walk behind me: this could make me ill. And there were a few instances where illness and death were attributed to a man having slept inadvertently in a Bena Bena man's house. Yet Gahuku did not perceive any of these differences as aberrations of human nature; other people did things differently, that is all. They were not to be blamed and far less corrected because their ideologies and some of their customs were not the same as those of the Gahuku. That they were different simply evidenced the existence of alternatives.

Gahuku also imported some essentials from elsewhere. Virtually all valuables originated outside their grassland habitat: shells, bird of paradise plumes, opossum fur and even the bamboo from which the sacred *nama* flutes were made. Salt came from the western mountains or from some springs in the Bena Bena region. On occasion, because they liked it, some men wore the Bena Bena style of male costuming.

These essentials reached them over extended trade routes. There was no direct contact between people at the extremes or along the midpoints of these routes, however. Trading partners who met face-to-face were not separated by any great distance; and for the vast majority of Gahuku the known world, the world seen for one's self, was little more than the area contained within the circumference of a circle having a radius of about ten miles from one's place of birth. Even within this world there were regions where it was not safe to go. The areas mapped by personal ties were much smaller.

Yet I do not think Gahuku were inexorably bound by tradition or adamantly protective of it. It was not conceived as being absolute, such that departures from it would inevitably wreak irreparable havoc. Dogmatic faith did not interpose an inpenetrable shield between realities as they were perceived in the Gahuku universe and the ways in which others may have perceived them, and when coupled with their pragmatism and basically materialistic interests and concern for the most advantageous line of action, it was a fertile and receptive climate for many of the things associated with whites, if not always receptive of their persons.

I don't think Gahuku could have been characterized as "philosophers." They were not overly concerned with abstractions or speculation or debating the finer points of the reasons why it was a rule to do this rather than that, why the rule existed. Yet this does not imply that they were therefore slaves to custom, their lives unthinkingly committed to a single course. Far from subtracting from them qualities of self-consciousness and self-reflection, it simply suggests that these qualities, which some men (and women, too) possessed to a remarkable degree, were employed for ends other than those in which we tend to think (and to hope) they are most plainly demonstrated. And as I have suggested, the leitmotiv of Gahuku culture sounds a loud chord of recognition, for I have often been tempted to conclude they had independently discovered the Protestant ethic.

Unfortunately, I have very little information from any Gahuku on their reaction to the sudden appearance of whites in the Asaro valley. It had been only about eighteen years before my arrival and there were many living men who had been present at the time or who had their first view and experience of whites only several years thereafter. Failure to collect this available information must be considered regrettable; my inadequate excuse is that I was not much interested at the time. Accounts of the expedition (led by the Leahy brothers—James, Michael and Danny—and James Taylor) that moved from Bena Bena through the Asaro and westward to the Wahgi Valley are available from the white side, but there is almost nothing presenting it from the point of view of the native populations, a single perspective characteristic of not only this but of all other subsequent explorations in the Highlands, even those conducted during my time. Some Gahuku (including the Ozahadzuha man, the rival of Makis) are alive and able to remember something of the period. I have heard them recounting to members of younger generations some of their astonishment when they first encountered whites and the material possessions they brought with them, and in 1950, both within and outside the Asaro Valley, I was personally exposed to similar curiosity. Even in that relatively sophisticated time, I was the first white person many people had seen or been able to touch—with whom they could sit down and talk, and whom they could ask to take off portions of his clothing (particularly shoes and socks) to see what was underneath. Because of my extremely fair skin and (at the time) red hair, these revelations were possibly particularly startling and, on the whole, I think produced not admiration but queasy distaste. In particular, the softness of my feet when removed from their protecting shoes brought reactions that were close to revulsion. Nowadays when old men, who surely will not live much longer, recall their own reactions to their first contacts with whites (and they are rare occasions) they tend to cast themselves in the role of the naive bumpkin, the country cousin, and present themselves in a light that reflects humorously and disparagingly on themselves.

As far as I know, the first white expedition did not pass through the territory of the Nagamidzuha, skirting it by way of Asarodzuha in its progress to the west and into the Chimbu

Valley. But the first government station, from which administrative control extended outward, was established nearby at Humeleveka, which meant that from the beginning the Nagamidzuha received not only a fairly clear perception of what was demanded of them under the new order but also of what might be useful to them. There is no reliable evidence of any opposition, even though in recording genealogical data the roster of the dead includes a rare notation—"killed by white men" (Gahuku: *gorohave*)—among the far more numerous deaths, from the same time, reported as "killed by Uheto" and so on. The former, as I recall, were mentioned in precisely the same matter-of-fact way as any of the others.

Despite its closeness to them, this period was already a completed segment of the motion picture of Gahuku life in 1950, unreeled onto the spool of their history; and the life I observed then, just as the life observed today, represented different stages of transition. Yet the advent of whites and what they brought with them is beyond question the most important externally generated source of change occurring in century upon century of Gahuku experience. It is therefore rather remarkable that even when it was much closer to them, Gahuku did not attach to it quite the same apocalyptic significance that our own ethnocentric disposition tends to persuade us it must have had.

Sometimes the reports from the white side of reactions to their appearance on the local scene may be tainted by a possibly understandable bent to see themselves, the intrepid "discoverers," as they thought others might have seen them: perhaps, because of their unheralded arrival and the novelty of their possessions, as deities or dead ancestors returned to their living descendants. So they may have misinterpreted some of the ways in which they were greeted. This is a commonly cited ingredient of "cargo cults" (millenarian movements) in many parts of Melanesia, but it is an oversimplified causal explanation, and in any case, there are no thoroughly authenticated or observed examples of such movements in the Highlands of Papua New Guinea. In some instances there are reports from both sides that people did suspect initially that the whites could be supernaturals, possibly the spirits of deceased kinsmen. In fact, I have heard some Gahuku say this was what they thought when they saw the first whites. But it was not a universal supposition; some people also surmised that the strangers must be "devils." In 1982, for example, I was sitting with a group of men who were laughing at an anecdote recounted by the Ozahadzuha man. He told how a woman (who is dead now) was clearing a patch of land for a new garden near the stream that separates the Nagamidzuha ridge from Asarodzuha, when the first white party mentioned above passed through that settlement. Using the customary means of communicating over distances, some agitated people from Asarodzuha called out in the direction of Nagamidzuha: "Oh, oh! All kinds of 'devils' are coming in your direction!" The terrified woman, not knowing how to escape, ran about in all directions, stumbling and falling, scattering the sweet potatoes she had dug earlier, and eventually remaining hidden in the kunai until long after nightfall.

It sometimes seems to me that whites are disposed to give too much store to these kinds of immediate reactions. After all, they are hardly more fanciful than many explanations advanced for strange phenomena in our own culture, and in any case, there is no evidence that they persisted for any length of time. The possibility, for example, that some people in the Chimbu area may have thought the whites were supernaturals (relatives returned from the dead) did not inhibit a few attacks on whites quite soon thereafter by other people. And, finally, my personal observations of first contact situations support my opinion that the attribution of supernatural characteristics and origin to whites, by some people, has been exaggerated and did not have the consequences that are sometimes extrapolated from it.

These personal observations are again one-sided, for I could not speak to or question the people concerned. But they may be worth recounting, since extremely few members of my profession have been there at the very first intrusion of whites, before any of the tentacles of government had touched them, when there were absolutely no visible signs of a different cultural presence, and its representatives were at best no more than vaguely rumored. The people I saw under these conditions were not Gahuku, but perhaps it is possible to extrapolate from the experience a little of the content of their similar confrontation less than a generation earlier.

2 The entire Asaro Valley had been pacified by 1950, though the alliances and reciprocal debts associated with warfare were still of major importance in ceremonial exchanges and other aspects of intergroup and interpersonal relationships. But not very far within the mountains to the south of Susuroka, there were people who were unaware of the pax Australiana and who had had no contact with any of its representatives or enforcers. There were air maps, dating from World War II, of this part of the country, but whites had not explored it overland and had no knowledge of what was on the ground, apart from the location of major rivers and mountains. Patrols set out more or less routinely from Goroka or the isolated patrol post at Henganofi

to map the terrain and to extend the authority of the central government.

The processes of extending government control did not proceed all at once. Beyond the Asaro Valley there was an area which was already pacified but whose people were not as familiar with the government's intentions and demands as the valley tribes. At intervals throughout this area government "rest houses" were maintained in a number of villages for the use of patrol officers when making tours of inspection. Christian missions also operated here. Farther out, there was another zone in a different and more recent stage of contact. Often the only representative of government was an experienced noncommissioned officer of the native police, headquartered in a village whose people had agreed to accept him. He had no official authority, did not speak any of the local languages and, except for his color, was as alien as any white person. He was expected to represent the new order of things, however, showing by example and counsel something of the future opening for the relatively new people with whom he lived. Beyond this intermediate zone, there were uncontacted and uncontrolled areas.

I should emphasize that the patrol I accompanied into the uncontrolled zone (as an unofficial member) bore no resemblance to the far larger Leahy-Taylor expedition through the Highlands in the thirties, but it was the same as many others, led by the assistant district officer (the late Dudley Young-Whitforde) and a young cadet patrol officer on his first tour of duty. In addition to an armed detachment of native police (about fourteen in number), there were about thirty carriers to transport tents, bedding, food, trade goods, and other necessities. We were not in communication with Goroka during the three weeks of the patrol.

I was with the patrol at the invitation of Young-Whitforde and with the permission of the district commissioner, the late George Greathead. I was staying with the Young-Whitfordes at Humeleveka at the time, waiting for the Nagamidzuha to build my thatched house at Susuroka, and Young-Whitforde suggested I might go with him, since I could not move permanently to Susuroka until the house was finished. He also told me he was inviting Makis. When I went to Susuroka to see how my house was progressing, I told Makis I had been invited. I gathered he had not decided (and he could have refused the invitation), but he said that if I went he would come to look after me, and I was frequently grateful for his help during the subsequent weeks we were together. His position, though he received a token cash remuneration from the government, was also unofficial. He had no duties other than to be there and observe, and, of course, he was as ignorant of where we were going and what we might see as any other member of the party. Indeed, for those who were native born it was, in a sense, a more hazardous journey. The whites knew they weren't stepping off the edge of the world, but the others (with the possible exception of the native police) were going into areas colored by folklore or which were completely blank, far outside the boundaries of their universe. As we progressed into this unknown, they surely recognized more that was familiar to them than we did. The observable features of the lives of the people must have contained recognizable themes, but despite this they were as alien and possibly just as unwelcome as the whites, and some of the dangers they perceived were more "real" since they were part of their own traditional attitudes toward strangers.

My own motives for joining the patrol were mixed. On the one hand, I knew I had been offered an unusual opportunity to observe a stage in the process of extending government control that not many anthropologists had witnessed, one that had generally receded into the past by the time they arrived on the scene. In the previous six years, I had also taught both senior and cadet officers of the Australian colonial administration as a junior member of the faculty of the Australian Army School of Civil Affairs and, later, the civilian School of Pacific Administration. My first tentative essay at fieldwork had been when I was an enlisted member of the Australian Imperial Forces in the lowland Markham Valley of New Guinea from 1944 to 1945, a time when Australian and American forces had only recently completed their offensive against the occupying Japanese invaders. Though I do not wish to imply it was the general attitude, some of those whom I taught were experienced and seasoned officials whose careers in the colonial administration went back to a time when the Australian equivalent of high school was not very far behind me, and I don't blame them for being skeptical of my qualifications to instruct them. Some had also distinguished themselves in the difficult period when the advancing Japanese had left the Allies with few footholds in Papua New Guinea and civilian government had been suspended.

Against this background, I must have seemed a naive juvenile to some, a perception possibly exacerbated in the army period by differences in rank, for all of them were commissioned officers and I was a corporal. But both before and after the war, the "old hands," whether civilian or government officials, were sometimes disposed to regard anthropologists with suspicion, their attitudes reflecting the common tendency to assume that those who have been there longer necessarily know more than newcomers: "How can *they* presume to teach us anything when we've lived the better part of a lifetime here and they come in for a year or so, then leave?"

This attitude ignores the caste system of colonial relationships. Their contention that they knew the native mind was based upon limited social contacts in which they did not question the assumption of their superiority, and conventions of interaction were mostly calculated to preserve it.

I do not mind recognizing that in some ways I saw my participation in the patrol as an admission card to a club whose members could not blackball me thereafter because I did not qualify on at least one important (and relatively rare) item on their questionnaire. But against this, I had to place my private assessment of my physical capabilities and my temperamental distaste for any military or quasi-military enterprise. Even during wartime in the Markham Valley I had been alone, in many respects even more alone than during my entire stay in Susuroka. In my ten months in the Markham I saw, on three brief occasions, only one other white person, and although I was a member of the Australian army, I was not armed and could have done nothing to defend myself. It was not necessary, and I don't think the possibility ever crossed my mind, even though the people (the Ngarawapum) with whom I lived did not want me at first, and despite the presence of the war in the flights of American bombers that passed overhead and local reports of Japanese stragglers in the Finisterre Mountains above where I lived. The Ngarawapum became the only protection I ever considered necessary. But I don't like the bluster and assertiveness of anything military. The ways in which self-reliance are generally thought to be demonstrated are not those by which I have measured it to my personal satisfaction, so this had led me to question such ways. Yet, of course, such self-reliance exercises a compelling attraction, if for no other reason than showing others you can do what they have decided you are incapable of doing and then leave it to pursue things that are more congenial.

Given the fact that this patrol was a minor and localized example of a genre, I may seem to be inflating its significance within the framework of these personal dialectics. Yet my decision to accept the invitation is unquestionably related to them and was not simply determined by anything I might have hoped to gain that would be of value to members of my profession or might advance my standing within it. I did not, in fact, anticipate I would return with much that might be valuable for furthering either of these ends, and I returned with even less than my most optimistic expectations had included.

After the first day, when we left Goroka later than the main party and were taken by jeep to meet them at the Bena Bena River, we were on the move for about ten hours every day except Sundays, breaking camp about six in the morning and stopping around about four in the afternoon, with a few brief rest periods in between. After leaving Bena Bena, it was arduous travel. There was almost no level terrain. We climbed up and down interminable mountain spurs and ridges over rudimentary tracks or, in the uncontacted and more remote areas, no preexisting paths at all. For the first two nights we slept in government rest houses, but there were none thereafter until we reached Lufa on the return journey to Goroka. When we stopped in the afternoon, tents were erected for the white members of the party, for the goods we carried, and for the native police. The carriers bedded down in lean-tos constructed on the spot from saplings and grass. I was mostly so concerned with the necessity to endure that I did not have much time to notice anything except where

I was going to place my feet in the tangle of roots, rocks and slippery soil. Since I have no head for heights, the occasions when we had to cross small ravines on the mossy trunks of fallen trees were particularly taxing. Yet, when I was not reduced to the undignified mode of straddling them (while everyone else walked across with upright confidence), Makis was there to walk in front of me and give me his guiding and steadying hand, as he was always there to push me from behind when I felt I could not manage the last quarter mile of an ascent to the top of a ridge.

When we halted in the afternoon, I was often too worn out to think of work. Usually I made some attempt, taking a camp stool outside our tent, opening my notebook and interviewing people. Except in the uncontacted areas there was no dearth of volunteers, but the farther we progressed the greater the difficulties of having even minimal verbal communication. We passed through about six different linguistic groups, requiring (if any could be found) almost as many interpreters before reaching pidgin English which, in any case, was known only to the police and a few of the carriers. The opportunities for making any systematic inquiries were nil, and I had to fall back on the little I could gain from observation only.

The journey through the controlled zone was uneventful. When we stopped in the afternoon, Young-Whitforde bought garden produce for the carriers and police and held an informal meeting with the villagers who, forewarned of our approach, had interrupted their work to assemble and listen to anything the government might have to say. Usually, he did little more than ask them if there was any trouble in their villages, and mostly their response was a resounding "no," which, as I knew from earlier experience in the Markham Valley, was not necessarily the case but sometimes merely a form of self-protection against the assumption that the white man would be angered by an indication of internal dissensions. Very rarely, a contentious matter was raised. As a magistrate, Young-Whitforde had the authority to deal with it, but he seldom gave judgment. Instead, he said the government should not be bothered by small disputes, which the people should resolve according to their own custom, an attitude which I think they found not only acceptable but reassuring.

The quality of our reception changed a little when we entered the semicontrolled zone. It was here we met the only display of overt hostility.

Two noncommissioned members of the native police had been stationed in different villages in this area to educate the people in the intentions and expectations of the government they represented. On the afternoon before we left Goroka, word arrived that one of them had been killed by members of the group with whom he lived. This could not be allowed to pass unpunished. The patrol was diverted from its intended route to apprehend the murderers and to bring them back to Goroka.

We arrived near the offending village early on Saturday afternoon and established camp a short distance from it on a level spit of land bordering a shallow stream. The village was out of sight on the other side, situated at the top of a fairly steep bluff which had to be scaled in order to reach it. Young-Whitforde made no attempt to enter it that day. Once the tents were erected, an interpreter was instructed to shout a request to surrender those responsible for the murder, commencing an inconclusive parlay between the camp and the bluff across the stream that continued intermittently until darkness.

There were signs of agitation on the bluff, frequent viewings of armed men among the trees or running across open ground. By the time we went to bed, the villagers had given no indication they were willing to talk or to comply with the surrender order, though we had learned that two men had instigated the attack against the policeman. That night, for the first time, the police detachment mounted guard over the camp, as they continued to do throughout the period when the patrol was in uncontrolled territory.

The parlay continued throughout the next day (Sunday), and armed men continued to appear on the bluff. About midmorning, the three whites and some of the carriers, escorted by police, went to bathe at a protected place in the stream. We were in the water when a shout from one of the sentries sent everyone scrambling in a highly undignified manner for the protection of the bank. Perhaps a dozen arrows flew toward us from the bluff, but all fell harmlessly short of their mark. I suspect that like the Gahuku, our opponents were by no means expert marksmen beyond a fairly close range. In their pitched confrontations they did not level their sights on a particular target but released a fusillade of arrows in the direction of the enemy, anticipating that one would strike home. I did not see Gahuku using their bows in combat, but this was what they told me when I accompanied them to disputes similar to the one described earlier, warning me that I was foolish just to sit there observing. When I replied that no one had any personal quarrel with me, they responded patiently, "Do you think they aim at a particular person? They shoot all over the place, and you won't be able to dodge."

The show of force at the river was not continued. At dusk, a party of men crossed the stream and surrended two of their number as the murderers. I don't know what had persuaded them, but apparently it was not a unanimous decision, for as we prepared to move forward the following morning the armed men were again running agitatedly along the top of the bluff. I imagine we were a fairly easy target as we began to climb it, but nothing happened. They had disappeared when we reached the top, and their village was deserted.

The two prisoners came with us for the remainder of the patrol. They were not restrained in any manner, though they were placed among the police, who were supposed to guard them. Even so, they made a brief attempt to escape later in the day. Quickly recaptured, they did not try again. We were probably well outside their territory by that time, and if they had got away their fate would have been just as uncertain as they may have thought it was with us. They were not tried in Goroka but were detained there until a subsequent patrol could return them to their home, their captivity hopefully providing them with experiences they would report favorably when they rejoined their people.

Recollections of the landscape through which we passed flow into one another in a more or less undifferentiated stream, punctuated here and there by a startling image. I remember vividly the unreal appearance of the village of Gono (Gimi tribal group) which we reached on the afternoon of the first day after our departure from the uncontacted area to return to Goroka.

We had seen the village briefly from our campsite the previous night and had glimpsed it occasionally from the crest of ridges as we progressed toward it the next day. Each of these sightings was breathtaking. A razor-backed ridge extended far out from the wall of mountains, high, poised in empty space like the prow of a ship lifting out of and cleaving the deep seas. The western face was almost sheer, a virtually perpendicular drop to the floor of a valley not yet revealed. The eastern face sloped more gently from the crest at an angle of about forty-five degrees. It was entirely deforested and quilted with gardens which were blindingly bright, yellow and green, against the more somber blues and purples of the ranges. Images of ancient fortresses, of Masada or the walled and towered medieval towns of Tuscany flashed across my mind with every view of Gono, intensified by the knowledge that the whole area through which we had traveled was also accustomed to the toll of incessant warfare, its pageantry and senseless loss.

We had to approach Gono from below, mounting to it by a rudimentary path up the western face of the spur. The ascent was like a nightmare, coming at the end of a day in which we had already climbed and descended some eight similar ridges. People from the village lined the path for the last quarter mile, a gantlet of squatting women and standing men who reached out to touch our legs and arms, a form of greeting which was staged for us almost everywhere in the semi-controlled area, calculated, perhaps, to give a false sense of importance to anyone disposed to interpret it as obeisance to superior beings, and a sharp contrast to the wary reception we received in the uncontrolled and uncontacted zone.

I am not sure how I made it to the crest of Gono, but it was worth it. Standing at the top, not far from the village, and gulping the cold air while every muscle quivered and for a while my eyes seemed unable to focus on anything above the level of my feet, I saw, through a watery blur that cleared and steadied gradually, a vast indigo sea whose waves were capped with wisps of mist and clouds. Shot with jade green as they lifted up and curved toward us, they seemed about to engulf the ridge, obliterating the huddled and insignificant village which was the only visible sign of any human presence in the turbulent sea-wilderness. Far below and in the distance, there was a glimpse of silver which Young-Whitforde identified as the Tua River, but it might have been merely fragments of spray caught in the troughs of the waves. It seemed impossible that there were other people in virtually all the troughs and along the slopes of the waves, people who had been there long before the short span of the recorded history on which we set such store, but the knowledge it was so increased my sense of awe at the mysteries that in one short lifetime you can barely begin to feel, far less comprehend.

For the greater part of our progress through uncontrolled country there was little open terrain, and no views similar to that from Gono. The wide expanse of the Asaro was a distant memory. We were in densely forested country all the way, where small glens were tucked inside the folds of the mountains and it was almost impossible to see any settlements before we reached them, coming upon them through scattered gardens that did not seem to be as intensively or meticulously cultivated as those of the Gahuku and their neighbors. The presence of the forest suggested that hunting was more important here than in the Asaro, where it was almost solely a pastime for novice youths and brought in little more than a few bush rats and small birds. Pigs were also far less numerous and were surely not the cultural focal point they were in the Asaro and all the major valleys west of it.

Settlements were characteristically small and relatively isolated from one another, a fair sized glen containing four or five among the trees on the lower slopes of the ridges. In turn, these local concentrations of people were often separated from others by deep ravines and turbulent streams crossed by suspension bridges constructed from forest canes. Wide enough for only one person at a time, they swayed perilously over rocks and foaming water, and on occasion had been severed deliberately at one end, necessitating a descent to the stream bed to cross to the other side. This was not to delay or prevent our progress, but a sign of either recent or current hostilities between adjacent groups. Palisades of varying height, constructed of roughly hewn timber, protected the villages, and there was other evidence of warfare in an occasional charred and deserted settlement, and once, indicating very recent action, the smoking remnants of a small hamlet which had evidently been under construction when attacked.

The signs of war visible throughout the whole uncontacted area must have reminded the carriers of their own recent past, a past which, as I shall show later, they did not regret. They did not look back on it as a heroic golden age despite the continual references to it in the evidence brought forward at intergroup disputes, and despite its importance in the mesh of obligations to be honored at ceremonial exchanges. We saw no actual fighting, however; indeed, it was impossible to observe or to obtain information on any important elements of the lives we interrupted so abruptly and left behind so rapidly.

Our progress proceeded in this fashion. For the most part, we were passed from one group to another. After an overnight stop in a particular group, Young-Whitforde tried to persuade someone to guide us to the next, and if he would not come all the way, to accompany us to a border where he could shout our request to be allowed to advance to those living in the territory ahead. Though languages changed several times, there were usually bilingual men who could do this, and different languages as well as differences in culture did not necessarily mean a complete absence of contact between the various groups. Within a particular group territory there were well-worn paths and trails we could travel, and sometimes less well known and far more rudimentary tracks connected people on opposite sides of completely uninhabited and heavily forested mountain country. Where they existed, these trails were used infrequently and were often revealed with the greatest reluctance, either because they were possible routes enemies might use or because they were secret, known only to a few trading partners at opposite ends of them. There were stretches of country where even these trails did not exist. Here, we cut our path as we went and camped at night in the forest.

The forest was dense, the canopy of the trees preventing observations of where we were and where we were going. The place was infested with leeches in some areas. We cleared our own viewpoints to take compass readings and to peer into valleys below, looking for signs of habitation: the light green of a man-made garden or perhaps a wisp of smoke rising from the trees on a distant ridge.

We never simply blundered forcefully into an inhabited area; our approach had always been marked long before we reached it. No one was taken by surprise, but their uncertainty showed in the numbers of armed men we could see through our binoculars as we came near. They tried to remain out of sight and gave no sign of their watching and waiting presence, neither shouting challenges nor asking who we were and what we wanted, but we could see them running from tree to tree with their bows and arrows and positioning advance guards in the way of our progress toward them.

At these signs of possible hostility, Young-Whitforde always halted the patrol in a relatively open place. The carriers unshouldered the baggage and sat down beside it. Three folding stools were brought to the head of the column for the whites, Young-Whitforde's positioned a little in front of the other two, so that the cadet and I flanked him. The armed police came forward and formed a semicircle behind him. Boxes of trade goods were placed at his feet. Then we waited.

Whenever it was possible, he instructed a man to shout messages to those whom we knew were watching us, telling them we wanted permission to pass, that we intended no harm, and requesting some of them to come into the open and meet us. We could not hear anything of their subsequent parlay, and they gave no answer indicating either acceptance or rejection of the request, but after some time a small group of men (three or four) usually broke cover and loped toward us. The police sergeant indicated they must halt and lay aside their weapons when they were about thirty paces from us. When they had complied (and they did not seem unwilling to do so), the boxes of trade goods were opened. It is possible they may have heard rumors of the bush knives and steel axes, but I never saw any among the uncontrolled people. The strangers were clearly sufficiently interested to come forward, without their weapons, to receive their gifts and to sit down only a few paces in front of us. They were always relatively young men, probably warriors in their prime, and their eyes were sharp, their demeanor not submissive but alert and watchful, uncertain and perhaps suspicious but nevertheless willing to gamble that we had stated our intentions truthfully. I was never sure if they had agreed to allow us to proceed, and I don't think Young-Whitforde could have been certain, but after allowing them time to examine their gifts he invariably made our intention known by ordering the patrol to its feet and starting to move ahead.

There was no resistance at any time. The men who had remained in hiding came forward and accompanied rather than guided us through gardens until we reached a palisaded settlement. These were always deserted, all the women and children having been sent to the forest, but we did not test our hosts by entering any village. We camped outside the palisades at night.

After dark the women and children usually returned. We could hear their voices (and sometimes their singing) and see the winking cooking fires, but none of them ever appeared in person. It was a womanless and childless country as far as we were concerned, though novice youths (identifiable because their hair style was similar to their Gahuku counterparts) began to appear later among the men, watching from a short distance as we erected tents and lean-tos while cooking details began to prepare our evening meal.

The observers were filled with curiosity and generally heeded warnings that they must not carry their bows and arrows when they came among us. Gradually, some of them began to lend a hand to the carriers and police, helping them to put up the lean-tos and fetching firewood. Even the more wary moved in closely, fascinated by the things they saw and sometimes trying out an axe under the watchful eyes of the carriers and police.

There was one highly embarrassing incident, at least it embarassed Young-Whitforde and shamed the police, and I thought it bordered on farce. After we had set up camp outside a village, Young-Whitforde bought a medium-sized pig. Intended as food for the police and carriers, he decided to demonstrate the power of our rifles by having it shot. The animal was tethered to sapling in front of an expectant audience, the whole patrol gathered on one side, and opposite them stood the villagers, who must have had no idea what the demonstration was intended to prove. Standing no more than twenty paces distant, the police sergeant raised his rifle to his shoulder, fired, and missed. Compounding the shame, he missed a second and a third time. The frightened animal continued to squeal and strain at the end of the tether; the villagers looked puzzled, perhaps wondering whether they were being treated to a peculiar ritual concerned with pigs, and the police and carriers stirred uneasily, doubtlessly feeling the honor of our party had been lost. Disgusted, Young-Whitforde took the rifle from the sergeant, and, holding it like a handgun, shot the animal from a distance of a few feet. It died immediately (without the usual squealing and prolonged staggering that distressed me when I watched Gahuku slaughtering their pigs for a feast), so I suppose some honor was regained, but I don't think the demonstration could have convinced the villagers that this strange weapon was more efficient than their own.

The forest territory was different from anything I had known previously; a green and almost silent world with hardly any birds, wrapped in a twilight where straying motes of sunshine shattered on the upper branches, their fragments sometimes falling to the ground to illuminate the vermilion flowers similar to garden impatiens: branch corals attached to the lower walls of a reef. The carriers from the open grasslands seemed to acquire the form and coloration of the undersea environment, draping their heads with trailing green mosses and moving through the half-light like the shadow image of marine creatures passing the entrance to an underwater cave. Sometimes when we stopped to rest they made strange flutes from bamboo canes and played them in pairs, one flute producing a deep and pulsing beat below an entwining embroidery of shrill cries that seemed to speak of some compulsive quest, of an unsatisfied and mysterious hunger that quickened both players and listeners with an excitement I did not begin to comprehend until many months later, when I heard the same cries winding across the grasslands at Susuroka and was able to relate them to their cultural contact.

I remember the nights when we camped outside villages at the edge of the forest. My tiredness was physical, not mental, and when we went to our canvas hammocks to sleep I was alert to a variety of presences, to the almost inaudible tread of police sentries making their rounds, to a few voices at the edge of sleep in the carrier's quarters, and to the fastening forest itself and to the vibrations of the unknown life behind the rough protection of the wooden palisade not far away. Makis usually came to our tent after we had had our evening meal, and sat below me on the ground. I studied the helmet of his hair, the planes of his face, his deep set and curiously beautiful eyes, dark brown in whites that had a faintly reddish tinge at their corners, and the finely molded straightness of his lips, wondering if I would ever learn anything of what passed through the mind behind them, if I would ever know what moved him from day to day and the moorings of ideas and values that provided him and his people with their particular human harbor; and my uncertainty was assuaged by his close presence and the way he seemed to have already admitted me a short distance into the harbor, with the implied promise that I could go farther.

These feelings subdued my physical tiredness. Layered over it, I felt a quiet confidence almost as secure as the canvas walls of my hammock that swung gently in space, seeming to move to the breath of the invisible presence outside, and I lay awake until my own breathing joined with them.

On one particular night, I left the tent to approach closer to this other presence, wanting to stand within it and to see and hear it without the muffling canvas of the tent—a night that has a particular significance because of the ways in which it became meshed with subsequent experiences and a relationship whose end I did not learn until thirty years later. I have described the night concerned but may be excused, perhaps, for repeating it now, for the description distills the essence of many others and of thoughts that were never far from me during the whole of our passage through the lives of people who had no knowledge of our coming and no way of knowing the legacy we would leave them.

> As I lay on my camp stretcher listening to the movements of the guard outside my tent, through the open canvas flaps I could see a triangle of silver light, for the moon was full; the mists that shrouded these mountain ridges had not descended yet. Except for myself and the police boy standing watch, the whole camp seemed to be asleep, and I felt the gentle tug of smallness, the intimation of mortality projected on an inner vision of the turning and evolving universe. At this precise moment voices rose in song—a sweet sound, matching my mood of quiet suspension, which took its measure from the stillness of the night rather than trespassing against it. I was so moved that I left my bed and went outside the tent. Several paces distant the tall palisade was dark against the sky. Its one entrance had been closed, and I made no move to enter it but stood watching the pale glow rising above it, the intermittent showers of sparks tossed by some invisible fire that burned and died with the lift and fall of the voices. Men and women were there, singing together, as I heard them later in Su-

suroka on many moonlit nights. The words had no meaning for me, but they rang then—and ring for me yet—with peculiar poignancy, the voice of people standing at the threshold of the future, perhaps beguiled by it already, intuitively drawn to each other and pausing for reassurance as they prepare to step across.

I do not know if this was the mood behind the palisade at the close of a day filled with alarms and sights which must have been beyond the imagining of those on whom we had intruded, even if vague rumors had reached them. At no time during the patrol could I get a clear indication of what they thought, what interpretations they were inclined to place on anything they saw. After their initial anxiety as we approached their homes, they barely said a word to one another. Perhaps there were no words in their language to describe the things before their eyes, and none of them could be sure they were seeing what their fellows saw. It was all too close to them; time would have to pass before the multitude of fragmentary and individual impressions could coalesce, after we had gone, and find an agreed upon place within the framework of their traditional worldview.

After their defensive reaction to our arrival, they showed no signs of hostility, and I remembered hearing experienced patrol officers saying that, as a rule, it was not the first whites who were threatened or attacked, that they had no place in the traditional pattern of hostilities, coming from outside the relatively narrow range of political rivalries and group identifications. Hostility to whites, they suggested, came later, often vented against those who followed the first contact patrols, and sometimes caused by resentment for incidents occuring during the first encounter. Attacks on the first major patrols through the Highlands seem to have been few, though in the period almost immediately following, some whites were murdered in attempts to take possession of their highly desired goods. Mindful of this, Young-Whitforde was careful to keep a close watch on both police and carriers, particularly the latter, who felt no binding moral obligations to the new people. He forbade them to enter any village or gardens or to fell any timber without receiving prior permission, and he warned them not to mingle with our hosts. As far as the latter were concerned, the purpose of the patrol was simply to make contact with them, to allow them to see us, and not to introduce them to any of the formal elements of government. They had no idea that these would follow later.

From the point of view of those whom we met, we were probably merely strangers who had come from somewhere far beyond the world as they knew it, and who would depart into equally unknown regions. There must have been speculation concerning our origin, our material possessions and the clothing and persons of the whites. They were as fascinated by the latter as by any of our goods, and when I removed my hat, my red hair created a minor sensation. Abandoning caution, they would rush forward to crowd about me to feel my hair and run their fingers through it, exclaiming with amazement when they discovered it actually grew from my scalp. Whenever we went to bathe, they followed in scores, watching in suspense from a short distance as we removed our clothes, when there was a concerted rush to try to touch us before we could gain the protection of the stream. Whatever they may have decided after we left, I don't think these reactions expressed anything more than natural curiosity. There was little indication that they were disposed to regard us as something more, or less, than human.

The first patrol through the Highlands in the 1930s had been at least five times as large as this localized example of a routine operation. It had brought goods in such quantities that our own meager supplies of knives, axes, and other items paled to insignificance by comparison, and it had also been supplied by air, which had necessitated the construction of temporary landing strips and radio communications. In every respect, its impact must have been far greater and observed by far larger numbers of people, for it passed through the most densely populated areas in the whole of Papua New Guinea. Yet the Gahuku who saw it did not perceive it as an historical watershed from which they dated all the changes that occurred thereafter. They were not historically minded. Genealogies beyond the level of grandparents or, occasionally, great-grandparents did not interest them. Past and present blended with each other, and their perception of time and historical processes was very different from our own, which includes notions of a primitive past abruptly separated from a contemporary present and a progressive future. So it is entirely possible that the people we contacted on this patrol do not recall it as an event that wrenched them from the past and set in motion an inexorable chain of subsequent events.

The goods we introduced clearly stimulated acquisitive interest, but beyond this, there were indications of other attitudes that are far less easy to identify since they apparently involve qualities subsumed by such terms as "receptivity," "openness," "foresight," and a "practical" (though by no means clear) perception of the "best advantage." Perhaps it was these qualities that had led Makis, seventeen years earlier, to cast his lot with the whites, not subserviently and not without questioning the more blatant aspects of caste relationships but simply because he was not locked into a closed worldview, where change and the possibility that there were other ways of achieving the values sought by Gahuku were not regarded as unspeakable heresies.

This surely must be counted as contributing to the decision of one youth, probably no more than fifteen, to leave his people in the uncontacted area and journey back with us to Susuroka. He came from the village where I had heard the singing and had watched the sputtering fires on the night described above. As we prepared to leave the following morning, Makis brought him to Young-Whitforde and said the youth wanted to come with us, and that he, Makis, would take him to Susuroka and adopt him. He subsequently lived there as a member of Makis' family and was given the name Susuroe, the final vowel being an affectionate diminutive of the name of his new home. Since he was a member of Makis' family, he was a member of my family, too, and he entered my house as freely as any of the others. The villagers liked to joke about which of us would be the first to learn their language, and of course he outstripped me, just as he adapted more rapidly to everything connected to their way of life. No one in Susuroka ever suggested he would remain there indefinitely; it was understood he would return to his own home eventually, taking back with him whatever he had been able to gain. He remained in Susuroka after I left in 1952, growing to manhood there, obtaining a job in the expanding economy of the nearby township, then leaving to go back to his people. I do not know the year he left Susuroka, or how long he lived after returning to the village, whose name I did not record when our patrol camped outside its palisade. All I was told in 1981 was that he was dead, killed by the sorcery of his own people.

 I am acquainted with five different age groups of Gahuku, though they do not correspond with that number of generations. First there were the generation of the father of Makis, who were the Nagamidzuha elders in 1950, old men like Sesekume, long past their prime, all of whom would be dead when I returned in 1981. They were the same age that Gihigute is now, many of them still active, always present on important group occasions, and listened to with respect because of their knowledge of ritual and of events in their lifetime that colored disputes while I was there. They did not stand out from the throng at gatherings called to discuss procedures or the rights and wrongs of any particular issue, but they were always consulted by those who played the more conspicuous roles, and the final consensus—the ideal basis of all decisions—owed a good deal to their unobtrusive counsel.

I think this was a rewarding time of their lives. They were respected because of their age and experiences, both of which are immensely important when knowledge is transmitted orally, and the Gahuku word for someone old in years (*ozaha*) did not carry any stigma of infirmity or uselessness but was more in tune with the term "elder." No special provisions had to be legislated to recognize their worth and dignity. Their status was achieved naturally by anyone who lived long enough, though those who had had distinguished careers in their youth exercised a greater influence than others. Men even granted special privileges to aged women. As a sign of their ultimate acceptance into the patrilineal group of their husbands, they were allowed to stand outside their houses (with closed eyes, however) whenever men paraded through the villages with the sacred *nama* flutes, the most carefully guarded symbol of male dominance. The women were quick to defend the rights they had finally acquired in their husbands' clans or sub-clans.

Males who lived to become elders were not pushed to the very periphery of the social system. They were no longer active warriors, which traditionally was the only fully acceptable and expected career for men, but I doubt that all of them regretted it, for there had always been young men who were reluctant warriors. At this stage of their lives they were also absolved of the severe self-disciplines considered necessary to produce and to maintain manhood and masculinity. They could interact more freely with the opposite sex, including their wives, and had closer, less inhibited and more affectionate relationships with their grandsons than custom and the superior-subordinate axis of relationships between members of proximate generations had permitted them to have with their own sons. This has a familiar ring, for relationships between alternate generations (grandparent-grandchild) in our own culture are generally characterized as less restrictive and more indulgent than those between members of proximate generations. But we also advance companionship as well as tutelage (and the discipline necessary to support it) as an ideal component of the father-son relationship. Companionship was not a component of the Gahuku relationship, however. Men had very little to do with their sons after their birth until they entered the men's organization as novices in their teens, and the sudden interest the boys encountered at this time was expressed in harshness, criticism, and traumatic violations of their persons.

The second age group consisted of all the adult men between approximately twenty-two and forty-five. These were men who were permitted sexual relationships with their wives, though traditionally they did not sleep with them in the same house. Some were already fathers of teenage children while the youngest were childless as yet. Makis, possibly a little over thirty-five in 1950, belonged to this group and Gihigute represented its upper age limit, approaching the status of elder.

This was the group upon whose shoulders most of the active responsibilities of men devolved. They were the warriors, the organizers of debate, the stringent guardians of male prerogatives, the cynosure of all eyes in their resplendent decorations at ceremonies, and the enforcers of the standards of conduct that prescribed both a social and a psychological distancing between the sexes. It was a brilliant company, a company that presented itself to the world in the ideological garb of superiority, even though this vaunted image concealed deep uncertainties. Its members were bound to one another by secrets hidden from males not yet admitted to it and, hopefully, always hidden from women. Despite the presence of more gentle hues, its palette drew upon the more violent of the primary colors and often placed them in clashing contrast. Its characteristic sound was agitated; metaphorically, the staccato beat of drums or the sudden eruption of trumpets were likely interruptions at any time. Like all associations in which particular conceptions of honor have become obsessions, it was compounded of suspicion as well as ideals of fraternal solidarity: suspicion of the motives of women, who were excluded from it but with whom it was necessary to interact, and animosities between its own members who were close to one another in age.

This was the company in which I had been placed by age alone in 1950, and I spent most of my time with its members. Thirty years later I had moved to the group of elders and had, perhaps, a slight entitlement apart from age to be included there, for I shared with the other elders some areas of knowledge not possessed by those who had not yet reached the "adult" age group in 1950, as well as all those who had been born since then. The children of people who had been my "children" were my "grandchildren" now, within the appropriate range of extending kinship terms. This is how they were presented to me and addressed me, and with those who were very young but not mere infants, it was an almost magic cure for shyness.

Youths from about sixteen to twenty-one in 1950 were not yet full members of the adult group. They had received their final initiation into the men's cult and were married, though they were allowed no contact with their wives and were not permitted to speak to them or sit with them. The final rite of marriage, granting them sexual access to the young women and establishing their own households, did not take place until older adults and elders decided their manhood was sufficiently secure to offset the risks involved in sex and more intimate contact with their wives, which was not until age twenty-one or thereabouts. It was a difficult period for them. Very few of the first marriages endured to the point of consummation, thereby threatening to delay admission to full adult status. Members of this group were not boys but neither were they fully adult men, though they had many of the latter's responsibilities. As I shall show later, they were particularly susceptible to contradictions in the dogma of male superiority.

Boys from around ten to fifteen wore a particular kind of headdress (*gene*) indicating their status: long streamers of bark cloth attached to their hair and reaching to their knees when thrown back from their shoulders. They were not members of the male cult and knew nothing of the secrets which would eventually wrench them into the ranks of its members with stunning violence and searing pain. At this period of their lives, they had almost no responsibilities. Day after day they roamed the group territory in small bands, out of sight but never far away. They were the principal reason why I was seldom alone. For, on my walks, they would appear suddenly from the grasses, and having nothing to do, would accompany me wherever I went, interrupting my thoughts with well-intentioned but irritating attempts to gain my interest by performing acrobatics in a grove of trees or darting into the grasses to bring me wild raspberries and other berries in order to teach me their Gahuku names. They filled the hours by hunting small birds and bush rats, by frightening and teasing younger girls, and by spying on unsuspecting adults. They often saw things their elders hoped to conceal, and their gossip frequently precipitated accusations and disputes that tore the fabric of domestic relationships.

Last, there were the children, all those younger than about ten. Their days were spent in the company of women rather than men. Their mothers or older sisters acted as nursemaids and were responsible for most of the discipline they received—far more, in fact, than anything shouldered by the children's fathers. Fathers showed greater affection for daughters than sons and, similarly, males were more closely attached to their sisters than their brothers, even though ideologies of gender separation emphasized oppositions between male and female.

The world of their fathers was observed only from a distance by male children, and from their earliest remembered years it was a menacing world, containing secrets that instilled fear into those with whom they were most closely associated. Though they gradually realized they would have to join it, they regarded the inevitable with justified apprehension, being told they were killed during the awesome rites (which they could not avoid) admitting them to the elite company of adult men. This prospect hung like a dark shadow just outside the brightness of years that were largely free of responsibility until they were fifteen.

There was not a comparable system of age groups for girls. The period of childhood lasted from birth to their first menstruation, and after this they were adult women. But in many respects their childhood ended long before menarche. During the years when almost nothing was demanded from their brothers by adults, they were already loaded with responsibilities. They cared for younger siblings, they fetched and carried and worked in the gardens beside their mothers, only rarely escaping to splash and laugh in a shaded pool with their peers. Little girls were wiser at a much earlier age then their brothers in the ways and expectations of the world designed for them. Though the prospect of marriage involved emotionally wrenching experiences that surely caused anxieties, the world of adults of their own sex was not invested by impenetrable secrets or mysteries whose audible manifestations struck fear into those excluded from them.

In the Gahuku world of the 1930s and onward, these age groups were formally recognized divisions of the population. Every individual's movement from one to another (saving only the transition from adult to elder) was marked in some public manner. What an individual did, what others expected of him, and the broad outlines of his daily experiences depended on where he was placed within the system. Elder and younger male siblings were not members of the same set until after they had reached the adult group. Postpartum taboos on sexual intercourse between husband and wife from birth to the weaning of children usually meant there was a three- to four-year interval between siblings and, ideally, they maintained this distance as they moved through the succession of statuses. Elder brothers were admitted to the male cult four to five years earlier than their younger siblings, and thus they were not only married and cohabiting but, with some exceptions, were also fathers before younger brothers achieved any of these essentials for respect and equal privilege. This subordination often rankled with some younger siblings, and the overriding ideal of male solidarity was not always equal to the animus it caused. The resulting rivalries contributed to the instability of relationships, though they were not as important as the other conditions and considerations I have mentioned.

There was no difficulty at all in recognizing these formal divisions in 1950. The boys who interrupted my walks wore the *gene* headdresses distinguishing them from the groups immediately above and below them. All but one of the young men I employed had been admitted to the male cult but had not yet established their own households, and the exception (Asemo) passed through the rites of initiation while I was there. All of this had gone by 1981, together with the ideological foundations of the system and most of the major institutions in which relationships between members of the various sets had been expressed. Warfare was only the most obvious of the missing links. It was undoubtedly a lynch pin in the ediface, and its prohibition under the pax Australiana removed one of the imperatives motivating adult men in molding the raw material presented to them in persons of younger males. Yet it would be a gross simplification to attribute the rearrangements to this single cause.

Compared with my return visit, living in Susuroka in 1950 had the quality of watching and being peripherally involved in a stylized pageant. In time, it had been possible to place everyone in their particular segment of the parade and to see the way in which each contributed to the grand ensemble. This does not detract from the individuality of anyone involved. All it means is that the component groups in the procession were more clearly marked and visible from day to day than in our own mass and largely impersonal society. The arrangements of a village, the line of low, round women's houses and the dominating edifice of the men's clubhouse, indicated the basic division between the sexes, which was repeated again and again, like so many refractions of the same image in a series of mirrors, in almost every walk of life. The way in which families sat outside their houses in the early morning, where the members went, what they would do, talk about and even see each day; their personal concerns and some of their anxieties—all these responded to a choreography that was more vivid because it was so different from anything in my own experience.

I could not recapture this daily sense of drama in 1981. Like the landscape under its new growth of trees, the broad sweep of the pageant and its startling highlights had passed into history, and the procession I watched this time moved to more familiar measures. Its participants were costumed in ordinary ways and, superficially, the entire ensemble often seemed no more than a variation on some urbanized themes I dislike whenever I find them.

This personal reaction (disappointment at the betrayal of a memory?) is a disservice to the Gahuku, however, for the drama lies in the very processes of change, and the stature of these people increases in proportion to the exceedingly short space of time they have had to accommodate to the breaching of a world that was surely little different from that of the uncontacted people through whom I passed in 1950. Certainly, my eyes may have been prejudiced by nostalgia for a time that, visually at least, had seemed to be braver and more resplendent. But if much that had been resplendent had gone, so had much that no dose of cultural relativism could persuade me to approve.

The achievement of the Gahuku lies in their demonstrated ability to alter so many of the contours of their life and to effect with relative ease a transformation other cultures have managed with greater difficulty. It is not an exaggeration to say that Gahuku have come as much as several centuries in the single lifetime of some men I know. How, I often wondered as I sat with them in the kitchen of Makis' house, do these men, old like myself now, look back upon the pageant I remember? Do they see their lives as having been wrenched from their moorings and cast adrift on a buffeting unchartered ocean? Do they appreciate the drama in which they were involved, or realize the extent of their accomplishments? As far as I can tell, the answers to all these questions are not what one might expect.

In 1950 the prohibition of warfare by the colonial government seemed to be accepted with relief, particularly by the group of youngest adults who would have been beginning their careers as warriors, and also by the youths wearing the *gene* headdress, for whom it would have been a prospect only several years ahead. Among the older adults, there were some hard men who behaved as though they chafed against the restraints preventing them from demonstrating their aggressiveness. Sometimes, too, older adults remarked that it had been easy to tell who was a man when everyone had to be alert to defend himself, women, and children from surprise attack. To demonstrate this state of perpetual readiness they pantomimed drawing their bows and snapped their fingers as though releasing arrows, but the simulated aggressiveness was often informed with a touch of humor rather than regret for the passing of a key form of manly expression. Even men such as Makis, whose warrior reputations were secure, did not flaunt this particular accomplishment or imply that the younger generation were becoming soft because they did not have to face the same tests, nor did the elders dwell on the past like veterans recalling the glories of old campaigns. The consequences of these campaigns were still lively ingredients of intergroup relationships, but that was almost all that could be said of them. I did not find anyone who wanted to see those days return, though in the heat of arguments some men boasted that their opponents would not be so presumptuous if they could be threatened with force.

Perhaps the most stunning of all the traditional institutions, the final initiation of males into the *nama* cult, was also on the brink of extinction in 1950. My reaction to this event is described fully in *The High Valley*, when I watched the youth Asemo wrenched into the fierce and harshly critical orbit of adult men. As I foresaw, he was the last of Nagamidzuha's youths to experience this violent climax to the long process of making a man. Initiation had not occurred since then and, I am sure, will never occur again. This does not invest me with the mantle of clairvoyance. The adults who arranged the initiation in which Asemo was involved knew full well it was the last expiring breath of a past already subject to questions. Maniha, Asemo's father, implied as much when in my house one night he tested me to see if I approved his decision to allow his son to be one of the company of violated youths. I am afraid I abdicated any responsibility, not knowing what this gentle and trusting boy was about to face, and perhaps even anxious for the opportunity to have a close view of something no other person of my kind or any other generation of Gahuku would ever see. Asemo is still in Susuroka and remembers everything, including my own ineffective efforts to teach him English, but he does not consider he is any different than those who never received the traditional badge of admission to the privileged order of men. Indeed, no one speaks about initiation nowadays. It is possible to provoke those who endured it to describe the physical ordeals in the briefest way, and when there is an audience of younger men they may do so in a manner that suggests "See how lucky *you* are!" Their reticence is not, I think, due to the possibility that the new generation may associate them with a barbaric past. Rather, they attach very little importance to it in their perception of their own identity in the present world.

In 1950 the domestic separation of men and women was also breaking down, clearly indicating incipient changes in ideologies. These are so important that I will deal with them later, but perhaps I may say that the stridently expressed superiority of men was maintained at a cost to them as well as to women.

There had also been indications of a different economic future for men who sought it. The opportunities were almost solely confined to unskilled labor or domestic service, but around the government station Gahuku saw a few other New Guineans driving jeeps, holding minor clerical positions in the post office and in the only trade store, or serving as foremen on various government and private enterprises. One Nagamidzuha man had also enlisted in the native police, but no one else showed any interest in following his example. The immediate ambitions of many younger adults, such as Hunehune, focused on becoming mechanics or licensed drivers. A few became wage laborers. It was the only readily available means of earning money, and necessity rather than preference persuaded some to accept it. Even then they seemed to recognize that such unskilled work was a dead end, and they looked for alternatives.

There were no ways in which they could acquire the knowledge and training necessary to achieve even modest ambitions. A Lutheran lay evangelist ran a school near the stream separating the ridge of Susuroka from Gehamo, but it provided entirely inadequate and desultory instruction in fundamentalist Christian dogma, as well as the bare rudiments of reading and writing in a language that was neither Gahuku or English and, therefore, no use at all for any kind of secular advancement.

Lutherans had been the first missionaries to follow on the heels of the white explorers, and they were the only representatives of Christianity then operating in the Asaro. Whether by statute or simply by pressure (I haven't checked any official sources), it seems to have been government policy to try to contain or avoid the sectarianism that may have accompanied the spectacle of different brands of Christianity competing for the souls and allegiance of people in the same area (and, of course, proselytization by any other kind of religious faith was out of the question). The result was that converts in Bena Bena were Seventh Day Adventists, Lutheran in the Asaro and predominately Roman Catholic in the Chimbu Valley.

The Lutheran lay evangelist near Susuroka was a Gahuku man who had been baptized and had attended a religious training school in Finschafen on the coast. There he had learned to read and write in *Kate,* a Papua New Guinean language the mission used for instruction and for translating biblical texts and stories. *Kate* and Gahuku are both Papuan languages, which means little more than saying that French and Italian are Romance languages, and learning to read and write in *Kate* was entirely useless for anything other than access to a few Christian texts. Ihanizo, the name of the lay evangelist, conducted services in his "church" on most Sundays and taught school for children intermittently throughout the week. He had not succeeded in making any converts and lived more or less on the periphery of society, tolerated but hardly respected. He had virtually no school supplies, no textbooks or writing materials except some slates and pieces of chalk, and he did not appear to be enthusiastic or dedicated to his job. A few parents sometimes berated small children for not attending his school, but I think this was more an expression of temporary impatience (wanting to get them from under their feet) than an indication of any ultimate value the children might have gained. Most of the children were not serious about school, regarding it as a novel pastime to fill part of a day now and then.

There were some whose attitudes were different, however. One of them was Asemo, who had learned the rudiments of writing from Ihanizo but who saw that an instruction confined to religion and the *Kate* language would not get him far, and who enlisted my inadequate help in an attempt to learn English. Though this was the only request of its kind I received from anyone, it exemplified more general and largely unarticulated attitudes. Many young men and older adults saw new goals in the world that was opening up to them, and they knew they would have to acquire new skills in order to reach them. Some, like Asemo, realized the advantages of being able to read and write, but they were also perspicacious enough to see these skills would not help them if they were confined to a minor language no whites used. Large numbers of older adults, for whom any kind of formal schooling was impossible, showed interest in new cash crops. They were understandably reluctant to devote much of their land and time to them, uncertain what the returns would be, but they were willing to experiment on a small scale. These tentative efforts brought in nothing or next to nothing, but they were evidence of speculative interest, and those who undertook them did so on their own initiative, receiving no help, encouragement, or instruction from the government.

There was a *didiman* (government agricultural officer) in Goroka who was in charge of a small agricultural extension program located on land that is now within the town boundaries. He ran a few dairy cows and bred pigs with imported Australian boars, ultimately, I suppose, with the intention of improving the local domestic breed. None of the Nagamidzuha received any benefit from the operation. Indeed, the agricultural officer was a fairly typical example of the old school of white government employees, regarding the local population as abysmal inferiors, untrustworthy and incapable of learning or assuming any kind of responsibility. He would not allow any of them (excepting those he had to employ) within the station area, and his attitude extended to his household servants, whom he forbade to enter his wife's bedroom even if she was not present.

The Australian amateur naturalist, philanthropist and re-frigerator magnate Sir Edward Halstrom had provided the financial backing for a landed trust at Nondugl in the Western Highlands, where sheep were being raised experimentally. (Incidentally, he was also a proponent of a view that the Highlanders, because the so-called semitic nose is a noticeable but by no means universal physical characteristic among them, could be the biblical lost tribe of Israel.) After I had been in Susuroka almost a year, I was surprised to learn there were two of these animals, obtained from Nondugl, on the ridge, given into the care of a man who kept them in a small enclosure and who hand-fed them like domesticated pigs. No one knew why they were there or what possible uses they might have, but their owner was prepared to try them as a novelty in much the same way as other men were planting a few coffee seedlings and passion fruit vines in their gardens, watching over them and wondering what might come from them.

There was interest in almost anything new. Young and old alike badgered me incessantly to explain how the things I used, and many of the tinned foods I ate, were manufactured. Since I am a technological ignoramous, my explanations were entirely unsatisfactory, yet I think that all but a tiny minority of us would be taxed to give an enlightening account, for example, of everything involved in getting the corned beef into the can. There are critical elements of any culture, including ideologies and symbols, that we simply use without reflecting on them, and of course, in our own highly technical culture, most of the things we rely upon daily are beyond the comprehension of the layman.

I did not report any of these intimations of change in my previously published accounts of the Gahuku-Gama, for in 1950 they were really no more than a surface vibration, an intermittent but premonitory flurry of wind across the deep waters of a lake. You could observe and also feel them, but at that time no one, not even those who had come there on the wind, could possibly foresee precisely how it would gather or to what particular places it would apply its pressure. Underneath the surface disturbance, everything continued to be as it had always been, that is for as long as any memory or experience could muster. Excepting only warfare, I did not have to reconstruct anything I described. The traditional institutions and ideologies of Gahuku culture were palpable realities.

The changes that are omnipresent now have occurred since I left the Asaro. The period of most intensive alteration was probably the sixties, when hardly any trained individual was there to record them. Not that such a person would have been present at any planning, however—the changes were not programmed social experiments. Apart from the new institutions imposed from the outside to further the ends of the colonial government, I think they came about more or less piecemeal as responses to situations in which some of the old ways simply could not be maintained or were impediments to achieving some of the new goals. I do not know any Gahuku who lived through this period who looks back on it as a time when the familiar world seemed to have been wrenched from its foundation and he and others perceived themselves as wandering in shock among ruins. Indeed, it is rather useless asking them what they felt, what the period meant to them personally. Gahuku are not given to introspection. I am reasonably sure that even before their traditional world had not changed greatly, very few of them looked back on their lives and wondered, "Did I do the right thing on that occasion? Would things have been different if I, or others, had acted differently?" Perhaps our propensity to review the events of our lives retrospectively reflects our conception of the linear progression of time and causation, in which the individual life is a microcosmic example of the grand plan. This was not the way in which Gahuku perceived themselves.

I do not mean to subtract from them the quality of self-consciousness or self-awareness. The feeling of "self"—of the idiosyncratic "me"—was strongly displayed by most of them, but particularly by the hard men, in whom it was developed to such a degree that they often seemed unable or unwilling to see much beyond their own self-interests. Yet the quality of self-direction, when tempered with other qualities, also sustained the careers of all those who rose to positions of influence in an essentially egalitarian society. It is this same constellation of traits that propelled some men rather than others into the maelstrom stirred by an event that, as far as anyone could tell, might have been little more than a ripple of water. All Gahuku who have succeeded in making a niche in their rapidly expanding world are clearly self-made men, but this is equally true of those who occupied the most respected and influential places in the less varied and less numerous niches available to them traditionally.

Yet the quality of introspection, the inward-turning eye that sees the self in silhouette against the patterned background of events, was not a noticeable characteristic of Gahuku. They were like swimmers who remain among the flurry and the foam of breaking waves, seldom venturing out beyond them to the deep waters from where you look back upon the inshore agitation. Occasionally, as when I watched Makis shoot his arrow into the evening sky, I received the impression that a man was treading water beyond the reef, momentarily separated from the beachside scene and assessing it against some unarticulated vision that was no more definite than the movement of the tasseled heads of grass and the fading colors of day. But perhaps this is projecting onto others something that I felt. Since I never became fluent in Gahuku (though eventually I could converse in it and understand most of what I heard), I may not have been equipped to penetrate these dimensions of self-consciousness, but I don't think I do a disservice to the Gahuku in placing them there among the breakers rather than beyond them. Their knowledge of their history was encompassed by the memories of the oldest living persons, and they did not place much store in the foundation stones that myths provide for other people. It is utterly impossible to imagine them ever becoming religious zealots, massacring "unbelievers" or indulging in more subtle forms of persuasion to propagate a faith. Their wars were not waged to extend political control or territorial sovereignty, and they were more tolerant of differences than those missionaries who felt it was their task to instruct them in what they should believe and how they should live.

This does not mean that the present was created anew with each succeeding generation, that the lives of those living *now* did not replicate the lives of those preceding them, but that their chronology did not reckon their existence in millions of years or even in centuries. The motion picture of their life flashed on the screen in short segments, each one, as it were, jumping out from a surrounding darkness. Each exemplified a tradition that an observer could assume to be far older than the time span of living memory, but Gahuku did not, for example, perceive that tradition as having been established at the Creation, when everything in the social and natural world had been appointed to a place in a hallowed and unalterable scheme. Life was governed by tradition. It wasn't anarchic, but neither was it locked into some timeless dimension, so that when the known boundaries of the world suddenly parted, people generally did not hesitate on the new threshold, fearful that the edifice of everything that had provided them with shelter would come crashing down.

In 1950, when the possibilities of change, rather than the product observable today, were in the air, there were almost no diehard traditionalists who prognosticated impending doom if there was any departure from custom. Instances of mission-inspired and directed public burnings and disavowals of the sacred *nama* flutes caused ripples of resentment among the older men in groups just beyond the area where the Lutherans were most active. Since the flutes were the supreme symbol of male hegemony, and also since male superiority and control was maintained against countervailing beliefs that it was threatened by the very nature and interests of women, it is possible to understand why burning them publicly might have been perceived by some as tantamount to opening Pandora's box and releasing several plagues. Yet the Nagamidzuha, who were among those who expressed resentment, did not brand the culprits as apostates, and certainly it would never have crossed their minds to counteract with force to return them to the fold of true believers and to expunge their errors. And though they still held fast to the sacred flutes as a symbol of basic male values, they seemed to be little concerned about departures from custom that were equally as radical repudiations of the traditional ideology. For example, the traditional domestic separation of the sexes virtually disappeared without raising any outcry or prophecies of imminent disaster.

I do not think that Gahuku held any truths as absolute. Today, for example, they do not distinguish between varieties of Christianity on the grounds that one is necessarily better than another or more true or pure, so that those who do not subscribe to the same institutionalized faith are in varying degrees of error. This also applies to the "pagans." The non-Christians of the Nagamidzuha do not regard the Christians as betrayers, any more than the Swiss Evangelical Christians of Susuroka look on Lutherans, Roman Catholics, Seventh Day Adventists and so on as being somehow less genuine or less elect than themselves. Similarly, Christians do not stigmatize the "pagans" for their "nonbelief" or, apparently, feel they have an obligation to draw them under the protection of the canopy of their own truth to save their souls. And for the most part, the non-Christians seem quite content to live side by side with the Christians. Their attitude toward them is open-ended and nonjudgmental, on the order of, "So, that's what they say. Well, it's all right. I can't really see it, but *maski* (that is, it's not of any real consequence)."

It is difficult to convey this essential sense of open-endedness since it is so contrary to the attitudes and moving forces of our own cultural tradition, and since it may seem to withhold from Gahuku the very keystones of what we consider to be organized social life, but the latter is not the case. At any point in time Gahuku moved in accordance with rules, yet even so, their rules were not based upon *universalized* absolutes. They were cultural relativists in their attitude toward those other people who fell within the limited range of their knowledge of different ways of life. They did not conceive of some abstract, common, or encompassing entity such as human nature from which you could derive certain rules of conduct applicable to an entire species. Even within their own system of rules and expectations, the extent of each man's moral obligation was ultimately determined by and varied with social obligations.

The Gahuku ethic was primarily secular. Unlike theistic ethics, its source was not externalized in the fiat of some watchful supernatural who had created mankind in a certain image and for a certain purpose and thereby enjoined on all its members an identical burden of obligation. They did not lack moral principles, but these were not derived from transcendental notions of the "good" or the "right." They would have found it very odd, for example, to be told that you should regard every man, simply as *man,* as having equal moral value. Similarly, they could not be fairly described as dogmatic. By this I do not mean that their world, both social and natural, was not ordered by beliefs concerning the proper forms of relationships and the existence of powers transcending human beings—beliefs concerning the ways in which such powers operated and in the ways of controlling or utilizing them—but such powers were not personified. Gahuku had no deities demanding worship on penalty of displeasure or misfortune either in this life or some other after death. Their worldview cannot be characterized as naturalistic; indeed, it was probably far less naturalistic than our own, for if you could put on the cultural lens of their vision you would see the operation of supernatural power in virtually everything affecting men. Yet these beliefs did not have the authority of calcified dogmas, so in an important sense there was little to challenge. There was no elaborate superstructure of dogma, worship, and priesthood intervening between men and the power on which they depended; and when alternative beliefs were presented, they did not have to contend with theological obstructions.

In concert, these various characteristics warrant labeling Gahuku culture as receptive rather than resistant to new ideas and to change. Certainly, there do not appear to have been major beliefs and practices which considerable numbers of people felt compelled to protect and preserve. The colonial government proscribed very few traditional institutions or customs. The changes it wrought stemmed from new ideas and institutions it introduced on top of those already existing, an enterprise which, from its point of view, did not entail repressive interference with the fundamentals of belief, practice, or organization—though any anthropologist or sociologist could have informed its representatives that what was introduced at the top would not float there like the separate layers of liqueurs in a *pousse-café*. Yet in 1950, Gahuku were already undertaking major changes on their own volition. They eliminated some traditional institutions and elements of ideology that did not fall under administrative proscription, so Gahuku were, in a sense, ahead of their time, since conditions then can hardly be said to have made them a necessity.

This is the general attitude I sensed among members of all the age-groups in 1950. It was not a time of turmoil, but neither was it a time of marshaling defenses to preserve the inner citadel of tradition. Tradition, in fact, was mostly intact—yet it was also clear that its gates had swung open, and almost no one looked with consternation on the prospect beyond them.

4   The prospect outside was not attainable in equal measure by members of the different age-grades, however. Irrespective of differences in aptitude or motivation, there were limitations to what those from different grades could achieve. Rather obviously, some of the opportunities available in the life of 1981—and presumably for the years ahead—belonged to those who are the same age (thirty-one) or younger than Lucy Makis, while the most disadvantaged were the young men beginning their adult careers from 1950 to 1952—the age-grade of Hunehune, Piripiri, Asemo, Hasu, Hutorno, and Lotuwa, who are the subjects of two chapters in *The High Valley*.

The age-mates of Makis appear to have kept the respect of others and a large measure of their influence and authority, despite the fact that none had any kind of formal education and might seem to be poorly equipped—because of their rural lack of sophistication—to appreciate some dimensions of contemporary situations. The arena of politics and competing interests is sometimes far larger than the stage on which they were accustomed to perform, yet I think they are generally able to comprehend broader issues. It could be that under traditional conditions influential men were necessarily manipulators, if this term is used without the pejorative implications it has come to have for us. It is true that their management of events contributed to their personal advancement and recognition, and though the arena is larger now, the same talents, which tend to include a certain skepticism of the motives of others, stand them in good stead. And in addition, old age is still no disgrace.

Javilo is one of these men. He belongs to Nagamidzuha but does not live on the ridge, residing on his clan land a short distance to the west near the boundary of a large coffee plantation. Short-statured and wiry—and, incidentally, there are no overweight Gahuku—he gives the impression of being hyperactive. He is seldom still, moving rapidly and incessantly, with mercurial changes of expression as he talks, and has an obviously strong sense of himself and his position as leader of his clan. I have no clear recollections of him from thirty years ago, but he remembers me, primarily through my relationship to Makis, whom he followed and supported with an admiration that has not diminished. He carries about with him a photograph I took of Makis, his three wives, and two of his children. Standing in the bare street of Susuroka, with my thatched house as background, they are wearing the customary dress of the time, though the addition of plumes and ceremonial shell valuables suggests I did not take it on an everyday occasion. Javilo brought the photograph out whenever I saw him, and when he invited me to a special meal on the day of my departure in 1982, he and his daughter dressed in the same style of clothing so I could make a record of him comparable to the fading image of his age-mate.

Javilo has largely withdrawn from the affairs of the ridge clans, his disassociation probably reflecting displeasure with the course of events following the death of Makis. People on the ridge still respect him, however, paying attention to his opinions and acknowledging his importance. He and other members of his group continue to have close ties with the "line" of Makis. In his own group, there is only one younger man—the son of a brother of Javilo—who seems prepared to disregard him and, as a consequence, has forfeited the support of its other members.

This man lives apart from Javilo in a small and relatively isolated homestead between Susuroka and Gohajaka. It contains two houses, one which he shares with his third wife and young daughter and another belonging to a grown son from a former marriage. The second house is rarely used, however. The son lives at the plantation mentioned above, where he is employed and being trained for a managerial position.

His father is Hunehune, who has a special place in most of my memories from 1950 to 1952 and whom I was so glad to find again in 1981. During that visit, however, he frequently irritated me to the limits of patience. He resumed our former relationship, leaving his homestead to live with me in Makis' house, and looking after me and accompanying me wherever I went. But I found out he drinks too much and is an importuning bore when drunk. Gahuku do not place our particular moral evaluation on alcoholism, though they may show impatience with habitual drunks, and I tried to overlook

The lower section of the village of Susuroka. The rectangular building on the left is the Swiss Evangelical Mission church (*haus lotu*).

Makis' house in Susuroka. His grave is to the right of the tree in the left foreground.

Namuri, formerly one of the principal supporters of Makis. Old men like to be photographed with their bows and arrows, with which they were always armed in 1950.

Some of the extended family of Makis (with friends) assembled in the yard of Makis' house for the family meal on the day of the author's departure in 1981.

The road along the ridge south of Susuroka. The village of Gohajaka lies under the trees in the left center background.

Ekuhakuka near the southern extremity of the ridge of Susuroka. The road on the left continues on to the floor of the valley, crosses the Asaro River, and runs into the distant mountains.

Lucy (left) and Lokilo Makis on the verandah of Makis' house in Susuroka.

Hunehune Opomari.

Zaho in 1981. He is holding a 1950 photograph of himself in the customary male costume of that time.

◀ Toho, daughter of Makis, in the yard of Makis' house. As a child of about ten years of age, she looked after the author's six months' old son thirty-one years ago.

The grave of Makis, flanked by two other graves with Christian crosses.
His memorial plaque rests against the base of the tree, center background.

Guma'e (left), biological mother of Lucy and Lokilo Makis, the author, and
Mukito (right) in the village of Susuroka.

Kopi Manove and his wife Claire (with their son Konrad in her arms) in the garden of his suburban house in Goroka.

Guests from Gama dancing at the *kantri* ceremony in Bena Bena. Their dress is basically traditional ceremonial costumes with some Western additions. The long vertical "wands" behind them are hung with paper currency which will be presented to them at the conclusion of the event.

Javilo and his daughter in traditional ceremonial costume on the day of the author's departure in 1982.

Hunehune's behavior, partly because of our past relationship and also because no one else seemed to judge it.

When I returned to Goroka in 1982 I was surprised—and a little disappointed—to find that only Claire Manove was waiting for me at the airport. Kopi, her husband, arrived half an hour later and took me to the Bird of Paradise Hotel, but neither of them explained why no one else had come. Before dinner that night, a knock on the door of my room announced the arrival of Hunehune. We had an affectionate reunion. He said he had come earlier in the afternoon and when I did not answer the door had assumed I was resting. Then he stated the purpose of his visit, telling me that Makis' house "stank"; it had deteriorated since the previous year, was infested with mosquitos breeding in the rotting tank, and had not been prepared for me. He had decided I should live in his homestead in his house, where I would be more comfortable.

Aside from the fact that his house is no more than a shack compared with the one Makis built—and even that had inconveniences that would not have worried me when I was young—living in the isolation of his tiny homestead was the last thing I wanted to do or had expected. Perhaps he sensed this reaction, for he said the people of Susuroka who were closest to me could stay there also. His suggestion ignored the fact that his house wasn't large enough for me and his family, let alone the others. I was worried. I did not know if he had described truthfully the condition of Makis' house; I wondered if others agreed with his proposal and, most important, if something had happened that would make it more difficult for me to return to Susuroka. So I did not agree, telling him I would decide after looking at Makis' house the following day.

Early the next morning, a call from the hotel's front desk informed me that "some people from the villages want to see you." I replied, "Send them up." There was a pause, then an apologetic and slightly troubled voice responded: "But there are so *many* of them." I brushed aside the obvious reluctance to admit them to the private areas of the hotel, and minutes later they were in my room—fourteen of them (with others waiting below in the hotel's garden), mostly members of Makis' clan but also including the Ozahadzuha man and his wife. Sitting on the floor, the chairs and bed, they came quickly to the point of their visit, explaining they had not expected me until later on the present day and had learned of my arrival only the previous night. This explanation given, they then announced that everything was ready for me in Susuroka. Makis' house had been opened, cleaned and was waiting for me. Any suggestions to the contrary, I was not to go anywhere else to live. Speaking for all of them, the Ozahadzuha man said in effect: "You are a Susuroka man. It's your place, it's where your family lives; it's where everyone knows you belong."

While his announcement reassured me, I sensed a disaffection with Hunehune that I had not been aware of the previous year. They had arrived early (waiting in the street outside the hotel since 6:00 A.M.) to counter his proposal before I accepted it. They did not mention his name, but since he alone of the villagers had seen me, it was clear they had him in mind. Their implied attitude toward him surprised me because no one had criticized him in 1981. During that visit I had blamed myself for wishing I did not have to see him daily, and I felt guilty of ingratitude on some occasions when I told other people I found him tiresome and irresponsible. They neither assented nor disagreed, which I found frustrating. I thought they must share my opinion, forgetting that Gahuku seldom make public judgments of the characters of others.

I saw little of Hunehune during the remainder of my 1982 visit. He was among those who took me to Susuroka and installed me in Makis' house—which had not deteriorated in the least since the previous year—but he stayed for only an hour. About sundown he returned drunk, and after hanging about for a while, making suggestions no one followed, went off to his homestead with the parting advice that he would be back the next morning. He came as promised around 9:00 A.M., having spent most of the night drinking at his homestead and causing a disturbance that resulted in court action against him. I did not know this, having heard nothing of the disturbance because of the distance between his house and Susuroka; but his behavior was intolerable and I eventually told him to leave, saying I did not care to see him in his present condition. No one else said a word, and I began to feel angry with them as well, wondering *why* they didn't *do* or *say* something to show he was behaving stupidly.

In the following days Hunehune came to the village a few times. I saw him occasionally among a group sitting in the street gambling at cards. We greeted each other pleasantly, but I was glad he wasn't around all day and every day. He was presently not only a member of the board of directors of the coffee plantation near Javilo's settlement but also employed there. When he arrived at my hotel room in Goroka, he had told me (and I confirmed it later) that the manager (Winston Jacob) had given him a paid leave-of-absence to be with me during my visit. Since he wasn't meeting this stipulation, I assumed he had returned to his job. This was not the case, and I suspect he was using some of his released time cultivating interests threatening the patrimonial rights to land of the clan to which he and Javilo belong.

Before this became relatively clear, however, other people on the ridge indicated a diffuse weariness with him.

Women from the settlements on both sides of his homestead complained to the Village Court official that he had abused and insulted them scurrilously during the drunken disturbance on the night following my arrival. The court official agreed and fined him the equivalent of U.S. $145. I have no idea what the average per capita income of the villagers is, but I am reasonably sure that Hunehune's fine was more cash than most of them can expect to earn in many months. There are some urban Gahuku whose standard of living may be comparable to the average lower-middle-class American family, and a much smaller number who are reputed to be wealthy, but the majority of the rural population are poor by Western standards. It is not the grinding and depressing poverty associated with urbanized, industrialized and overpopulated countries, however. The rural peasantry have little cash to spend on clothing, and their houses lack virtually everything we consider bare necessities, but they own the resources on which they depended traditionally and which may also provide them with seasonal income from introduced crops (principally coffee in the Asaro Valley). The amount of cash assembled for some traditional exchanges is sometimes astonishing, but it represents the contributions of many people who share the obligations involved. The average villager appears to have little ready cash from day to day.

Hunehune could not pay the fine from his own cash resources, but he could expect his relatives to help him, and the day following the verdict he was in Susuroka asking their assistance. I saw him from the veranda of Makis' house, guessed his purpose and also that he would try to include me among the contributors. After a while he came into the kitchen where I was boiling water for tea.

"Morning Goroha Gipo," he said affably, sitting on the floor. "I haven't come to see you for several days."

Since that was obvious, I let it pass. "Is everything all right?" he asked.

I told him everything was fine and asked if he would like some tea. Yes, that would be good, so I made it in the only other mug I owned and gave it to him. It didn't have enough sugar, but I wasn't to disturb myself. He would find the package in the cardboard box where I kept my few groceries.

His tea sweetened to his taste, he came to the point without delay, telling me (as though I may not have heard it) he had been taken to court for "a little trouble" and fined. He had only twenty dollars of his own and others had promised to contribute an additional twenty-five dollars. Would I help to make up the remainder? I said "No," telling him it was his fault: he wouldn't be a nuisance if he didn't drink too much. I was reasonably confident my refusal wouldn't be questioned by anyone, and after he left (with no attempt to press me) I found that the majority of other people he approached had also declined.

Unable to raise the amount of the fine, Hunehune returned to the court to obtain a reduction, but the plaintiffs' only concession was an offer to accept a large pig in lieu of some of the cash. He did not have a pig and, again, those whose help he sought declined to contribute. The matter had not been resolved when I left, but other events before my departure indicated that far from being chastened, he was pursuing a course that might have more serious consequences.

The land for the coffee plantation near Javilo's settlement had been acquired on a ninety-nine-year lease from several different groups—clans as well as tribes—while I was there from 1950 to 1952. I was present when the money for the lease was distributed. Javilo's group were the Nagamidzuha most directly involved: a portion of the property is part of their landed patrimony. But other ridge clans received small amounts. The original leaseholder, an Australian, had begun to clear and plant part of the property and to build a home on it before I left in 1952. He subsequently sold the lease, and later the original contract was terminated under the provisions of the Land Redistribution Act of Papua New Guinea. Immediate title reverted to the original owners, with the national government acting as trustee and the National Development Bank providing large interest-free loans to develop the property. When the loans have been acquitted, full control and income from the plantation should be shared by the landholding groups. The plantation's present board of directors is controlled by their representatives. Its powers are limited in everyday matters of planning and management but the owners' title is apparently secured by the Land Redistribution Act, provided they are not persuaded to relinquish it. Recent events suggest this could happen.

A major shareholder is a Gahuku man who bought into the property at considerable cost. He is not a member of any of the original landholding groups—though he is affiliated with some of them—but his cash investment and wealth are a base from which he is able to apply pressure both locally and, allegedly, at higher levels of the national government. He has proposed buying out the other shareholders, which would mean relinquishing their rights in perpetuity. The price offered is over U.S. $200,000 at current exchange rates, and there is no doubt he can raise it, but there are suspicions he is acting in collusion with wealthy interests prohibited from owning land under present law.

Three things must be accomplished before his proposal succeeds. First, the board of directors must vote on it; then the minister (parliamentary head) of the relevant government department must transmit the vote and his recommendation to the prime minister for final review. In late September 1982 the directors met and voted, dividing evenly because Hunehune Opomari abstained. This impasse apparently gives the minister the discretionary power to make a tie-breaking decision.

While I cannot divulge all the information I have—and a great deal of it is unsubstantiated in any case—Hunehune's role is on public record, and so is Javilo's response to him. Several days before the vote, Javilo and others opposing the sale confronted him, demanding him to state his position clearly. People who were present reported he assured them he would vote in accordance with the wishes of his clan. His subsequent fence-straddling action was not precisely a vote against Javilo but it could have the same effect, leaving the next step to a minister who is said to want the sale of the property.

Javilo reacted angrily. He forbade Hunehune to come near his settlement and threatened him with bodily harm if he even so much as entered the plantation area. He had no legal basis for this, but until the time I left, Hunehune was sufficiently concerned to arm himself with an axe whenever he left his settlement.

Hunehune's personal motives for rejecting his closest kinsmen are not part of the public record, and he never confided them to me. I asked him about that proposed sale on several occasions, and I'm sure I said I agreed with Javilo that the interests of his clan would be served best by retaining their rights in an excellently managed, flourishing, and developing operation. I remember he never looked at me directly and never stated his position unequivocally. He listened, studied the floor, seemed to nod in assent and murmured vaguely, "Yes, that is so," but I wasn't greatly surprised when I learned of his abstention. There are allegations he was bribed by Javilo's opponents, but if this is so, they must also be annoyed with him. His action may give the minister discretionary power to decide the issue in favor of the purchaser, but such a move would almost surely warrant closer scrutiny at higher levels of government.

I do not think it is difficult to understand what Hunehune's motives may have been, however. The prospect of immediate cash for his interests in the land is surely one of them, and in addition there was the possibility of obtaining other benefits from an association with wealthy and influential people. For example, he was said to have been constantly in the company of the purchaser and the minister—who had arrived from Port Moresby to be present at the meeting—for several days prior to the vote. He has, perhaps, a frustrated wish to be important. He had been an elected member of the Village Court in 1981 but lost the office to an opponent in 1982, and he is prone to inflating his influence with others, bragging about his accomplishments, and giving himself credit for a respect he clearly does not have. I don't think he is sufficiently acute to have seen that his abstention served none of his purposes, merely making the situation more difficult for everyone and truly isolating him in the middle. Rather, it seems typical of his indecisiveness and lack of direction coupled with an underlying need for recognition. I think he expected to reap some advantages in the regional political system by aligning himself with the purchaser and those supporting him—at the cost, however, of alienating those who were his natural supporters. The certainty that this would follow from casting an equivocal vote led to his abstention and the unforeseen consequence of antagonizing everyone with whom he wished to remain in good repute.

I was disappointed with Hunehune and also saddened by the difference between my memories of him as a young man and the person he is now, but looking back to that earlier time, I sometimes wonder if the flaws I attribute to him were apparent even then. I can see that he tended to be irresponsible as a young man, that he was sometimes opportunistic and also prone to giving himself airs, lording it over those who were younger and wanting the admiration of those who were influential. Yet these qualities were tempered by his youth and what seemed to be an endearing frankness and readiness to mend his ways. In the end, I was deeply grateful to him. If I had been asked, and if the conditions of Gahuku life had not changed, I don't think I would have forecast an outstanding future for him, but I'm sure I never expected to find that his faults outweighed his other attributes.

This makes me wonder if, in 1981, I would have found in Makis the qualities for which I remember him. My own perspective on others has surely changed in thirty years, and perhaps I cannot recapture the vividness of the less complex vision I had then, or the confidence I discovered in realizing I was apparently both liked and accepted. These owe something to both the enthusiasms and uncertainties of a period when a great deal has yet to be proved, and when there is enormous satisfaction in accomplishing things without having any certain guidelines. I am tempted to say that in later life a degree of secularization is almost inevitable: the mountains change their color and become no more than hills; the light is no longer an astonishingly bright shaft but is diffused uniformly throughout the landscape. Yet I don't think I would have found a great discrepancy between my memory of Makis and what he had become. He would have changed in appearance, as everyone has changed, perhaps losing some of his physical grandeur in the soiled trappings of Western clothing—becoming more ordinary, just as life appears to be more ordinary, more secularized, and even depressing compared with the period when I knew him.

This implies neither total approval nor neutrality in my judgment of Gahuku culture when I was there thirty years ago or when I look back on it now. The traditional culture may be appreciated as one example of human creativity without necessarily assenting to all of it. The rites of male initiation were only one climactic expression of ideologies having cruel consequences in many other relationships, and the institutionalized expression of ideas involving pain, strident assertions of dominance, and the demeaning of others involves errors as well as creativity.

By the same token, I don't admire some of the alternatives presented to the Gahuku. Fundamentalist Christianity—which is the kind to which they were exposed—is a bleak and repressive faith, replacing one kind of fear with alien concepts of sin, fire, and eternal damnation. And since it professes to have a monopoly on truth, it ultimately suppresses the prerequisites for creativity which are man's unique endowment. There is little reason to be jubilant over the alternatives to the traditional political and economic system, either. For the vast majority of Gahuku the future can amount to little more than marginal participation in a global system distinguished neither for its altruism nor its equity. They may have been poor by the standards of that system, but that is not the same as being impoverished, which is an increasing likelihood.

These personal values color my reactions to the present as they colored my responses to the past. Anyone who knew the Gahuku thirty years ago is bound to be depressed by much that is observable today. Sitting on the veranda of Makis' house on Sundays and listening to the voices coming from the Swiss Evangelical Mission's church only a short distance from his tomb, I found few reasons to offer those inside the building or their spiritual mentors unqualified congratulations. It wasn't simply that "My Darling Clementine" struck me as a singularly unfortunate aesthetic choice for the context, but also because the openness and adventurousness I have admired in Gahuku appears to include an uncritical willingness to embrace the vulgarization of many other aspects of their lives. Two days before I left the valley in 1982 I visited an Australian who is surely the most famous white man living in the Highlands. It was not our first meeting. I had visited him in 1981, had met him briefly during World War II, and he had been a neighbor from 1950 to 1952, although I cannot remember speaking to him at that time. He deserves the liking and respect he receives from all segments of the population, and his place in the historical record of the Highlands is secure and unblemished by the superiority that was unfortunately the hallmark of many of his colleagues during the colonial period. Since he and I are among the relatively few living whites having a close association with the Asaro Valley thirty years ago—though his association is far longer and more continuous than mine, dating to the first exploratory expedition to enter the region—it was inevitable that much of our conversation consisted of reminiscences, and I remember he prefaced some of his comparisons between then and now by saying: "Before these people degenerated." I did not—and do not—agree that this is the right word to describe the contrast that probably less than a handful of non-natives living in the valley are able to appreciate, but I knew what he had in mind. It is the generally dismal consequences of secularization and—from my personal perspective—the vulgarization of life through the unselective adoption of many of the elements associated with the only alternatives offered to the Gahuku. For there were no alternatives to the spiritual poverty of fundamentalist Christianity and participation in a world political and economic system whose harvested fruits are likely to be bitter. And yet there is a distant hope. It lies in the manifested resilience and creativity of the Gahuku—and, very likely, of all Melanesians—in their adventurousness and their openness. These valuable qualities coupled with education and the awareness of some common strands of cultural tradition and national identity—which is now barely in its infancy—may result in a new and more or less autonomous consciousness, even though there is no drawing back from a commitment to the impersonal forces of global politics and economics.

5 But Makis and his age-mates were not the principal heirs to the future discernible in 1950. Their age at that time insulated them from some of the problems and challenges confronting young men who were at the threshold of their adult careers. It was the members of this age-grade—the age-mates of Hunehune—for whom the world had truly begun to open and expand, revealing new horizons and the possibility of alternatives. The pressures and enticements outside the boundaries of tradition affected them more deeply and personally than their seniors, and they were by no means as well prepared as the generation of their own children to achieve what they sought. This is the reason for referring to them as the most disadvantaged segment of the population. They had no sustaining foundation of accomplishments in traditional pursuits, and they not only lacked but had no means of acquiring the skills necessary to advance beyond a peripheral participation in the new world.

I knew a handful of these young men well. They were not the same chronological age—Asemo was the youngest, being separated from the eldest, Hasu and Lotuwa, by about five years—but they had a common social status, had similar responsibilities and obligations, and, if the world had not changed, faced an identical and limited future. They were individuals, however, as different from one another as any randomly selected sample of young men sharing some basic elements of status in our own culture. I preferred some of them to others, particularly Hunehune and Asemo, the former for the endearing qualities I mentioned earlier and the latter for his seriousness and because the violent events of his initiation seemed such a poignant commentary on the direction in which the world they had inherited was moving. The preparation that he and the others before him had received was directed toward a way of life that was slipping away even then, but nothing I or anyone else could do would provide him with sure directions for the path he wanted to travel.

I don't think these young men would have achieved equal distinction in the kind of life for which their elders had tried to prepare them if times had not changed. I could see Hasu and Hutorno earning a name for themselves as warriors. Asemo seemed less suited than all of them for this assertive and dominating role, and Hunehune might have attempted to claim a greater reputation than he deserved. Not one of them expressed any regret that they weren't called upon to be tested in this way, however, and all of them had ambitions in the enlarged world represented by Goroka.

With the exception of Piripiri, all are living, though only Asemo remains in Susuroka. They are now members of the age-grade to which Makis belonged when I met him. All but one have been married more than once—Hunehune's present wife is his third—and all have children, but none have achieved any particular distinction. Hunehune and Hutorno alone have sought any public office in local government, and the former was a member of the Village Court until he lost to Hutorno in the 1982 Provincial Elections. This is a minor position, however, the court officials having a limited jurisdiction in some civil complaints such as the episode of Hunehune's scurrilous verbal attack on women living near his homestead, when Hutorno found him guilty of defamation and imposed the fine.

In 1950, none of them had a voice in the decision-making processes. Unless their own behavior was under questioning, their views weren't sought. Now that they belong to the grade that previously provided the managers, they appear to have assumed some elements of their predecessors' role. Members of the younger generation are still mostly silent participators in internal governance; the visibly active and more vocal roles fall to the age-mates of Hunehune, though those who are elders continue to influence decisions in most situations involving traditional practice and precedent.

I don't think I would have expected to find another Makis in the ranks of these young men. What he had built fell apart at his death and perhaps the necessity for such men has diminished with the relative stabilization of intergroup relationships beginning with the imposition of the pax Australiana.

The pax Australiana was imposed and maintained by agents of an outside power that arrogated to itself—as all colonial regimes must do—the sole right to resort to force. Its power was not legitimate, but in a way—over and above the simple reality that it had more efficient and effective means of enforcing its order—its external origin tended to invest it with a mystique the present institutions and representatives of centralized government do not have. The central government—no less than its colonial predecessor—monopolizes the use of force as a last resort, and the means of implementing its authority are presently in its sole possession, but I think it may be said that decisions made by its representatives at the local level are more open to attempts to decide some matters by traditional measures. The legitimacy of a representative central government is not completely understood, and simply because its authority is ostensibly more indigenous—not remote and unassailably authoritarian—there may seem to be more room in local matters for the overt expression of abiding enmities and suspicions through direct action.

But despite this, the forced stabilization of geopolitical relationships under the pax Australiana remains a basic fact of life, in the sense that there is no foreseeable return to the kind of force that compelled large numbers of people to vacate their territories and bide their time in exile, waiting for the swing of the pendulum to favor them again.

This new element in the external relationships of different tribal groups has had internal political consequences. It seems unlikely, for example, that the present situation of the ridge clans of Nagamidzuha replicates anything that occurred to them in the past. Clans scattered and their membership changed, but virtually always as a response to warfare. Since warfare is no longer possible and intertribal relationships have been more or less stabilized—for any recourse to force cannot have the consequences formerly associated with it—a basic imperative for fostering and maintaining internal cohesion, and favoring what is often referred to as the big man type of political leadership, has been removed. Under the old conditions, I don't think it would have been possible—or it would have been improbable—for the ridge clans to survive and maintain their territorial integrity with their present attenuated relationships. It is also likely that the Ozahadzuha man's behavior would have been more restrained. Whatever his personal motives may have been, his actions encouraged—some say he even demanded—the dismantling of the edifice Makis had constructed, thereby reversing the direction of policies which were of paramount concern to the traditional leaders and to younger men who may have sought such positions. The fact that the ridge clans submitted passively also indicates an essential change in external political conditions. Stating it succinctly, it is presently possible for groups to keep what they have, even if they are small, without the necessity for the kind of strength that was vitally important in the past. Changes in the area of intertribal politics have allowed a degree of clan—intratribal—autonomy or separation that would have been contrary to survival interests, and have diminished the need for the type of leadership Makis represented.

This does not mean that there is no cooperation between the ridge clans or that their identity as members of the tribe Nagamidzuha is not important to them. They appear to be proud they are Nagamidzuha. Even young men who were

only children or weren't born thirty years ago express satisfaction that the tribe isn't as small as it was, and there are
occasions that marshal the whole group. These are relatively
rare, however. Many institutions that were tribal in scope
have disappeared. Male initiation—clearly connected to warfare—is one of them, but hardly less conspicuous to anyone
who knew the Gahuku three decades ago, the greatest ceremonial exchanges of wealth are missing. Some traditional
exchanges, involving truly large transfers of wealth, have not
lapsed. These include marriage and one called "paying for
the head of kantri" in pidgin, but they involve clans and
smaller segments of kin groups rather than having the tribal-
wide significance of those that occurred in the context of the
pig flute (*idza nama*) ceremonial cycle.

The attenuated intratribal relationships do not mean that
the personal qualities possessed by traditional leaders are un-
important for today's most successful men. All it implies is
that some of the ends to which they are directed are no longer
imperative, and some others involve a constituency that ex-
tends beyond and may also cross out some of the lines that
mapped intertribal relationships in an earlier time.

There are a few Gahuku men who have been outstand-
ingly successful in the enlarged political and economic world
of today. I know only one of them personally, and it is no
more than a slight acquaintanceship. He is chronologically
several years older than Hunehune and is not a member of
Nagamidzuha—indeed, none of the few and reputedly truly
wealthy men belongs to that tribe—but his tribe is a traditional
friend, and he was also the third husband of the woman
whose first marriage is described in *The High Valley* (chapter
five). Soon after Papua New Guinea received independence
from Australia, he became an elected representative to the

national house of assembly from the Eastern Highlands Province. He had also developed sizable coffee plantations, being among the first Gahuku to undertake large-scale production of the crop. Subsequently, he lost his seat in the legislature, as well as control of his coffee holdings. Alcoholism is reportedly the cause of his financial eclipse: his plantations were neglected and mismanaged, forcing the National Development Bank to place them under temporary receivership and approved management in order to recoup its investment in the loans extended to him.

This is the only case I know in which alcoholism may have contributed to the termination of a promising public career, but alcohol is recognized as a problem, particularly in urban environments.

In Susuroka and other rural areas, alcohol has become a ubiquitous presence in social life. My attitudes toward it are not morally pejorative, but there is no denying that it has contributed a frequently unpleasant and often boring element to some domestic and public occasions—not to say possible dangers. It was not available in 1950 and, as far as I know, Gahuku did not possess any traditional substitute, except perhaps the extremely infrequent use of betel, but nowadays it is consumed both privately and publicly. Cases of beer are included in every exchange of wealth and almost every small formal meal marking events that are socially significant to kinsmen. It is relatively easily obtained from legal sources by people living close to towns, but throughout the countryside it is also available from black markets at inflated prices. I don't know whether these sales are illegal. They were never concealed from me, and I was often in houses where the supplies were in full view and the purchases conducted openly.

As far as I was able to observe, almost no hard liquor is consumed in the villages. I had small quantities of both beer and scotch in my house in 1981 and 1982 (but none from 1950 to 1952), and in the evening I usually offered a drink to the men and women who were with me. None of them ever chose the scotch. Whenever my clansmen celebrated, my contribution to the occasion was a case or two of beer. I was never asked to provide hard liquor.

The quantities of beer consumed at public ceremonies have added to some of the irritations and frustrations I experienced during my first fieldwork. Until I learned to accept it philosophically, the Gahuku's characteristic vagueness concerning the programming of important events was annoying to someone accustomed to more precise timetables. First, there wasn't much forewarning. They would advise me that something would occur "soon," which could have meant the next day or a week later. If pressed to be more precise, they would simply say—not without exasperation—"It will happen when they are ready!" Since I could not be sure I would have the opportunity to observe the same event again, I was often torn between wanting to be present whenever it occurred and the need to follow some other line of inquiry which might take me to some other place. I was often informed only at the last minute—that is, the day of the event—and even then the seemingly endless hours of waiting in the hot sun or the thin shade of trees drained away some of my anticipatory enthusiasm and excitement.

I suppose these periods of inaction were instructive, at least after I had learned some of the language. Sitting or lying with increasing discomfort on the ground among the men, I could listen to what they were saying and also observe the women and children from a distance, but people were not disposed to speak slowly for my benefit or to explain their jokes and the topics of their conversation. I lost interest and closed off the desultory chatter and occasional laughter, withdrawing into a personal world where I tried to find words for the contrasts of light and shadow or the motionless canopy of leaves and spiny, vermilion fruit a castor-oil tree threw across the sky above my head. And even when things got under way, spurts of activity were punctuated by long intervals of inactivity and seemingly disorganized discussions I was unable to follow.

Waiting around is an even more tiresome component of gatherings and ceremonies today. In 1981, Kopi Manove took me to a *kantri* ceremony at which members of his clan (Meniharove) were the principal recipients in an exchange of wealth. It was held by a Bena Bena group whose members were the descendants of refugees who had gone into exile with the Meniharove more than thirty years previously and had only recently returned to their clan territory, which had remained unoccupied in the interim and was more than twenty miles distant, on the northern slopes of the western Bena region. I went with Kopi, around 10:00 A.M., to the Meniharove village where the guests were preparing for departure. Two trucks were waiting to transport them when the principal recipients had completed dressing in ceremonial regalia. Women outshone the men on this occasion—the ceremony recognized maternal connections and intergroup relationships through marriage. Their faces were brilliantly painted in reds and yellows and their heads dressed with a profusion of bird of paradise plumes—decorations women do not customarily wear on other occasions. A few were bare breasted, but others wore Western bras, alone or outside a blouse, and all of them had added yards and yards of glittery Christmas tinsel to their ensembles. They were already drinking beer. Indeed, judging from the way in which some of them met me, I surmised they were already tipsy.

I left with Kopi, his wife, and some other people in his Mazda truck at about 11:30 A.M., going ahead of the main guests, who, as far as I could see, had finished dressing and were standing around drinking. It was about an hour's drive along the Highland Highway, through country where I had not been in 1950. After an hour, we turned north from the highway along a track that became more and more rudimentary as it climbed the deforested foothills of the Bena valley's wall. We crossed a stream, and Kopi parked the truck beside the track. Everyone got out. Claire Manove had made some sandwiches before leaving Goroka, and I shared them in the fitful shade of some casuarinas bordering the road. Some other members of the party walked a short distance toward the stream we had crossed, sat down, brought out their tattered playing cards and began to gamble. Kopi said the main party would not be long behind us: he had delayed our departure from the Meniharove village until he saw they were ready to leave.

Hours passed. It was a beautiful day, bright and immensely clear. From the fringed shade of the casuarinas, I looked across miles of empty countryside toward the southern wall of the valley, and, farther out, to the steel gray shape of Mt. Michael. I was the only member of the party who had ever been closer to it or had seen the stretch of country on the other side of the distant mountain wall, and for a while, I forgot where we were and the increasing boredom and discomfort as the hours passed. The others played cards or lay down in the brittle grass and tried to sleep, stirring sometimes to complain and to listen for the distant sound of approaching vehicles. I looked at the mountain and recalled my journey around it, when I had been with the first of my kind to go there, contrasting those experiences with the Mazda truck behind me, with our sandwiches of store bought white bread and processed meat, and the knitted woolen cap and cotton dress worn by my daughter Lucy Makis.

It was near the beginning of the rainy season, and I saw that swollen clouds were gathering in the east and above the mountains behind me. Even if you know people as well as I knew some of those who were with me, it is difficult to pass the time in customary small talk when you hardly know their language—even though Kopi, his wife, and Lucy Makis spoke English. You are, perforce, an outsider who cannot ever be completely familiar with the texture of the life they share with one another. For example, I can be reasonably sure that if I had been sitting with someone from my own culture I could have described to him what I saw as I looked across the valley, and I could have expected him to understand my vision, even if he did not share it fully or was relatively disinterested in the personal interpretation I placed on the natural composition. Yet I could never be certain that my Gahuku companions would see what I saw, would be able to experience, even vicariously, my vision, as I, of course, could never delude myself that I experienced the one they had. Even the conventions in which we describe the external world are provided by the lens of our own culture, and the inner world of subjective experience is even far more difficult to enter across the boundaries of different ways of life. Under these circumstances, it is difficult to start a conversation. You cannot simply throw out some remark or observation and expect it to be taken up and returned, beginning the embroidery through which you find and place the other, even though you may discover you do not care for what you have found. Casual conversation with strangers is hardly possible, and discursive discourse, even with those with whom you are well acquainted, is difficult to sustain. Almost inevitably, it assumes more of the characteristics of a formal interview—mutual, no doubt—which requires a greater effort to find the connecting links that will keep it moving forward.

I was thinking of this as I sat beside the road with my friends and my children. Lucy and Lokilo Makis, watching the gathering rain clouds, becoming more and more irritated by the delay, and wondering if the event would be aborted. Lucy stirred, sat up and yawned. I looked at her, smiled and said in English, "Patience is a virtue."

She returned my smile, knowing what I meant, lay down again with her back toward me and went to sleep.

All the others were also sleeping on the ground among the sparse grass. Farther down the road toward the stream, the card players continued their game in a dappled clearing. I continued to sit there, staring across the now visually familiar valley and trying to accept the sentiment I had voiced to Lucy.

At half past three Kopi sat up, cocked an ear in the direction of the road on the other side of the stream, and announced he could hear the sound of trucks. He called out to the card players, who, without interrupting their game, replied they had heard it too. People around me stirred, stood up, and stretched. I did the same, immensely relieved that *something* seemed about to happen. But no one seemed to be in any hurry, and another half hour passed.

I asked Kopi what could be delaying the trucks, supposing he had heard them. He called to the card players, held a brief exchange with them and said, "They've probably stopped down there to straighten their decorations after the ride, and to drink some beer."

Shortly after this—and still with no sign of the trucks—he suggested we all get into the Mazda. We proceeded up the track, farther into the foothills, until it ended at a clump of scrubby pine trees. Everyone got out, and once more settled themselves on the ground. I sat down alone, resigned but also unreasonably angry, wishing I hadn't wasted a whole day for such little profit. I told myself that I had seen the same ceremony many times when some of the people with me hadn't even been born. I knew what it was about, and how it fitted into the mesh of Gahuku socialties and ideologies. Indeed, as soon as people had told me we were going to a *kantri* ceremony I had been able to assign a place to it in the general context of Gahuku life, even if I did not know the precise connections between the groups involved on this occasion. But I had also thought it incumbent on me to observe how it may have changed. Now, preparing to endure another period of waiting, I thought it would have mattered little if I hadn't bothered to come. It was probably enough to know that the ceremony still had a place in a world that had altered in many dramatic ways.

There was still no sign of the trucks when, suddenly, everyone rose and began to walk forward. Kopi helped me to my feet and told me to follow him, and now it was like many other occasions I remembered and on which I had found myself disadvantaged: a rapid, uphill climb along the crest of an exposed ridge, stumbling on an uneven track, clutching at grasses to prevent myself from falling ignominiously, and eventually arriving out of breath on high ground above a small village of traditional thatched houses.

The interval of waiting was only brief this time, hardly sufficient to regain my breath and steady the muscles of my legs. Farther down the track, in the direction of the clump of pine trees, the grasses were topped with a moving, blossoming array of multicolored tassels, and the sound of singing rose toward us through air already faintly brushed with dusk, a premonitory breeze and the smell of rain in clouds that had been gathering since the early afternoon. Once again, I admired the theatrical flare the Gahuku brought to their ceremonies. All the long and boring hours of "waiting in the green room and the wings"—though I don't suppose it seemed like that to the participants, who knew in advance when their call to go on stage would come—were worth it when the curtain rose. The natural setting—here, the bare ridge dropping away to the valley floor, and the bulk of the mountains behind the foothills where I stood—seemed to demand this sudden eruption of sound, color and orchestrated movement.

As the moving blossoms took on form and stature, we turned away and hurried down the slope ahead of them into the waiting village, where crowds of people lined both sides of the street. Kopi led me to an elevated grassy knoll occupied by more than a score of boys, youths, and young men.

Below the knoll—about fifteen yards from where we sat—two long wands of bamboo, each more than twelve feet tall and stripped of leaves, had been erected in the ground. Both wands were covered with a double row of one *kina* currency notes. Fourteen cardboard cartons of beer—each containing two dozen bottles—were stacked on the ground at the base of the wands, and in front of these there was an array of bird of paradise plumes and some traditional necklaces of large white cowries. All this, together with quantities of cooked pork that had not yet been removed from the earth ovens, would be given to the visiting Meniharove.

Kopi asked me to guess the amount of currency. I estimated twelve hundred *kina*. He studied the wands for a moment. "No," he said, "I think it's more than two thousand." Others joined the game; all their guesses were much higher than mine, some higher than Kopi's, and I think two thousand *kina*—the equivalent of U.S. $3,000—would not be far from the mark. I was surprised by the size of the gift, but later I was told it had been a relatively small exchange. On a similar occasion concerned with Kopi's small son Konrad, he had included a truck as well as currency, beer, and valuables; but he said he would not hold another one, though traditionally the "head" of *kantri* had to be "payed for" more than once during a person's lifetime, the occasions coinciding approximately with stages in the maturation—and changes in social status—of the individual concerned.

Meanwhile, the Meniharove guests entered from the opposite end of the street. No Gahuku dances were able to hold my interest for long. Those that weren't primarily a headlong rush of men were, like this one, a relatively slow jog-trot of men and women advancing to midway down the village, turning and retreating, and repeating the same sequence over and over again, while their hosts jogged forward to meet them at a short distance on either side. The plumes and paint and the singing—the song, like the dance, was repeated endlessly—were initially stirring, even though, as far as I was concerned, the spectacle was marred by the incongruous addition of portions of Western clothing and the tawdry festoons of "Woolworth" tinsel. Each dance set lasted about five minutes; then the guests broke ranks and retired to the "wings."

This was customary, but now they occupied the intervals with drinking beer—rather than chewing sugar cane—provided by their hosts. After the time out, they regrouped in the street and began another set.

By the time they had completed several sets, some of the women were breaking step, stumbling, and colliding with each other in their ranks. The light was fading, and the sky and landscape were far more pleasing to watch than the deteriorating progress of the dance. To the west, in the direction of Goroka, the countryside was blurred by columns of falling rain, separated from one another by luminous patches of yellow and green where the sun reached the valley floor through apertures in the massing clouds. The purpling storm behind the village to the north had spilled over the crest of the mountain wall, pushed forward slowly but inexorably by the wind that had changed from a premonitory breeze to a steady blow. Yet the village, in its isolated bowl, still held the light—an amphitheater bathed in a effulgent incandescence in which grasses, the needles of casuarinas, and the thatched roofs of the houses quivered with an intensity of color like the guttering flames of candles against the darkening sky.

And still the staggering dance continued, monotonously and repetitiously, on the stage below me.

Kopi turned to look at the approaching storm.

"When will they stop dancing and distribute the money and beer?" I asked.

"They'll soon be too drunk to do anything," he said laconically.

One of the women dancers staggered, fell, picked herself up and, laughing, swayed to the sidelines, where she grabbed a bottle of beer, tilted her head and gulped it, one hand grasping the thatch of a house to steady herself.

Large, cold drops of rain began to fall. Kopi signaled to Lokilo. We rose, descended from the knoll and pushed through the crowd of onlookers in the street, collecting other members of our party as we went. I was delayed momentarily by the drunken woman who had fallen in the last set. I knew her, and when she saw me leaving she grabbed me, clutching me to her and almost bringing me down beneath her, stroking my face, mouthing the customary greetings in a thick, almost incoherent stream, and insisting I couldn't leave yet—all this to the vast amusement of the crowd.

I got away from her eventually, joining Kopi and the others, who had waited for me on some high ground at the entrance to the village. We reached the Mazda before the rain had begun to pour steadily, but it was a wet and uncomfortable journey for most of the return journey to Goroka.

This exhibition of public drunkenness was not an unusual sight, but in fairness to the Gahuku—or at least to those in the rural areas—there is no population of derelict, indigent alcoholics comparable to anything existing in our own culture. In a sense, it is hardly appropriate to speak of "public drunkenness" as we customarily use the term. Most areas of life we consider private are far more public in a Gahuku village. Houses are close to one another and are not soundproof, and except when it is raining or after dark, they are seldom occupied. Domestic life goes on outside, in the village street or in the gardens, which, in turn, are not separated from one another by high fences. A premium is not placed on privacy— which is one of the more trying facets of living there. The attitude that "it's none of your business" is more or less irrelevant when most private business is also public knowledge, for it is difficult to conceal many things we try to keep within the home. Moreover, most of the inhabitants are related to one another in some way. The life in a village, its intensity and the knowledge of others that is shared by everyone, is more like that of a large extended family living under one roof than a city or suburban neighborhood or even relatively small rural communities from which so many people in our culture wish to escape. Everyone knows—even if they don't discuss it openly—the current state of relationships within a particular household; they know, and hear, when a married couple are quarreling, when a husband has beaten his wife— and this, too, is often public—or when he, or she, is drunk.

Most public ceremonies involving people from different villages are also different from our own comparable events and from large celebrations of recent introduction, such as the observance of Independence Day or the Eastern Highlands Show. The latter commenced as a Christmas event under the colonial regime prior to independence, when the district commissioner summoned representatives from all the tribes in the controlled and semicontrolled areas to appear in ceremonial regalia at government headquarters in Goroka and to perform their own dances and songs. At that time (1950– 1952), the various contingents received food and gifts—salt, rice, and some valued trade goods—at the end of the command performance, which was primarily an opportunity to impress the native participants with the "global" sway and paternalistic concern and largesse of the central and alien government, incidentally also bringing together groups that were often complete strangers to one another—foreigners from the unknown regions on "the other side of the world." The Goroka Show is not an annual event now. It alternates with the Western Highland Show held at Mt. Hagen, is no longer associated with Christmas, and includes displays of agricultural produce as well as crafts for sale, but the earlier

Christmas "sing-sing" is clearly its progenitor. It is a major tourist attraction, and most of the startling photographs illuminating the pages of *National Geographic* magazine and coffee table types of books have been taken at either this or similar nontraditional events in Papua New Guinea.

The point is this: You cannot apply our standards of what is seemly public conduct to events such as the *kantri* ceremony described above. These traditional ceremonies are public only in the sense that—unlike some others—they are held in the open and, therefore, aren't private. All the principal participants, and even a majority of those who are merely looking, are either known to one another or are linked by personal ties. Seeking for an analogy from our own culture, it would be similar if we held most of our private celebrations and anniversaries where everyone could see them, not excluding our cocktail parties, at which some guests occasionally behave abominably.

Yet even allowing for this qualitative difference, alcohol seems to have exacerbated the tensions in some relationships or, at least, has contributed to less contained or more spontaneous—and possibly irresponsible—expressions of both festering antipathies and reactions to temporary and passing causes for suspicion or complaint. I think that in some instances it has advanced to the flash point of relationships that were always volatile, which again is not outside the range of our own cultural experience.

6 Though alcohol is now a commonplace element of social life, a great many Gahuku—both young and old—do not drink. Lokilo Makis and a number of other members of his age group do not touch it, though as

far as I know there is no institutional or family pressure to abstain. Most of the elders, my own age-group, are teetotalers or drink beer sparingly, and I did not observe any drinking among the teenage population of Nagamidzuha. I am reasonably sure this does not mean it doesn't exist, though it is probably on a small scale. Alcohol or addiction to it were not among my primary interests, and in any case I was not there long enough to make any systematic investigation of its social and personal consequences. Yet it was new and, therefore, I was bound to notice it. The population I observed is not a scientific sample, yet given my position and the quality of my interaction with its members, my obervations may not be worthless.

Chronic drunkenness seemed to be far more common among the members of the age-grade of Hunehune than among the members of the one above it, the grade of Makis, or the generation below, the grade of Lokilo Makis and Kopi Manove. This does not mean that all the members of these older and younger grades abstained from drinking alcohol: Makis, for example, clearly drank to excess occasionally. I do not know if drunkenness had become a characteristic of his behavior since the time when I had known him, but basing my judgment on his character then, I am reasonably sure that the circumstances of his death were not an isolated incident. I have no evidence that he was frequently drunk, however. The Ozahadzuha man does not refuse a beer when it is offered to him, but I have never seen him drink more than two bottles. Indeed, his wife drinks far more than he does, and I think his abstemiousness is characteristic of his generation. Similarly, alcohol is clearly not a personal problem for all age-mates of Hunehune. Asemo, for example, drinks no more than the Ozahadzuha man. But all the other members of his grade whom I know as more than casual acquaintances are reputed to drink heavily, which does not mean they are alcoholics. Gahuku have no word for the addiction, but I think they clearly see a difference between occasional bouts of excessive drinking and drunkenness and chronic intoxication. Of the five living members of this grade with whom I had close relationships when they were young, two probably qualify for the latter category.

I know less about the grade to which Lokilo Makis belongs and those who are several years younger, in their late teens. In many ways, I am more familiar with the interests and the lives led by their parents when they were the same age. Thirty years ago, the teenagers—those nearing their final incorporation into the *nama* cult—were left very much to their own devices during the day, roaming the ridge with a modicum of responsibility or adult surveillance. Yet they were almost always underfoot, the range of their movements being restricted by the map of group relationships, and they had nothing comparable to the variety of interests and activities from which the young may choose at present. Nowadays, many of the latter are also attending school, and some may be employed outside their village. Similarly, their elder brothers lead lives that are less circumscribed than their counterparts in that earlier time. Their mobility has increased enormously, and their reaction is often found in the town or even farther afield. For example, it is relatively commonplace for them to go on overnight jaunts to places as far away as Kainantu.

The opening of both the geographical and social worlds means that it is less easy to observe these young people from day to day. Some of their activities are not only beyond my capacities but, being adaptations of Western mores, are also events at which someone of advanced age tends to be out of place. The same age difference did not separate me from the novice youths and young men in 1950. I was by no means out of place at their gatherings, but "grandfathers," though shown respect, were hardly appropriate participants or even spectators in some of their grandchildren's social activities. I observed some entirely new institutions which are primarily the concern of the current generation of young people, and I learned a good deal more through my familial relationships with many of them, yet I cannot say that I know them—their interests, problems and motivations—as well as I knew their fathers in a more restricted, repressive, and less mobile world. I shall have more to say about them later, however. Momentarily, it is the predicament of their fathers that interests me.

I don't think it is a misjudgment to characterize their generation as the most disadvantaged in the historical context of their time—either in terms of the changes occurring or foreshadowing them or in the directions they took. Clearly envisaging the expansion of the world for which they had been prepared, already experiencing alterations in its contours and motivated to move out, the majority of them lacked even the rudimentary skills necessary to obtain more than a tentative foothold on the periphery of accelerating events and would live to see many of their children overtaking them. In itself, I don't suppose this is at all unusual, and I did not detect any envy or resentment on the part of those whose sons and daughters—and there are a significant number of them—are far more at home in the material and social order beyond the boundaries of traditional life. But this rather commonplace situation in changing times is not the core of their predicament, which was, rather, their inability to match opportunity with aspirations.

Clearly, this was not an equal measure of experience for all of them. Just as today some young people seem quite content not to try to make a position for themselves in the world outside the village, or even to avail themselves of opportunities they possess, so there were members of their parents' generation who showed little interest in trying to pursue any kind of career among their more limited range of new choices. Yet I think it is possible to say that the expanding world beckoned the young men of 1950 in a substantially different way. Younger generations have grown up *within* it. From their early years onward it is part of their everyday experience, not a trumpet call outside the gates but an integral element in the orchestration of life, and this means there are important qualitative differences in their perceptions of it, attitudes toward it, and even ambitions in it compared to those of their fathers.

The life symbolized by what was observable at Goroka thirty years ago represented the great adventure to many young men. Not so long before this, warfare had been the principal testing ground for manhood. It dominated the pattern of life. The imperatives and restrictions it imposed, and the values associated with it, permeated the greater part of cultural experience. Life had other dimensions to it, of course, but warfare encapsuled the whole of it. It limited movement, and placed a premium on fostering a particular kind of masculinity which, in turn, colored the relationship between men and women. It was the only career open to young males and was, in a sense, the ultimate adventure.

This adventure had gone by 1950, however, and for many young men it had been replaced by another which in some respects held greater hazards, since those who embarked on it had no formal preparation for it. Virtually everything connected with it was unknown; indeed, it is not being over fanciful to say they were not even as well equipped for the enterprise as the European navigators who set out to enlarge the boundaries of the world in the Age of Discovery. Carrying the analogy further, those who returned from the adventure were received at home in much the same way as the explorers who had passed from the ken of families and countrymen in search of knowledge or with the acquisitive ambition of finding the riches of Eldorado.

Only a small number of Gahuku had been outside the Asaro Valley by 1952. One or two of these, including the man who ran the Lutheran Mission "school" below the ridge of Susuroka, had received some religious instruction at centers on the coast. The handful of others had been indentured laborers, signing on for work—for a stipulated period—on copra plantations in coastal areas or offshore island groups. This was before the colonial government—because of its concern about the introduction of malaria—imposed a temporary ban of the recruitment of Highland laborers for coastal work. I was present when two of these young men, one of them belonging to Gama and the other to Uheto, returned to their villages following a period of compulsory quarantine and treatment with antimalarial drugs at Goroka. At that time wages were fixed by the government; people in the private sector, including myself, were cautioned not to pay more than the official scale in order to avoid the "contagion" of increased demands. My memory is uncertain, and I have not bothered to turn to official documents to refresh it, but I think the monthly wage for domestic help was in the neighborhood of thirty Australian shillings, the equivalent of about U.S. $1.00

at today's rate of exchange. In addition, employees had to be provided with a legally enforceable minimum of food, tobacco, clothing, and some small personal items. Apart from the experience, what these pathfinding adventurers were able to save or purchase out of this largesse were the fruits of their quest for Eldorado.

Yet these meager fruits were carried home in tin boxes like trophies in a Roman triumph. The returning laborers, dressed in Western shorts and shirts, were greeted by crowds of kinsmen with the clamorous excitement that welcomed new members of the *nama* cult at their "rebirth" following their adventure of initiation. Indeed, their reception may have been informed with a greater measure of feeling than the ritual expressions of emotions that heralded the new status of the latter after their separation and symbolic death. And the following day, the laborers were honored with a large feast, highlighted by the distribution of the spoils of their enterprise. When I met these young men later, people always informed me of their accomplishment as though it was not only deserving of special mention but, in some way, had also made them members—possibly even representatives—of the life to which I belonged. And the laborers had tales to tell which most members of the audience found as curious and beyond their comprehension as those recounted by seafarers returned from journeys beyond the known boundaries of the world. They often made a point of coming to see me and demonstrating their familiarity with my culture, watched by silent and openmouthed observers who shook their heads and murmured "ayee!" in disbelief.

None of Nagamidzuha's men who were the same age as Hunehune and those who were my companions, employees, and helpers more than a generation ago have achieved any noteworthy distinction in the modern world. It is true that the relatively few Gahuku who have acquired nontraditional wealth—much more of it, it seems, than I shall ever possess—and recognition in the enlarged arena of provincial and national politics apparently belong to the same age-grade. They are not the generation of Makis—that is, those who are elders now—but chronologically they appear to be several years older than members of Hunehune's age-set, for the members of any particular age-grade were separated from one another by anything from one to seven or more years: the cycle of initiation into adult status, and the assumption of its responsibilities, occurred at no less than five-year intervals. As far as I know, these truly wealthy men have had no more education than Hunehune and his age-mates, and perhaps less than Asemo, who belongs to the same grade as the young men I described in *The High Valley* (chapter three) but who was initiated into it probably five years later than them. Asemo can print his name and can read a few words from a book. None of the others are able to do this, and I don't think the modern capitalists belonging to the same age-grade are more skilled in these particular accomplishments. Moreover, I don't think they were among those who were enticed to undertake the adventure of leaving their villages to broaden their experience of the new world.

It is probably futile to speculate why they have prospered so obviously compared to others belonging to the same generation. Individual differences in the skills of management and entrepreneurship, which were also important in traditional times, must be recognized. In addition to these imponderables, their tribal groups are all far larger—both numerically and in landed patrimony—than Nagamidzuha, giving them, perhaps, access to more primary resources and a large constituency of supporters. The reputation of Makis, for example, his recognition and the name he had, was out of proportion with either the size or local importance of his clan and tribe and was based partly on the recognition he received from the representatives of the colonial government. His clan is by no means landless, but it is not as well endowed as others in Nagamidzuha, and despite his relatively imposing frame house, which was certainly not built entirely from his personal resources and those of his direct descendants, he was not as wealthy in contemporary assets as the Ozahadzuha man who attempted to fill his shoes. He left no legacy of permanently developed, income-producing resources. He had not engaged in coffee production, apart from a few small plantings in mixed gardens, which provides the foundation of most of the contemporary fortunes of men who were younger yet whose lives overlap with a time of relatively unaltered tradition and the shape it has today. And this—apart from anything they possess in aptitude, acumen, and access to resources—may also have to be considered in comparing the few eminently successful members of the same age-grade with Hunehune's set within it: being older by some seven years or more, they were more firmly established in the network of social ties and obligations so necessary for advancement.

The young men of Hunehune's age-set cannot be classed as failures in the context of their time, however. They had no opportunity to acquire any formal schooling, and none of the white-collar or semiprofessional jobs some of the younger generation hold were available to them. Outside of the commercial production of coffee, which was then a speculative and unproven crop, the only avenues they possessed for enlarging their experience of the world that was overtaking them were the limited roles of domestic servants, laborers and, representing the height of ambition, drivers and motor mechanics. None of the six whom I employed from time to time continued in domestic service after my departure. They can hardly be said to have received from me the kind of training that would recommend them for such positions in other European households. There were always too many of them— my house didn't have hardwood floors or anything else that had to be kept spic-and-span; my meals were cooked on an open fire on the ground until I eventually obtained a kerosene stove; my few clothes were washed in the stream below the ridge; my water was stored in a forty-four gallon kerosene drum and replenished by either catching rain in a couple of galvanized buckets or by being carried from a spring on the hillside in long, hollow bamboos. I accepted at least twice as many helpers as I needed, thinking the village was entitled to some return for what they gave me: the land for my house and garden and their willingness to let me live there, to answer my questions, and to share a part of their lives.

None of the members of my household had any interest in making domestic service a career, in joining the police, or in being day laborers on plantations or various public works; indeed, I had the distinct but unconfirmed impression that laboring jobs were filled mainly by people from outside the Asaro Valley, perhaps principally from the less developed and more heavily populated Chimbu area to the west. At one point during my first fieldwork I attempted—on the advice of Makis—to employ an itinerant Chimbu man when I was particularly annoyed with my Gahuku helpers, who seemed to have so many local distractions and so little motivation that they were seldom there when I needed them. It was a useless effort, however: the villagers never accepted the Chimbu man, but complained about him, treated him as an unwelcome foreigner, and browbeat him constantly, until I was forced to dismiss him for his own sake as much as for mine.

Whenever they spoke about their futures, Hunehune and his age-mates said they wanted to become drivers, and all of them did. After I said good-bye to him, Hunehune was accepted by a European employed in the Department of Civil Aviation, received driver instruction, and obtained his license. His job took him to Lae for a time, as well as to other parts of the Eastern Highlands; he was employed at Henganofi when he received word of Makis' accident in 1969. Some time later he acquired a secondhand truck of his own and used it for hauling and passenger service in the neighborhood of Goroka. He says he still has it, though he has not used it for at least two years because it is unserviceable and is being held at a service station in Goroka until he can pay for repairs. He asked me to lend him 800 *kina* (the equivalent of U.S. $1,200), the estimated cost of putting it back on the road. Since it was an impossible request, I did not bother to verify his story, but I'm skeptical that any garage would store it for this length of time. It could be nothing more than a rusting and abandoned piece of junk, one of an increasing number of derelict vehicles that are beginning to appear beside the roads and on the outskirts of villages.

The other age-mates had similar careers after I left in 1952. All spent some time outside the valley. All have been back for a good many years, and like Hunehune, they have nothing material to show for their various enterprises. It was one of them who bought and subsequently lost a truck with a share of the wealth distributed after the death of Makis.

I have no way of knowing whether this group of adventurous young men recognize any discrepancy between the little they have now and what they may have hoped to achieve when they accepted the challenge of the expanding world thirty years ago: this kind of introspection appears to be no more characteristic of Gahuku now than it was in the past. They had high ambitions for their time—higher than many others of the same age—and with the pragmatic acuity that distinguished notable men in a more traditional era, they eschewed more readily available unskilled and dead-end jobs for more venturesome occupations that were light-years removed, in relative terms, from any preexisting models.

It is possible, of course, that the way in which I characterize their personal situation is not how they see it. I may be justified in believing that I know a good deal about the values, beliefs, motivations and the structure of relationships forming their traditional cultural environment, and, almost certainly more than any other person of my own kind possesses. But I am an outsider; and the discrepancy I see between their opportunities and aspirations may be colored by unjustified extrapolations from my own culture—that is, from its particular orientations and perspectives on both individual and social problems. Because of this, I may be inclined to exaggerate the "tragic" dimensions of their situations, expecting they *must* recognize and subjectively experience what I see when I place them against the unfolding panorama of events. If they do see and feel it, it is not articulated. They do not rail against circumstances that might be held responsible for their failure to achieve more than a small measure of the expectations they may have had when they set forth. They recount this portion of their lives in a relatively bland manner or in a way that is sometimes informed by a tone of pioneering pride, and I do not possess the necessary skills or specialized knowledge to judge whether this may merely camouflage or compensate for deeper feelings of frustration.

If I am correct in suggesting that chronic drinking is more prevalent among the members of this middle generation than the ones above and below it, remembering that my observations are confined to the rural population only, it could be correlated with such subjective feelings, however. I have absolutely no evidence that it is a problem among those who are elders now. In the years that have passed since I first went to live with them, these old men have had to accept truly dramatic changes in the life they knew and were passing on to others; indeed, the alterations that have occurred in their lifetimes are far more drastic than anything experienced by members of other generations. The ideological foundations of major institutions have either crumbled or disappeared, and the very form of some relationships responsible both for the feeling and the patterning of life have changed almost beyond recognition. In their lifetime, these old men and women have seen and participated in a revolution—or evolution, perhaps—whose dimensions transcend anything experienced by younger generations. They did not try to forestall it, using their established reputations and authority of their positions to erect defenses around the tradition they knew. Rather, it might be said they foresaw, accommodated to, and even instituted some of the changes that are aspects of life at the present. But the new world did not confront them with the same challenges and aspirations it presented to the young adults of 1950; their adventure was qualitatively and substantively different. Perhaps one can say they were not the front line troops called upon to go out and test their mettle, and thus were protected against some of the personal experiences of inadequacy and frustration, if not defeat.

Similarly, the generation of those who were children in 1950 have a different experience from their fathers, and some of them are preparing their children for a life, if they want it, that is now an integral part of their heritage. It may not be a heritage that is attainable by all the youngsters, just as it wasn't attainable by all who are young adults today, but more of the necessary means to claim it exists for them compared to the middle generation of Hunehune, Asemo, and the others: few of them need go forward into an unknown world without preparation. The adventure has changed, and if the gap between opportunity and aspiration has not been closed, it is not as wide as it was for the young adults whom I watched when they were starting out and whose service with me was their first step on their journey.

FOUR

THE NEW GENERATION*

| 1 | The first time I heard the sound of the sacred *nama* flutes in the context of Gahuku life is one of the most vivid memories from my earlier fieldwork. It is as fresh as when I recalled it in *The High Valley* (pp. 113 and 118):

> I awakened one morning with the feeling that something new had been added to a familiar situation. The village was completely silent, yet the air seemed to vibrate uneasily against my ear, prompting me to recall the unidentified sound that had

*Some of the material in this chapter appears in more extended form in: Kenneth E. Read, "The Nama Cult Recalled" in *Ritualized Homosexuality in Melanesia*, Gilbert H. Herdt, editor, (Berkeley, Los Angeles, London: University of California Press, 1983); chapter three of *The High Valley* provides a description of the rites of male initiation, including nose bleeding and cane swallowing/vomiting.

broken into my sleep. For a while I lay still and listened intently for anything that would give it a recognizable shape, but there was nothing to which I could fasten an explanation. The day had barely begun. It was far too early for any movement in the houses, and the sound that had left its track on my mind must have come from outside the settlement. I started to dismiss it as imagined when suddenly it came again, lifting me up to my elbows with a sense of shock.

In later months the same notes came at many times of day, but they always carried the quality of this first encounter—the predawn air chilling my arms and shoulders, the glimmer of light in the empty street, and the whole valley lying exposed and unsuspecting as it slept. Their sound eludes description. It had too many different elements and contradictions, and the music was based on an entirely alien scale. The clear air offered it no resistance, and the notes, coming from a distance, seemed to wind at will through an echoing void, tracing such a capricious path that their origins were successfully concealed. They struck with a hollow, pulsing beat in the base register, a continual explosion of notes like a cry of hunger torn from a distended, disembodied throat. More shrill cries played in and out of this rhythmic background in repetitive patterns that after a while could be identified as tunes. Both elements were deliberately joined, contrasting and complementing, designed to produce a unified effect. The shrill notes fluttered avidly around the deeper cries, possessed of the same need and urging the stronger on to fulfill it like vultures wheeling in a cloudless sky, dependent on their predatory fellows. . . .

In the following weeks the sound of the *nama* were threaded through the background of every day. The Gama flutes could be heard quite clearly from Susuroka, but as the season progressed other tribes and villages signified their intention to hold the *idza nama* festival, and on any morning the calls seemed to speak to each other from a dozen different places, harshly insistent from the grass-lands to the south, thin and troubled like the last notes of an echo, from the hanging valleys in the western moun-tains. Though they became a customary part of experience, I was never able to sleep through their cries, always waking as their notes beat at the threshold of dawn and carrying the memory of them in my mind as I waited for them to return in the blue and golden air of evening. Their inaudible vibration hung upon the intervening hours, pulsing in the sunlight and the purple underside of clouds, following a breeze along the leaves of the cane fences, filling the land-scape with the quickening tempo of life.

The cries of the flutes are heard no longer in the Asaro Valley. Some of the new generation of young adults may have heard them on the occasion described above, but it is probably no more than a vague infant or childhood memory. They listen for a different sound now.

One afternoon, around five o'clock, I left the veranda of Makis' house, passed his grave and walked to the back of the yard to stand for a while at the fence separating it from a newly cultivated garden and, farther down the hillside, the new road running the length of the ridge. I had been writing up some notes in my room, sitting uncomfortably on the floor with my tablet on my knees. My eyes were tired and I needed to stretch, to feel the air on my face and to think of something other than the people of Susuroka. I had heard Lucy walk across the veranda and go into her room two hours previ-ously, and I knew she was still there from the sounds she made as she readied packets of rice, cans of fish, and bottles of kerosene she would sell in the evening to people on the ridge who patronized the family grocery she operated from the house.

The village was deserted, and I wanted to have some time alone before people began arriving home from work and I had to light my lamp and begin preparing a meal for those who decided to visit me.

I had been standing at the fence for only a minute or two when Lucy joined me.

"Hullo, Daddy," she said. "Have you finished work?"

"Yes, Lucy. For the time being," I replied, probably not without a note of irritation.

"It will soon be time to light the lamp," she said.

"I suppose it will."

Pause.

"I'll have to go to Goroka tomorrow," she said. "I'm almost out of kerosene."

"You know, Lucy," I said, turning to her and smiling because I felt I had been abrupt with her, "if you'd buy some beer and go into the black market business, I might go into partnership. Both of us could make a fortune."

She laughed. "How do you know I'd send your share to America?"

"Well, if you didn't, you'd have to give me free kerosene when I come back again. Charging your father twenty *toia* a bottle seems like profiteering!"*

At that moment the jumping, bumping sound of Western band music, faint but clear, reached the place where we stood from the direction of Goroka, alternately fading and then

---

*Twenty *toia* are equivalent to about U.S. $0.35.

returning with increasing insistence. It seemed to be approaching along the Highland Highway. At the bottom of the garden below me two women, who were tucking cuttings of sweet potato vines into mounded hills of soil, straightened and stood listening, exchanged a few words, then bent to their task again.

Lucy said, "It's the band coming out for a 'six-to-six' tonight."

"What's a 'six-to-six'?"

"You know—disco," she said, executing a few swaying dance steps. "They're having one tonight at Namuri's place."

I didn't know, so she explained it to me while we listened to the steadily approaching sound of reggae music.

A "six-to-six" is a dance that lasts from six in the evening to six the following morning. It is organized by two or more entrepreneurs who charge an admission fee of two *kina* to a roped-off enclosure in the village street where it is held. The price of admission entitles those who pay it to "disco" to the live band hired from Goroka. Black market beer, cooked rice and tinned fish are sold throughout the night by the entrepreneurs, who hope to make a profit on their outlay of capital. The participants are mainly young, unmarried, and married people who "disco" dance with each other Western style. Older folk may sit around and watch outside the enclosure— and buy the beer and rice if they wish—but even if they prefer to remain in their houses, I doubt they get any sleep. The sound of the band, which seems to be familiar with only one tune, beats back and forth along the ridge and must be deafening to anyone who has to suffer it at close quarters all night. I was glad it began to rain a few hours after this particular "six-to-six" began. It didn't stop the dance, but at least it meant there were longer intervals between sets in which I could sleep for a while in my bed in Makis' house which, unfortunately, was only about two hundred yards from Namuri's place.

The provincial government apparently tried to ban the "six-to-six" for a time, citing outbursts of brawling, exacerbated by drunkenness, as the reason. I don't think the ban was ever successful, and there is no attempt to enforce it now or even to discourage the dances. They are still potentially volatile events, however. The trouble is mainly over women, which is not a new or particularly noteworthy departure from traditional times, when a good deal of village and intergroup litigation centered on women and pigs. Lucy said that the "six-to-six" brawling is precipitated mostly by young husbands who suspect other men are paying too much attention to their wives and begin a fight, either attacking the man or the wife, whom they may accuse of having encouraged the advances. I listened to Lucy discussing the brawls with other women. The burden of their comments was always this: men were to blame; women, even wives, should be free to dance and interact with any man they choose; it was old fashioned to try to limit their freedom and keep them in their place.

I don't think Lucy would object to me calling her a feminist, possibly one of the first Gahuku women to openly question the traditional authority and hegemony of men. She showed her independence publicly when she was only nineteen and voiced her resentment at the distribution of her father's personal wealth and belongings, asserting her right to his few former possessions which she keeps in her room in his house. Indeed, I think she is generally recognized as owning the house. She may not have a legal title to it in either a customary or Western sense, but she has the only key to its door, and it is not used by her full brother Lokilo or other direct descendants of Makis. People speak of it as "Lucy's house" or as my house when I am there.

By her own account, Lucy's outspokenness has caused some animosity. Her criticism of the Ozahadzuha man for his part in the unseemly scramble for her father's wealth, and her continuing championship of the rights of his descendants, have led her to suspect that sorcery caused a series of illnesses she suffered a few years ago. She is not the eldest of Makis' publicly recognized direct descendants. Lokilo is the only male, however, and he is several years younger than Lucy, mild mannered and nonassertive. I can see the physical heritage from Makis in all his children. Watching Lokilo, I often thought I must be looking at his father as he must have been when he was young, before I knew him. He has the same strong nose, fine and deeply set brown eyes, the same firmly defined brows, and lips that curl upward to light his high-cheeked face when he smiles. When we were sitting silently together, I sometimes felt an echo of the vibration that had passed between myself and Makis on the evening I count as the real beginning of our friendship.

Despite the difference in our years, I was more comfortable with Lokilo than any other person. He was not an encumbrance when I wanted to be alone. I did not have to talk or ask questions to bridge the silences that fell when we were together either in the house when he was holding his sleeping infant son in his lap or when we were walking along the roads traversing the ridge. He did not seem to think it strange when I turned aside to sit and look across the valley for a while. He could not have known what my memories projected on the warm sun, the sea of almost motionless clouds, the dappled shadows of the distant mountains and the honeyed scent of crotaliria, but he seemed content and understanding, not impatient and wanting to share his thoughts or mine. When I rose, often with his unsolicited help—his arm through mine as he helped me up a hillside—we exchanged smiles in an almost conspiratorial fashion and continued on our way, conversation resuming in an unforced and undemanding manner.

Lokilo does not speak English. He has had no schooling because, Lucy says, his mother Guma'e—who is also her biological mother—"fastened" him to the village: she did not want him to go to school and possibly move away from her to take an outside job. From all accounts, Makis was filled with pride at Lokilo's birth. This was his first and only son from any of his three wives, and he gave the child a name that reflects both his pride and expectations. "Lokilo" may be freely translated to English as "smoke from feast fires rising," referring to the columns of smoke—plainly visible when the valley was deforested—drifting into the sky from piles of firewood burned to heat the stones for earth ovens at major celebrations. Makis signified by the name his ambition for his son, saying that when people saw such evidence mounting the air from Susuroka they would say to one another, "Ah, it's Lokilo, the son of Makis!"

I do not know if Makis resisted Guma'e's decision to keep Lokilo in the village. Guma'e was his youngest and favorite wife and perhaps he did not want to deny her. But Lucy says she had to obtain her own schooling—she has graduated from high school—without any encouragement from her parents.

Lokilo shows no sign of harboring any resentment for the opportunities he may have lost through his parents' attitude, but I doubt that he would have met his father's expectations even in relatively unchanged times. The introspective and quiescent elements of his character are more prominent in him than in his father, and this may be one of the reasons why I responded to him more than to his sister or other Gahuku belonging to his generation. Saying good-bye to him for possibly the last time, I felt the same unarticulated sense of present loss and future deprivation which has been one of the threads of my life since I embraced his father on the day I left him more than a generation ago.

Lucy, far more than Lokilo, represents the other side of her father's character, its assertive, dominating, and eminently practical traits, though the expression of these qualities are tempered by some cultural restrictions that are still imposed on women. These restrictions are less sharply defined and less harshly imposed than in the past, however, and Lucy's public assertions of her rights and her advocacy of those of her clan trespass on areas that would have been roundly forbidden to members of her sex—not that women had no means other than outright public confrontation of protesting the status to which they were assigned. Their behavior frequently forced men to do what they wished by defaulting their prerogatives as members of the grand gender.

Some of the changes that have occurred in relationships between men and women are implicated in juxtaposing the sound of the *nama* flutes and the "reggae" band playing in an open truck to announce a "six-to-six." I don't think anyone seeing the Gahuku now would be able to appreciate the contrast suggested by placing them side by side, however. They wouldn't hear the *nama* flutes now—or any other kind of flute for that matter. They would probably conclude that the "six-to-six" music is not traditional, and anyone from the West would recognize the "disco" style of dancing, but they would not recognize what the style—young men and women dancing face-to-face and occasionally touching in public—conveys about changes in intersex relationships. It was a startling departure from anything I had seen previously, but to appreciate the contrast it is necessary to stop the reel of the film of contemporary life and replace it with one from an earlier life.

2 | Two passages from work I published in 1951 and 1952 are important in trying to understand the ideological underpinnings, and their institutional expressions, of the polarities between men and women in traditional Gahuku culture:*

> Men like to see themselves as superior both physically and intellectually to women . . . But in actuality, for their own security, they are continually compelled to reaffirm their supremacy in ritual. (Read, 1951)

> In the final analysis, the idea men hold of themselves is based primarily on what men do rather than what they have at birth. They recognize, indeed, that in physiological endowment men are inferior to women, and characteristically, they have recourse to elaborate artifical means to redress the contradictions and demonstrate its opposite. (Read, 1952)

These statements focus attention on two interwoven and largely contradictory themes of Gahuku culture. First, the folk biology of gender differences, in which women were perceived as being inherently better endowed than men at birth to fulfill their destinies. Second, the necessity for men to rit-

---

*Kenneth E. Read, "The Gahuku-Gama of the Central Highlands," *South Pacific* 5 (8): 154–164; and "Nama Cult of the Central Highlands, New Guinea," *Oceania* 23 (1): 1–25.

ually promote and "complete" less certain biological processes in males, while, at the same time, bonding them to support and adhere to the values and ethos of male superiority and the preeminent importance of their roles and contributions to the welfare of the group.

In the everyday public domain, the social ascendance and dominance of men was a matter of palpable experience. Domestic living arrangements traditionally separated the sexes. Adult men slept in a clubhouse, apart from their wives, other women, and their uninitiated sons, an immediately observable example of gender distancing that would prompt all anthropologists to inquire into folk notions of female pollution; but it was also clear that this physical separation—after a certain age for males—was carried over to other major areas of social life.

Women had no official, public voice in secular or sacred matters. They were not excluded from the "gatherings" called to air and decide *some* internal public issues, but they were present only as spectators who were not permitted to express their opinions. This subordinate place (sometimes enforced by physical means) characterized the status of women in public life. It does not mean that they had absolutely no influence and could not in certain circumstances (for example, in matters of divorce or the termination of arranged betrothals) behave in ways that compelled men to actions they wanted them to take. And when they were old and long past childbearing age, they were given some special marks of respect even in the context of the male *nama* cult, old women being allowed to stand *outside* the village houses (not hiding inside them) when men paraded with the flutes in the street, though they had to close their eyes as the procession passed to the men's house. Their important role in the husbandry of pigs was also recognized. Theoretically, a man could dispose of his pigs as he wished (that is, apply them to any one of a number of culturally recognized ends), but I noticed that men usually consulted their wives before committing themselves, and when they did not do so, they sometimes encountered protest and more than usually strained relationships. The wives of men who had made noteworthy contributions of pigs to the *idza nama* festivals were also accorded a kind of reflected glory, being allowed to wear some characteristically male decorations and to accompany the men's dances of welcome and assertions of pride.

From the standpoint of the objective outsider, it seems obvious that the subsistence tasks assigned to men and women were complementary, but this is not the equitable way in which men perceived them. Women's work or women's sphere (excepting their childbearing capacity) did not begin to match the importance of what men did and were expected to do. The Gahuku-Gama were a warrior society, and this past was so close to them in 1950 that although there was no longer any need to do so, most adult men still carried their bows and arrows when they walked the tracks to the gardens or went visiting. Old enmities persisted. The honoring of blood spilled by friends and allies was an important obligation recognized at the distribution of pigs in the *idza nama* festival, and a great deal of the formal oratory at intergroup gatherings centered on fighting.

The ideal qualities of maleness subsumed by the concept of "strength" did not imply mere physical vigor. It meant demonstrated excellence in all the activities in which men were dominant, as well as forcefulness, aggressiveness, pride in one's self and one's masculinity, and, in the extreme, a refusal to recognize that others were your equal. Men did not attach a great deal of either private or public importance to the things women did, except when their behavior seemed to be challenging. They recognized that women possessed some knowledge that was closed to them, but as a rule they tended to dismiss it in a cavalier fashion. In short, masculinity was *the* focus, *the* lynchpin of cultural pride; the supreme cultural achievement.

Ritual centered on men. They were obviously dominant in everything concerned with the *nama* cult (which, in turn, occupied the dominant place in ritual), but there were also few collective rituals that focused on the persons of women. Possibly, the persons of women could be ascribed a central place in first menstruation and first pregnancy rites, but even in these it was the significance of the events for men that was ideologically emphasized. Men not only managed all the ritualized aspects of life but most of them also concerned men, on whose welfare (using the word in its broadest sense) the welfare of society itself depended.

The major values of Gahuku culture were weighted on the side of men. Whatever a group achieved was primarily of their doing and making, and therefore they were responsible for the general welfare. Women had a reflected glory only—a shine they achieved only through their subordinate and dependent relationship to the ideal public image of the grand and noble sex, and this is not so unfamiliar that it should be startling or even controversial.

But why, in this clearly male-dominated society, should Gahuku insist that it was particularly hard work to make a man? The question is rhetorical, but it is one the Gahuku recognized and to which they would have provided an acceptable answer in the context of their ideology. Summarizing and also extrapolating from the data, it boils down to this: all of a female's basic potentials were given by sex at birth, and this was by no means the situation for those who were born male. Both males and females had certain biological potentialities at birth, but the fruition or fulfillment of the potentialities required very different courses of action. Indeed, the development of immature girls into adult women required almost no assistance, being a natural (inevitable) process as contrasted with a cultural process.

At first glance, this seems familiar. After all, we tend to give more attention to turning boys into cultural men than we do to making cultural women out of girls, encouraging (not to say forcing) the former into activities that are characterized as manly and masculine. Both, of course, are enculturated to accept the roles our culture (like all cultures) assigns by sex, yet I think our attitudes suggest that ensuring that males become masculine requires more encouragement (and is therefore more doubtful) than its opposite.

This was clearly one of the functions of the men's secret *nama* cult.* Like those of many other Melanesian cultures, Gahuku initiation rites were sequential and developmental, beginning at about a boy's eighth year and continuing at intervals for fifteen years thereafter. Along the way, the most violent of the events were those I observed when Asemo was admitted to the *nama* cult, but the path of full manhood included yet another, occurring when each new batch of cult members were permitted to cohabit—that is, have sexual relationships—with girls to whom they had been betrothed. Speaking of the Sambia—another people in the Eastern Highlands—Gilbert Herdt remarks that their "male initiation is a

*Gilbert Herdt, *Guardians of the Flutes: Idioms of Masculinity*, New York: McGraw-Hill, 1981, pp. 204–205.

rigidly structured form of inculcating manliness step by step. It begins when boys are seven to ten years old and, in the ensuing ten to fifteen years, effects the transition from childhood to adulthood." This is also true of Gahuku initiation, though the processes of making Sambia men include some striking differences.

Herdt uses the concept of *masculinization* to aid his description and analysis of his Sambia data, and in the Sambia context the dictionary glossing of the term is appropriate, since semen (to the Sambia) is analogous to a biochemical androgen. Semen, taken through ingestion, is necessary to modify a boy's body (thus making him a complete man) as well as imparting to women, through the ingestion of smaller quantities, the "strength to bear and suckle children" (Herdt, 1981, p. 205, note 1). This does not apply to the Gahuku-Gama, but it is possible to use the term "masculinization" in a less specific sense than Herdt to characterize the cultural intent and direction of the rituals associated with the *nama* cult. The extended series of rites were concerned with marking and promoting stages in male maturation, but this was by no means all that was involved. Biological gender was assigned at birth: one child was male because he had a penis, another was female because she had a vagina. But a child born with a penis (and therefore biologically male) had to be induced to acquire a constellation of secondary sex traits in order to be not only male but also masculine. This was the crux of the rites of incorporation included in the *nama* cult.

I have said elsewhere that the Gahuku-Gama seemed to be preoccupied with the physical attributes of the person, and in the same context, I noted that the physical growth and development of children was a major concern and a focus for ritual treatment and recognition. On one of these occasions both boys and girls (ages about eight) were included. The ceremony, with its bestowal of gifts, was an obligatory recognition by a male parent (and his kinsmen) of the residual rights and interests of his wife's kinsmen in her offspring, interests that did not end until their death; but its visible focus was to note and admire the physical development of the youngsters. Following this, however, there were no further rites concerned with female maturation until first menstruation, whereas concern for the maturation of boys increased as they were drawn farther and farther into the orbit of the *nama* cult, a concern that continued for years beyond puberty.

It may be a simple observation, but I think the Gahuku-Gama noted that the signs of sexual maturation are more obvious (visible) in females than in males and seemed to constitute an inevitable sequence from the gradual development of female breasts to the dramatic event of menstruation: women appeared to be more basically endowed than males to complete and fulfill their biological destiny without assistance. Cross-cultural studies have also shown that girls tend to acquire speech and motor coordination abilities earlier than boys, and presumably these were among the visible, observable phenomena persuading Gahuku men that they "outgrew boys."

I have no doubt that this is how men saw things and that they also fastened upon menstruation as a critical watershed in the disparate development. They did not hesitate (without any prompting) to liken the nose-bleeding rites of the *nama* cult to menstruation, explaining that both were necessary to complete the processes of maturation and also acknowledging that men had to simulate (ritually induce) an event that occurred naturally in women. But more than this was involved in ritualized nose-bleeding and vomiting for men.

Boys were introduced to nose bleeding and cane swallowing in the next-to-last ritual concerned with making a man (around about the age of thirteen to seventeen), and while the former may clearly be viewed as a simulated menstruation, both were also purification rites, necessary not only to promote the physical growth and well-being of males but also to effect their masculinization.

Transposing once more from Herdt (1981, p. 205), "Men believe the maintenance of (biological) maleness is arduous, its resulting masculinity tenuous." To accomplish both ends, males had to be purified or cleansed of their pre- and postnatal contacts with women. This was foreshadowed as early as between ages six to eight, when on the occasion of the dramatic initiation rites of teenagers in the great *idza nama*, boys were ritually separated from their mothers and other women and washed in a stream by adult men. This rite was physically separated from the events involving the older youths. The children were not allowed to see the *nama* flutes or any of the other events occurring in another section of the stream, and after their ritual bathing they were returned to the custodial care of mothers and older sisters. But most of them went through the experience one more time before their final initiation.

The long period of "prepubertal" (that is, prior to residence in the men's house) contact with women was detrimental to the development of biological maleness and masculinity. Nose bleeding and cane swallowing were the most dramatic examples of the care men had to take to ensure that their welfare (in the very broadest sense) was not affected adversely by their inevitable contacts with women, and it must be remembered that they were not once-in-a-lifetime occurrences. Following the compulsory introduction to them, both became self-administered rituals that men were expected to perform to preserve the integrity of their maleness and masculinity, a bonding duty that increased following the assumption of sexual relationships with their wives. Even during the period of 1950 to 1952, a majority of adult married men wore canes looped around their waists as a customary and relatively inconspicuous item of everyday apparel. I was told that women did not know their significance; they were part of the secret lore of men. And I was also told that men always used them before undertaking a hazardous masculine activity such as warfare. But they were also used more frequently, especially by strong men who had a heightened sense of their masculinity and a sometimes overweening attachment to the extremes of behavior in which this important quality was expressed. But men who were less strong but by no means weak also bled their noses and swallowed the canes from time to time. Both were necessary to maintain their manly vitality.

Manly vitality was sapped by a male child's association with women, including not only the period from birth until he was weaned (about two to three years old) but also during gestation. Men knew nothing about the actual procedures followed by women in childbirth. Special circumstances enabled me to witness birth on several occasions. Men knew this. Indeed, it was always they who requested my attendance, but they never once asked me a single question about the event I had witnessed and which they had never seen. I have no data that suggests that Gahuku-Gama men had any of the fears or suspicions of Sambia men concerning what women might do with a new-born child (Herdt, 1981, pp. 206–208); but they believed women did not want to bear children (because of the pain and danger to them) and knew ways to prevent conception as well as to induce abortions. If a new bride, following the assumption of sexual relations with her husband, seemed to be visiting her mother and female relatives too frequently, older men characteristically warned the young husband that this is what she was doing: learning from them ways to prevent him from achieving his masculine right to fatherhood. In the same context, it was never suggested or, apparently, thought possible that a man might be to blame if a couple were childless. This unfortunate state could be attributed only to female perversity—to their general inclination to challenge the interests and the social welfare of men.

But such assumed or suspected social challenges were grounded in more basic physiological differences and oppositions between maleness and femaleness. In the womb, a fetus developed in and was nourished by a coif of female blood and came into the world covered by it (so much, at least, men knew or suspected). Semen, too, was necessary to make a child, but the manufacture of a fetus required cumulative amounts of semen (apparently from the same male), and semen loss could adversely affect manly vitality. Thus, the very act of procreation was potentially hazardous for manliness.

It was, however, the assignment of sex at birth that determined the general direction of the respective paths the newborn would take toward maturity. The mother's blood and milk as well as infant dependence on females could affect the progress of a boy to manhood. Thus, these pre- and postnatal influences had to be "washed" away or expelled by purification rites and an increasing social separation of boys from women and their incorporation into the society of men who were responsible for masculinizing them. The oppositions between male and female were, at their root, the expression of antipathetic biological principles whose future implications were established in the womb.

What was at stake at the birth of a male child was not only his growth (assuming he survived) but ultimately his manhood—his masculinity. Gahuku did not disentangle these concepts, for the first was a necessary, and problematic, ingredient of the second. Not so for female children. I do not think Gahuku saw much need to "feminize" girls, apart from introducing them (at a much earlier age than boys) to the round of tasks they would be expected to perform in adult life. As noted above, minimal ritual attention was given to their maturation. Clearly, they outstripped boys in this respect. Youths were betrothed to girls (about their own age or a few years younger) during the *idza nama*. Thereafter they were required to avoid each other for about four years. These betrothals were almost notorious for their instability, and in explaining why they did not endure men always said the girl "outgrew" her intended spouse.

At least two things are involved here. One is that women became sexually mature earlier than men. Both reached puberty (it must be assumed) at about the same stage in life, but a boy was not ready for his male role in reproduction for many years thereafter, whereas a girl did not have to wait. This is another facet to the antipathies between men and women. Gahuku men found sex pleasurable, and judging from men's attitudes and remarks, so did women, but males had to forego such gratification until their elders decided that the development of some secondary male characteristics made such relationships safe or, really, relatively safe for them.

Women were not disposed to wait. In a sense, they were more naturally sexual creatures. They were also, from the male point of view, characterized as sexually demanding and even irresponsible. Young men accused of making a girl pregnant always insisted that she had initiated the encounter, and this was also the invariable defense of a married man accused of adultery with another man's wife. In neither case was it necessarily true, but the defense was at least publicly appropriate and more or less acceptable given the indoctrination that males had to exercise self-discipline in sexual activity (for the sake of their manhood and masculinity), whereas there were no such inherent inhibitory restrictions placed on the expression of female sexuality.

Gahuku-Gama boys, youths, and young men were confronted with this dilemma during their incorporation into the *nama* cult. All of its activities glorified maleness and the superiority of masculinity, yet neither manhood nor masculinity were certain and their production required a great deal of surveillance, harsh criticism, and self-discipline. Since intimate contact with women was harmful for the development of manhood and the maintenance of masculinity, it was necessary to effect both social and psychological distancing between the sexes. The former was effected by gradual but regimented stages, beginning with the first "washing" of male children (above) and ending with their reception into the men's house, at which point the traditional domestic separation was established. The psychological separation (and I must say that I know virtually nothing about such mechanisms) included instruction that males should resist the "precocious" sexuality of women until they were sufficiently mature to reduce the risk to the achievement of masculine strength. Paradoxically, however, the masculine ideal included instruction that a sign of a male's maturity and strength was his ability to draw women to him sexually.

Both sides of the coin were present in the institutionalized courting parties initiated by girls.* From the male perspective, it is difficult to avoid concluding that such activities fitted one aspect of the public image of women—as sirens enticing initiated youths and young men into hazardous situations (ibid., pp. 191–192). But at the same time, older men encouraged and expected them to participate and often questioned, with a good deal of acerbity, the masculinity of young men who, following the termination of a first betrothal, had not been able to induce girls to "run away with them" (ibid., p. 156). Young men were entangled in more than a two-way bind. Among other things, they were taught that the promotion and preservation of their masculinity (and therefore the preservation of male superiority) required not only social separation from women but also harsh kinds of self-discipline (nose bleeding and cane swallowing) and a self-denial in gratifying sexual drives that was not as strictly imposed on women (at least until their marriage). But the "catch-22" was that males, as members of the grand gender, *should* be sexual objects women desired (they were less than masculine if women did not desire them), and this was by no means certain. Youths who went to the girls' courting parties entered a situation that was charged with this ambiguous excitement and always went armed with magical substances (revealed to them by men following their reception into the men's house) that were supposed to make girls desire them. The frequent breaking of first betrothals (almost always by girls) and the subsequent long, tedious and frustrating attempts by youths to

*The "courting parties" are described in *The High Valley*, chapter five.

induce a girl to run away caused a great deal of anxiety to young men.* For, contrary to their precautions and to the ideal of masculinity presented to them, a male was not fully masculine without a woman, and women could (and apparently did) withhold from men, or threaten to prevent them from achieving, their full masculinity.

In far many more ways than one it is possible to say that women were perceived as the enemies of men, but enemies who were as necessary to the ideal of masculine strength as were the traditional enmities between adjoining tribal groups. This ideal resisted the notion that anyone was your equal. True strength (that is, true masculinity) required individuals and groups to assert their ascendency over others. Equality was antithetical to the grand ideal of masculinity and masculine pride, and the constantly recurring chronicles of intertribal warfare epitomized one aspect of the dominating ethos; for warfare proper (*rova*) as distinct from feuding (*hina*) required no precipitating event (though some were often cited). Warfare did not lead to conquest (in the sense of extending boundaries or imposing sovereignty over others), though one of its aims was to destroy the villages of enemy groups and force their inhabitants to seek temporary sanctuary elsewhere. But in the course of time, the defeated (who always intended to return) were commonly invited back to serve once more as a foil for testing and demonstrating the ultimate expression of strength and masculinity.

As the contest of strength seesawed back and forth between enemy groups (and also in the context of ceremonial exchanges between friendly groups in the *idza nama*), so it also teetered on the fulcrum of ideologies of sexual oppositions.

*The High Valley, chapter four.

Notions concerning the polluting characteristics of femaleness are themselves rather commonplace cross-cultural data, but for Gahuku they were the ideological watershed on which the opposition divided, though Gahuku did not carry them as far as some other Melanesian groups. They were clearly an important underpinning in the social distancing of traditional domestic living arrangements, but they were also expressed in other less conspicuous forms of social (and, presumably, psychological) distancing. For example, it was a grave trespassing on the personal boundaries of a man for a women to step across his legs, walk too closely behind him while he was seated or touch his hair or his nose. Elsewhere I have suggested that Gahuku paid far more attention than we do to the physical attributes of personhood.* I tried to show that "the part stood for the whole," and in this light it is far easier to appreciate the affronts to male personhood occasioned by any of the above behaviors on the part of women.

I do not have (since I was not equipped to obtain it) any psychological data to support my statements that male hostility for women was a basic element in relationships between the sexes, but in addition to anything I have noted so far, it seemed to be obvious enough in some of the usages to which women were subjected: sticks thrust into a vagina as a punishment for adultery; public whippings with canes if women presumed to speak from the sidelines at gatherings; and stomping on them in the heat of marital disagreements. I should make it perfectly clear, however, that such dehumanizing treatment did not preclude the development of apparently rewarding and enduring affective relationships between

---

*K. E. Read, "Morality and the Concept of the Person among the Gahuku-Gama," *Oceania* 25, 1955.

individual men and women within the distancing boundaries of sex. In any culture, individual relationships are not cut to the same precise and invariant pattern or from precisely the same piece of cloth, and those who had recourse to these extreme measures (saving, perhaps, the public whippings) represented extreme characterological examples of the ideal of masculine strength.

Yet women were presented as a potential threat to masculinity and possibly even to life, for the most virulent recognized form of sorcery required some of the intended victim's semen and women were assumed to be the sorcerer's agent for obtaining it, not entirely excluding a man's own wife (at least until she had proved her identification with his interests and those of his patrilineal group by bearing him a child).

For obvious reasons, I know virtually nothing about a woman's subjective experiences of being female or of her sense of self or person in relationship to males. But I doubt that the latter, at least, conformed entirely to male ideas of what it ought to be; for men were quick to see or suspect challenges from women, who were opposed to them not only in a fundamental biological sense but who could use their biological endowments to jeopardize male interests and even to question some of the ideal components of masculinity. This is the covering sense in which women might be said to be the enemies of men—the very enemies, or possible enemies, and inhibitors of the development of masculinity. No wonder, then, that Gahuku men were misogynists in many ways. But their misogyny was not all of one piece either, for women could not be simply excluded and given no attention. On the contrary, they were a constant source of trouble and a focus for anxiety and competition.

The male ideal often foundered—like all ideals—on the practical exigencies of living, but it was no less important because of this.

Like all rituals of incorporation, the rites of the *nama* cult were intended to produce, seal, and maintain a social and psychological bond, in this case to produce a community of men whose common interests were set apart from and, ideally, above the community of women. In order to accomplish this, it was necessary to inculcate in each generation of males a subjective awareness and experience of what it meant to be male: to secure their adherence to a sense of maleness shared—the almost ineluctable bond that transcended most other personal bonds. This also required, as the other side of the coin, measures to ensure that women were reminded of the subordinate position of their sex through the customary usages reported above and the ritual wounding of brides prior to the assumption of sexual relationships with their husbands. Yet it also seems clear that from the male perspective the community of women, their common interests and sense of a shared female self, was a more natural social and psychological entity. This fundamental difference constituted the unstable sands beneath the edifice of male superiority, and the ritual communicating it, the subjective recognition and sharing of it, and the measures to support it firmly were the bonding interests of the cult.

3 The *nama* cult is not even a memory to the youngest generation of Gahuku today. To the outsider who observed its rituals and heard the cries of the flutes throughout the day at a particular season, who saw the overwrought responses to them reflected in the faces and voices

of men, and who passed by the closed and silent houses where women and uninitiated boys hid from their threatening calls, the final curtain has descended on an awesome event. But I have no personal regrets. Participating in the climactic ritual of making men was one of the most exciting experiences in my life. I stood just inside the periphery of the ritual, separated from it because I had no active role in the rites yet also entangled with it; observing the rites objectively, yet engulfed by the sounds and smells: the intermittently shrilling music; the clamorous voices, as agitated as the tossing plumes on the heads of the warriors; and the odor of blood and vomit threaded sourly through the overheated air of noon. And I was subjectively joined to the immature youths who were the focus of attention. For, on three occasions, between ages ten and eighteen, I had been forced to participate in rites of incorporation into masculine associations of my own culture, the last occurring in my freshmen year as resident of an upper-class Church of England College at my university, when the collective rite for members of my class included being immersed in and struggling through a foul-smelling bathtub filled with a concoction based on sump oil, and crawling naked down a cloister with a cake of soap between my legs. This "civilized" rite may say something about the insecurities beneath the hypermasculine (and also somewhat misogynist) Australian ideal of male bonding; but apart from this, the revulsion I had felt formed an empathetic link with the Gahuku youths who were forcefully confronted with harsher violations of their persons.

It is more than likely that a majority of Gahuku youths incorporated the experience of their ordeal into their sense of self, into the common bond of maleness—with all it implied in the way of cultural privilege and dominance—linking them to other members of their sex, just as, I suppose, there must be some of my own age-mates who, following our test, incorporated the revolting ordeal as an invisible sign of election to some kind of an elite. The Gahuku who in later life became the "reluctant warriors" probably had some comparable temperamental aversions for the masculine role their culture assigned to them, but they were less fortunate than I, for they had far fewer alternatives. In fact, there were only two: to be strong or soft, and only those whose behavior placed them toward the strong pole of the continuum could hope to acquire prestige and influence.

Gahuku women were also placed in a cultural straitjacket at their birth; indeed, its straps were even more confining. The one possible shape of their lives was subordination to men. Even in old age their proven worth as producers of children or their accomplishments in other areas of life did not modify substantially the cultural limitations placed not only on their choices but also on self-expression. Employing a phrase that is possibly more appropriate to their opposite gender, "reluctant women" were perceived by the dominant sex as a greater threat than the apostates among themselves, and indications of unwillingness to comply with their assigned role prompted harsher and more brutalizing sanctions against women than any imposed on men.

I do not know what some feminist anthropologists may be inclined to make of these remarks. Thirty years ago, I had no more than a fraction of the personal interaction with Gahuku women I have today, and age combined with my honorary kinship status are not solely responsible for the difference; for I think the increased opportunities for interacting with women, being in their company, talking to them casually, and asking them about their lives indicate a substantial shift in the traditional boundaries separating the sexes.

There is unquestionable truth in the judgment that the vast majority of ethnographies, since they have been written by men, provide an essentially one-sided perspective on the cultures recorded, but to suggest that this reflects the gender biases of their authors is another matter. In the tribal societies with which I am personally familiar—and most of the others I know only through the literature—even the outsider is inhibited by the formal restraints of being an identifiable member of a particular sex, and these restraints apply no less to women anthropologists. It is therefore not deliberate neglect, or even unconsciously biased oversight, which must be held accountable for the relative richness of our data on men compared to women. Anthropological biographies of women are virtually nonexistent. There are none that I know of from Papua New Guinea, not even among the small body of autobiographical materials published by native New Guineans—and, incidentally, at least one contemporary spokesman for a "Melanesian Way" assesses the traditional status of women in an apology that is far more chauvinistic than any Western anthropologist would care to be identified with.

My own published account of a Gahuku marriage has been cited by one colleague as a rare instance where some attempt has been made to highlight the event from the girl's perspective and, by implication, to suggest the subjective place the experience may have had in her life experience. I do not doubt it was traumatic, though this element might well have been offset by the public attention she received, and possibly by some pride in what it signified: her change in status and the achievement of one of the acceptable goals sought by men and included, however remotely, in their calculations for her from the time she was born and identified as female.

I would not begin to suggest that I can speak to the subjective experience of women during 1950 to 1952. They were there, right under my eyes, so to speak, but separated by a distance that was not of my choosing but which expressed their formal separation from all men after the latter had crossed the boundary line between what might be referred to as "childhood" and "incipient adulthood." Contacts with them, even opportunities to question them, were limited by cultural restraints on what was proper for them to do and for me to expect from them, and it wasn't for lack of attempting it that I did not get to know them personally. Only the wives of Makis and a few others about the same age came inside my house for any other purpose than to bring me something from their gardens, and those who sought me when I was alone were usually prompted to do so by some personal crisis that seemed to recommend me as a temporary sanctuary and a possible sympathetic ear for their tearful and overwrought complaints about their husbands' treatment. I was also present, always at the request of men, on several occasions when the women gave birth. These men woke me in the night and instructed me to go to a nearby settlement—on two occasions a Gehamo village some distance from the ridge of Susuroka—where a woman was in labor. I don't know why they asked me to be there, but perhaps it had something to do with the role I played when Guma'e gave birth to my daughter Lucy, and I don't know what the women thought about my presence. I knew there was absolutely nothing I could do, but I put on my clothes and stumbled through the dark countryside, guided by a man who always left me when I reached the woman's house. Neither the mother nor the other women attending her objected when I came through the door on my hands and knees. I couldn't talk to them, but they smiled, said my name, made the customary welcoming gestures with their hands and offered me a place among them on the ground beside the patient. I did not take my notebooks on any of these occasions, an oversight which I am sure many of my colleagues would regard as particularly remiss, but I knew that what I was watching was a woman's secret, that I was a trespasser. My own reticence inhibited me from seeming too curious and asking importuning questions they may have thought I had no right to ask and may even have made them suspicious of what I might recount on returning to the men who had sent me there.

I suppose this attitude should not be recommended to anthropologists doing fieldwork, who in their quest for information may often appear to their subjects like bulls in a china shop, barging into their lives with a heavy tread and showing little concern for the delicacy of the materials surrounding them. The lacunae in my own fieldwork—and be sure there are many—owe something to this possibly unprofessional reserve, but then, there is always a personal equation contained in the data collected and recorded, in the significance a particular mind attaches to it even in the manner in which it is marshaled and the theoretical framework within which it is placed. And I'm not sure that despite its shortcomings the less aggressive and more passive approach doesn't pay off in the long run. It seems likely to me that interpersonal confidence grows in proportion to the extent you show you are not there solely to collect and record information for purposes that are usually beyond the comprehension of your subjects; that your interest, in short, is not merely to understand them in some abstract sense but also to know them as persons, to touch them as individuals playing out their lives within the confines of a particular worldview and its definition of the human condition. When this kind of confidence is established, it tends not only to bring information in a natural way but also allows you to participate in many situations as something more than an observer, for you have a kind of right to be there: your presence is not based on tolerance only but is a dividend of the intangible connections you have made without really planning them or forcing them. The relationships of people in all cultures are not forged from steel; rather, they are strands of glass that will bear only limited weight applied to them.

This kind of attitude cannot be dignified as a method, and it cannot be taught. It transcends technique and any of the mechanics—the necessary tools—that can be acquired in the classroom, but this does not mean it is an essential quality to possess any more than it absolves those for whom it may be congenial from employing the methods for collecting and interpreting data that are transmitted formally within a discipline. But for the very reason that it is unteachable, I suppose it is open to the charge that it is nothing more than a mystique. If this is so, then I venture to say that most anthropologists—far more than sociologists—are aware of it, respect it, and, to varying degrees, of course, tend to be far more sensitively attuned to people and the differences between human populations than the members of any other social science. This may be because anthropology is comparative, not simply the study of a single case, which is usually the case of sociology. Human variation on a worldwide scale is the focus of anthropology. And in itself this may be instrumental in selecting those who elect it as a career: they have a temperamental affinity—beyond the formal problems they investigate—for a personal knowledge and experience of lives that seem to be completely different from their own. In this sense, there *is* a mystique involved in anthropology, not in its formal methods, many of which it shares with other social sciences, but in the motivation to engage in it and to place one's self in the kinds of situations it characteristically involves.

Given the limited contacts I had with Gahuku women from 1950 to 1952, I don't have subjective data from them to support my generalization concerning intersex antagonism consequent upon the institutionalized gender cleavage. I do not assume its existence simply from instances of husbands mistreating wives, however—though up to a point this would not have been considered mistreatment by Gahuku—or from the tearful complaints and expectations of sympathy some women expressed to me personally and in private. Rather, the gender cleavage was exemplified in quite ordinary domestic arrangements and in virtually all areas of public life, and the rituals of rebellion included in marriage ceremonies and the climactic rite of making men may be viewed as a formal expression of the antipathies inherent in the folk ideology of biological differences and its ramifications in a society dominated by men and their collective interests. Though ultimately contained by conventions of what was allowable—which really meant "allowable by men"—the rituals I observed often seemed to teeter at the edge of disaster, the women pressing their ritual license beyond the point where it was recognized as simply conventional.

None of this implies that men could afford to disregard women or that they attached no value at all to their contributions to group life. Far from being able to ignore them, the folk ideology summarized in the section immediately preceding this suggests the more or less *constant* attention they were compelled to give to them, even if the direction of this attention was ensuring that women were kept in their place and that the social and psychological distance between the sexes was maintained. There is no doubt that relationships between the sexes were not sharply black and white. They had elements of a dialectic, though it was one in which men were bound to prevail, since they commanded the ultimate sanctions to enforce the supremacy of their point of view.

I cannot be sure how much of the traditional ideology of biological differences was known to women. I don't think they accepted at face value the men's explanation for the cries of the *nama* flutes. There were numerous occasions when the instruments were paraded along exposed ridges, when the processions were surely visible to anyone looking upward from gardens on bottom land below. Men broke off branches of crotalaria shrubs and carried them to form a screen around the players when they reached the elevated portions of the tracks, but the screens were mostly ineffective. In their excited state, the men seemed to forget their purpose, inadvertently lowering the boughs and leaving the players fully displayed in silhouette against the sky. But the fact that all women probably knew how these reverberating cries were produced does not detract from their power as symbols of male control and the enforcement of the supremacy of male values and interests.

Other elements of the folk ideology were also male secrets. They were not discussed in mixed company but were part of the lore adult men imparted to youths when they took full charge of them, but women were perfectly aware of their social consequences, since the limitations on cross-sex interaction they imposed were palpable components of their life experiences with men.

I remember an incident in 1982 that indicates not only an alteration in my personal relationships with women but also more noticeable changes in intersex relationships generally. It happened one afternoon shortly before I left Susuroka. I had taken one of my yellow tablets to the "kitchen room" of

Makis' house and sat down on a pallet belonging to the husband of Toho. He slept on it every night, just outside the door to my room, and left it there for me to use during the day because I had no chairs. I did not close the door to the veranda and the yard below and beyond it, and I was barely seated when an old lady mounted the ladder to the veranda, entered the room, and sat beside me.

We exchanged smiles and greetings. Composing her legs, she took some colored string and a bone needle from the equivalent of her reticule and began to weave a *bilum*. She is a charming lady, not much younger than I, who is the wife of one of my clan brothers. I had known her slightly thirty years previously, but never as someone to whom I could talk. Now, as she sat beside me, her fingers flipping back and forth as she wove the colored strings, she said to me,

"You're working, Goroha Gipo?"

"Yes," I replied, though I wasn't writing anything on my tablet.

There was silence for a while as she continued with her weaving. Then, without looking up, she asked, "You are going back to your other place—America?"

"Yes, I must go back soon."

"Is it a long way?"

"A very long way," I said, and tried to explain I would be traveling for more than two days.

"They say that when the sun goes down here, it is morning there. Is that true?"

"Yes, it is like that. It is a very long way."

"Ayee!" shaking her head. "It is too hard to hear," that is, to understand. "Why must you go? We say this is your place."

"I must do my work," I said. "I must find money to buy food and clothes. My son must go to school."

"But isn't he a man now, like Lokilo?"

"He is older than Lokilo, but his school takes a long time."

"He is married?"

"No, he isn't married."

"Well, it must be different in America. All of us are married quickly."

"Some marry quickly in America. Some wait."

"Well, I don't hear it," she said.

It was about half past three. Beyond the open door, the sun was bright in the yard of Makis' house, but the air seemed to be gathering itself together, its weight increasing in the face of some threat from the sky toward the northeast. Now and then the spent flowers of bougainvillea rose several inches from the ground, stirred momentarily into life by the down draft of gusts of wind passing through the upper branches of the trees. It had rained heavily during the previous two nights, and almost until noon on the present day. Lava, returning from her work at the Goroka Base Hospital, told me that no planes had come in or out of the airport, and I was a little worried that the rain might delay my departure to Port Moresby.

The old lady interrupted these thoughts by suddenly becoming still, dropping her weaving into her lap, raising her head and listening to something beyond the door.

"Do you hear the bird?" she asked quietly.

I listened, and thought I could hear a few bird calls, though they were carried away on a gust of wind before I could be absolutely sure.

She picked up her needle and colored strings and began to weave again. "It's Makis' bird," she said.

I knew immediately that if I asked she would tell me something no one had ever mentioned, not because they did not want to or were prohibited from telling me, but simply because it was so commonplace that it had never occurred to them, and none of my questions, or any of the situations I had observed, had prompted them to explain and enlighten me about this particular element of ideology.

"What is Makis' bird?" I asked.

"Oh," she said, "you know. It's been here all the time since you came back, but it's often here when you're away. You know the manner of birds," she said, as though instructing a child. "Birds cry before sunup and before sundown. They don't cry in the sun. But Makis comes here to that big tree outside and cries in the sun. We hear that bird in the sun. It cries in the big tree when there is trouble. We hear it shake the leaves up high when people fight, when they are angry. People have heard it every day since you came back."

"Perhaps it's angry with me?"

"No," she said, shaking her head and chuckling. "We listen. We can tell. You see, it doesn't shake the trees on top. It says, 'It's all right now; you live in its house.' But I think it may be angry today, because it doesn't want you to go. We know all birds aren't the same. Some are like this one."

"Perhaps it was only the wind shaking the top of the big tree."

She shook her head. "We know. Birds don't cry in the sun."

The place this piece of casual information has in Gahuku eschatology does not matter in the present context, and in any case it was far too late for me to collect additional data on the relationship between birds and men who had died, or, perhaps, only certain dead men. I mention the incident mainly because I cannot imagine being placed in a similar situation during 1950 to 1952. Gahuku men who were my present age at that time encountered fewer restrictions in interacting with women than those imposed on younger males. Their manhood established, they were no longer compelled to prove themselves and were no longer active participants in the more physically aggressive aspects of life: they had retired. They did not have to bleed their noses or induce vomiting to purify themselves of the harmful physiological consequences to manhood and masculinity involved in contacts with the opposite sex. Traditionally, they continued to sleep in the men's house, yet there were observable differences in the quality and extent of their informal associations with their wives and other women.

It is not that the quality of relationships between men and all women was precisely the same. Fathers were far more closely associated with their daughters than their sons, for example, and men seemed to have strong affective bonds with their sisters and other female members of their clan. Sisters were important to young men who were placed in the unenviable position of being compelled to find wives for themselves (see *The High Valley,* chapter four), for the groups into which clan sisters had married contained the girls who were the most suitable potential brides. The sisters' houses and their hospitality provided such young men with an entry to groups where their search was most likely to succeed. Male suspicions and the need to protect and conserve manhood focused primarily on wives or women who were possible sexual partners, yet the relationships between all males (after a certain age) and all women were colored by the imperatives of the social and psychological distancing described above.

Though I was an outsider during 1950 to 1952, I was also only in my early thirties and was therefore at a stage in my life when the social distancing between men and women was most heavily pronounced and strictly maintained. Even if I may have wished it otherwise, neither men nor women considered it proper for me to ignore the rules. Indeed, it would have been a breach of etiquette, if not a serious affront, if I had chosen to sit among the women and observe the men from their viewpoint when the sexes divided formally at public gatherings.

It was different now. On public occasions—such as the Village Court proceedings held at the boundary of the disputed land described above—I often left the men and joined the women choosing to do so partly because I could usually find some shade where they were seated, and also because of the more relaxed and gossipy atmosphere on their side and of their enlightening comments on those conducting the debates. No one questioned or seemed embarrassed by my choice. The fact that I am old now and have almost universally recognized kinship ties with many women may have something to do with this, but I think it also reflects some alterations in the ideologically prescribed and formally maintained boundaries between the sexes.

Women came as frequently as men to my house on my recent visits. Either alone or several of them together, they seemed to come simply for company weaving their *bilums* and laughing and gossiping. Sometimes when they spoke only Gahuku I would interrupt them and say chidingly, "Now, that's enough! You know I've forgotten most of your language. Do you expect me to sit here getting bored?" They took it in good humor and willingly explained what they were talking about, though there were also times when they gave me sidelong furtive glances and lapsed into Gahuku again; then I often reminded them I hadn't forgotten Gahuku completely and could gather from words here and there the subjects interesting them, particularly when they had something to do with myself. Most of them were my relatives—either consanguineal or affinal—but they were a wide variety of ages, from very young granddaughters, who often went to sleep in my lap, to young wives and unmarried girls and elderly ladies. Some of them slept in the house almost every night, not in the same room—for I made it clear that when I closed my door I expected to be left alone—but separated from me by no more than several feet and a flimsy wall. Whereas I had lived largely in a world of men before, it was one of more or less casual mixed company now. Rather than being merely a dividend of age and general recognition of my "place" in the system of interpersonal relationships, my observations suggest my experience followed the direction of a more general trend.

In the contemporary world, young people meet in far more numerous unsupervised situations. Though the courting parties of the past may seem to have been licensed occasions for youths and girls to engage in sexual activity, they were not entirely unsupervised. They were initiated by girls in the dry season, the period of the year for most major rituals. Small groups of girls, usually led by an old woman, paraded through the village street and along the garden paths in the early evening, wearing fresh string aprons and yellow everlastings tucked in their hair and giggling rather self-consciously between songs that signified a "party" would be held within the next few nights in an unoccupied house in the village which was designated a "girl's house" (*moho numuni*) for the occasion. The event, lasting the entire night, took place in the village and therefore among adults, though their presence was largely invisible. But as far as I could judge (I never stayed for an entire night), at least one adult man was always present.

Apart from this single event, all other meetings between youths and sexually eligible girls had been furtive. Their physical separation on all public occasions did not prevent winged glances passing between them, and it is also clear that such expressions of interest sometimes led to clandestine assignations. Even young people who were officially betrothed were kept apart from one another. They were not supposed to meet, converse or have any other kind of contact until after the ceremony (years following their betrothal) which gave them permission to cohabit. Even in this, young men sometimes "jumped the gun," however. When such breaches of rule were discovered, usually because a girl became pregnant, there was a public investigation. The young man always denied his responsibility. I do not believe he was always telling the truth, but the denial was consistent with the ideal of the sexually self-disciplined male guarding his manhood against the offered enticements of the sexually aggressive woman. No punishment was exacted on the youth though it was said (I have no verification of it) that the girl could have been killed by his age-mates.

These folk notions of the sexual characters of men and women were clearly shibboleths. The men of my acquaintance were obviously interested in sex and were not the protesting though apparently vulnerable models of virtue men were given out to be. They discussed the sexual charms of particular girls and married women with the kind of libidinous interest that is quite familiar to us, and they planned encounters and recounted them with a good deal of relish. Yet this does not mean that the official ideology can be dismissed as having no consequences. It was maintained in the domestic separation of husbands and wives, in the zealous guarding against affronts to the male person, in the voluntary but expected purifications following initiation, in the rules limiting contact between the sexes, and in the rendering of judgments and the assessment of penalties when breaches were brought to public attention, when, of course, men were always the presiding judges.

Today, the ideologically imposed boundaries are not nearly so obvious. Young people patronize meeting places not available to them previously: Goroka's movie theater, "disco" tavern, markets, and many others. During my recent visits they also made excursions in mixed groups in trucks to Kainantu, staying there overnight and returning the following day. The "six-to-six" brings this more relaxed atmosphere into the village where, indeed, even everyday interaction shows less formal inhibition than thirty years ago.

The large number of young children in today's village population is unmistakable evidence of the breakdown of many of the rules associated with the traditional ideology of sex. I noticed it almost immediately on my arrival in 1981, not needing to have it brought to my attention by virtually all the older people whom I had known previously, though they continually pointed it out to me. Indeed, there were two things they seemed to think I should notice as significant contrasts with the past I had shared with them: the reforestation of the valley and the number of children. Time and again when old acquaintances and kinsmen sat with me in the company of members of younger generations they remarked on these differences between now and then, though there were others I thought no less remarkable. Invariably, their stock explanation to the younger audience cited the demise of warfare as the principal reason for increased family size, pointing out that in the "old days" too many defenseless children needing protection had been a burden to both men and women. I was willing to accept this up to a point. It is quite possible that many of the sexual rules contributed to population control and that too many defenseless infants and youngsters could have been a liability. By the same token, a large number of able-bodied males was an advantage; so considerable effort was expended on the recruitment of adults referred to earlier in this book.

Improved health and health facilities are surely not solely responsible for doubling (by my admittedly imprecise calculations) the child population of the Nagamidzuha villages. Whatever connection it may have with the cessation of warfare, the fact remains that many of the controls on sexual activity have gone, and thus many of the ideological justifications for such controls are no longer relevant or part of the instruction received by young males.

When I ventured to point this out to older people, citing for example the former postpartum prohibition on sexual intercourse between husband and wife and the restrictions on sexual activity young men encountered following their incorporation into the *nama* cult, they generally agreed, but they would not discuss them and even seemed disturbed if I tried to mention the traditional rationale. For their part, young men often seemed bemused or bewildered when I made such comments. I gathered not only that their elders had never mentioned the former rules but that they were also a little embarrassed, if not unbelieving, to be confronted with them by someone who was, after all, an outsider.

The old lady's remark that Gahuku "marry quickly" is only partially correct if it is applied to the past. First marriages occurred around the median age of about eighteen for boys, but they were not permitted sexual relations with their wives until possibly twenty-three, and since these first marriages characteristically did not endure to the point of cohabitation, it could be a year or so later until they were established in a legally recognized sexual relationship with a woman. First marriages today may be a little later, perhaps around twenty, but there is no obligatory period of waiting to consummate the union: this does not ride on the decision of older men concerned to foster and safeguard manhood. Thus, the customary procreative role of men begins earlier, and furthermore, children are often born with much shorter intervals between them.

Today's more relaxed sexual mores are a striking departure from the past. Gahuku misogyny is no longer such a conspicuously encouraged and reinforced ingredient of male bonding, which does not mean that the social distance between the sexes or the ultimate control of public matters by men have disappeared entirely. This has not happened even in our own culture in the last several decades, despite far more vocal and organized efforts to eliminate male prejudice. It does seem, however, that there is a greater readiness among Gahuku women to protest openly some of the controls men used traditionally to "keep them in their place."

As I have tried to point out in this book and elsewhere, it would be entirely wrong to swallow whole the reiterated male view that the opinions of women were inconsequential, not worth considering in any of the decisions they made. Women could influence some matters in the direction of their own personal interests. Yet this was not equivalent to exercising any "constitutionally" guaranteed rights, but rather the by-product of their roles in economic subsistence and biological reproduction. For in both cases, disregarding the official attitudes, men were dependent on them for many of the things that affected their honor closely. And it is possible that this discrepancy between reality and ideology is also an important component of the tensions I have attributed to traditional male-female relationships. The image of themselves men presented to the world wasn't as firmly based as they depicted. Women could not be ignored in their calculations, including such important matters as marriage and the disposal of their accumulated wealth, particularly pigs, which women had helped produce.

It is more appropriate to speak of women's influence in these matters rather than their rights, however, for it was pressure exercised largely within the family and not in the public arena, where they had no official voice in the processes of making decisions.

Times have changed for the younger generations of both men and women, and to a lesser extent even for some women who are closer to me in age. You could not call these changes a revolution. Rather, it is more like the surfacing of an influence that had been largely submerged or kept submerged by the instruments and ideology of male dominance, and I think the colonial regime of over thirty years ago may have made some contribution to this.

Most of the colonial officers I knew then (and during the six years prior to 1950) were responsible men. Few of them had any depth of knowledge of the cultures of the people for whom they had administrative responsibility, but this was not solely because of a total lack of interest: there was a kaleidoscopic array of different cultures in each administrative district, and officials were transferred fairly frequently from one district to another. Their attitudes toward the native population could be characterized as paternalistic and condescending, but they did not display or express their conviction of superiority as arrogantly, unfeeling, or exploitively as a large number of whites in the private sectors (though I certainly encountered a few officials whose behavior was a match for any of the most bigoted private individuals). In general, those who had magisterial powers were genuinely concerned with implementing the equities embodied in the pax Australiana which, on the whole, attempted to safeguard the rights and heritage of the governed. And I think it may be said that they were generally disposed to listen more favorably to a woman's side in litigation and to accord it greater import in their decisions than it may have received from male judges in her own culture (though again there were some colonial officials whose mistaken conceptions of the insignificance of women in the native cultures seemed to be an amplified echo of their own attitudes and whose judgments, in a few cases known to me personally, were harsh and even brutalizing to an extent which scandalized men).*

The colonial courts also operated *outside* and over the traditional system and were often used as courts of appeal from decisions reached within local communities or, as some people saw them, alternatives to traditional processes. Local colonial magistrates attempted to respect indigenous custom and often declined to hear many minor complaints, referring them back to native authorities to settle, but the number of cases appealed to them from 1950 to 1952 indicates that disgruntled litigants realized the colonial courts could be an instrument to modify if not reverse unfavorable decisions or even to bypass traditional procedures. Women used the co-

---

*The worst of these occurred in the Markham Valley during the war, when the newly reoccupied area was administered by military officers of ANGAU (the Australian New Guinea Administrative Unit). Some of the officers of this unit had been members of the Australian civilian administration before the war, but others had not.

lonial courts rarely on their own behalf, yet there were cases when they did, overcoming the embarrassment of exposing themselves in public before strangers and also risking the possible consequences of their action in their own communities.

The trend begun in colonial times had continued and indeed increased since independence. Most minor litigation is referred initially to an elected member of the Village Court who, roughly speaking, represents a tribe on that larger body. He has authority to dismiss charges or to impose some penalties (fines) if they are proved, but in both cases his decisions may be appealed to the Village Court as a whole and thence to the District Court, and conceivably upward through higher levels of jurisdiction. Each member of the Village Court is elected to office by both men and women and may be replaced, which makes him more vulnerable to the fluctuations of public opinion than those who guided the decision-making process in traditional times, and also opens the door to the possibility of greater amount of contention over his decisions. Both these developments provide women with advantages they did not have previously. They are not only part of the electorate to which the Village Court official is responsible but he also depends on them as well as men to keep his office; and his decisions are not necessarily binding, for they can be appealed to higher levels by those who are dissatisfied with them. I don't think that as yet there is anything like an organized women's caucus at the local level or the national level, but many women are aware they have formal avenues of protection and channels for expressing protest and dissatisfaction which are additional to those previously available to them.

Women in the more remote countryside may be less aware of this than the people of Nagamidzuha who are semi-urbanized and more familiar with the institutions of both the previous and present forms of central government. Their greater sophistication was recognized even in the time of Makis, who often gave advice to litigants journeying to the District Court of Goroka from more remote places in the Asaro Valley and even from areas on the far side of its surrounding mountains. But some Nagamidzuha women also hold back from taking allegations of mistreatment to their representative on the Village Court. Three such reluctant litigants were taken to task by other women in my house in Susuroka recently. One had sustained a bruised eye and upper arms, the others showed no confirming signs of the mistreatment they alleged, but all were presented with the same argument: they shouldn't remain mute, their representative on the Village Court was compelled to listen to them, and if he was derelict they could go over his head to other authorities.

The man representing the ridge clans of Nagamidzuha on the Village Court held four formal hearings during my brief visits in 1981 and 1982. Women were the plaintiffs in all four, and men were the accused in three. Only one of the three alleged physical mistreatment, the others being accusations of verbal defamation similar to Hunehune's scurrilous attack mentioned earlier. Perhaps the number is not adequate statistical confirmation of my impression that nowadays women are more ready to publicly protest male attitudes toward them, and also realize that the present judicial institutions are required to give them more formal and serious attention, but I don't think any of these cases would have received a comparable degree of notice in 1950. It is very probable they would have been stifled or dismissed as inconsequential.

This raises a question asked most recently by Langness: Were women *typically* mistreated in the past?* If mistreatment means more or less daily examples of the *physical* abuse of most women by most men, then the answer is no. I have frequently pointed out that across the ideological and ritual boundaries separating them, the relationships between men and women ran relatively smoothly. I have given a few examples (but there were others as well) of apparently deep affection between husband and wife (Namuri and Mukito, Makis and Guma'e) and have pointed out that fathers had warmer relationships with their daughters than their sons, brothers with sisters rather than male siblings and sons with mothers rather than their fathers. Apart from wives, none of these women were possible sexual partners, however. Excepting mothers, they were all natal members of a man's own group. Although wives (or potential sexual partners) were almost invariably members of friendly groups, they were outsiders—considered to be more closely identified by loyalty, interest and affection to their own consanguineal kinsmen than to a husband and his people. It was wives who bore the brunt of mistreatment and suspicion and who, initially at least, lacked support in the group into which they had married. But this could change in time. A wife could prove her identification with her husband and his group by not running away, by bearing his children, and by skillful management of her economic tasks, and in the long run she could achieve

*Lewis L. Langness, "Discussion," in *Sexual Antagonism, Gender and Social Change in Papua New Guinea*, Fitz John P. Poole and Gilbert H. Herdt, editors (*Social Analysis*, 12, 1984).

virtual incorporation into it. By the time she was old, or even earlier if she had borne children and generally behaved herself, she could count on an increasing measure of support from her husband's kin if he mistreated her arbitrarily.

I observed the public lashings with canes to the backs of women if they ventured to interrupt the deliberations of men. This punishment was directed at *all* women rather than specific individuals, but in a two-year period I also saw numerous examples of the latter, probably more than would be regarded as usual in a population of comparable size in our own society. *Physical* mistreatment was not by any means a day-to-day occurrence, but there is more to the question of mistreatment and the judicial status of women than this. Langness, for example, refers to the "number of abused children and battered wives in the United States," resulting from male behavior which we *currently* deplore, which is common enough to be a recognized problem but which is hardly typical of the general conduct of male-female relationships, and this makes him wonder "what standard might be applied" to Gahuku.* The cases are hardly comparable, however. For it is not solely a matter of the number of cases observed by or reported to the person who was on the spot; it is also a matter of the attitudes and responses of authority to them—that is, a question of the latitude men had to use or threaten to use physical force to control women and the means of protest available to women if it was used. In both respects the ideological and institutional climate of our *contemporary* society and *traditional* Gahuku society are appreciably different. In the latter, force or the threat to use force was a recognized instrument of male control over women in domestic and public relationships. Its

*Langness, *Sexual Antagonism*, p. 81.

legitimacy as a sanction was not questioned, though there could be doubts about the severity with which it was applied and whether its use was appropriate (proper) in some circumstances. In other words, it did not have the same moral or judicial implications it has in our society at present; and saying this does not place the Gahuku outside the perspective of our own moral and social history.

I have recently been reading for a second time Barbara Tuchman's account of moral and social conditions in Europe in the thirteenth and fourteenth centuries, and time and again I was struck by parallels with the conditions of women in Gahuku society in 1950.* Allowing for some necessary changes in wording, there is a distant echo of the official view of Gahuku men in the characterization of women in the *Speculum* of Vincent de Beauvais (whom Tuchman tells us was "the greatest of thirteenth century encyclopedists"), namely that woman is "the confusion of man, an insatiable beast, a continuous anxiety, an incessant warfare . . . a house of tempest."** This is probably putting it rather too strongly for most Gahuku men and, as Tuchman says, it was no more true to thirteenth- and fourteenth-century life than the romances celebrating courtly love.† There are also parallels in the manual of conduct the Ménagier of Paris composed for his wife. "She should not be arrogant or answer back or contradict him, especially in public, for [the Ménagier continues] 'it is the command of God that women should be subject to men . . . and by good obedience a wise woman gains her husband's love and hath what she would of him.'"‡ And the same Mén-

---

*Barbara W. Tuchman, *A Distant Mirror: The Calamitous 14th Century*, (New York: Alfred A. Knopf, 1978).
**Tuchman, *A Distant Mirror*, p. 211.
†Ibid., p. 211.
‡Ibid., pp. 213–214.

agier cites the cautionary example of "a husband who was harshly criticized by his wife and 'being angry with her governance smote her with his fists down to the earth,' and then kicked her in the face and broke her nose so that she was disfigured ever after and 'might not for shame show her visage.' And this was her due."*

Tuchman does not suggest that such extreme behavior was commonplace, but in concert with other legal disadvantages of women and a host of additional homilies, manuals, and popular tales these examples surely say something significant about societal attitudes toward using force in controlling the behavior of women and supporting the dominance of men. Similarly, the threat of force was a recognized sanction in traditional relationships between men and women in Gahuku society, whereas it was not a legitimate instrument, under any circumstances, to use in disputes between men who were members of the same clan or, possibly, between women. No punishment, other than some criticism, was exacted from men even if their behavior was considered too severe or inappropriate by other males of their group.

Force no longer has the same legitimacy as an instrument for controlling women, and the judicial system provides them with avenues for protesting and securing the punishment of offenders which are additional to any they formerly possessed. Other traditional instruments of male control have also gone, including the *nama* cult; for whatever else it was, and whatever women may have thought of it privately, the cult was an instrument for keeping women (and also youths) in their proper place. The disappearance of warfare (which does not mean there are no circumstances under which it might return) and the *nama* are linked, and both were im-

*Ibid.

portant to men in controlling youths as well as women—in transmitting and perpetuating the ideologies of distance and opposition between the sexes. The social environment in which young people are reared has changed greatly since 1950. Nowadays, women receive an education with men. They have opportunities for employment outside the villages, they may travel within and outside the Eastern Highlands Province, and the existence of a market economy on their doorstep gives them opportunities to use their talents and managerial acumen to earn a cash income which they may control themselves despite some opposition. And finally, they have the additional protection of the formal judicial institutions of central government.

4 At the southern extremity of the ridge of Susuroka, at a place called Ekuhakuka, there used to be a tiny cluster of dilapidated houses where the track descended to the valley's floor and continued on to the principal village of the Meniharove. I was fond of walking from Susuroka to Ekuhakuka when I wanted to be alone during 1950 to 1952. The ridge is not greatly elevated above the valley, but its height, the openness of the track, and the motionless sea of grasses were a lifting release from the pressures of village life.

Standing among the tumbled houses of Ekuhakuka reminded me of times I had spent in Roman ruins along the southern coast of Turkey. While the car which had brought me there waited out of sight far down a hillside, I used to sit on the fallen capital of a column in the scented haze of wild thyme and sage growing among the ancient paving stones, the broken arches of a once populous arcade rising against the clear, blue sky like a fading echo of the busy life they had sheltered. Such moments are a time for turning inward, for pausing to consider one's own purpose; and in the sun-drenched ruin of Ekuhakuka, with the same quality of light and sky around me, I had tried to imagine the fortunes of the people who had lived there only recently and the direction of the lives of those whom I had left temporarily, wondering what was foreshadowed for them by my own presence; for I knew I would not have been there except for the gathering momentum of events whose origin was far beyond the boundaries of their known world.

No one walks from Susuroka to Ekuhakuka now. Trees clothe it for most of the way, and the main road to Lapigu and Siane has supplanted the track I used to take. Here and there along it a derelict automobile rusts among weeds inside the wire fence enclosing a hamlet, and "ruined" Ekuhakuka has been replaced by a cluster of new houses and a neatly lettered billboard inscribed "Giligilipaka Planatation." Virtually the entire western side of the ridge is planted with young coffee trees, where once there had been nothing but kunai and scrubbly crotalaria. The prime mover, organizer, and manager of this development is Kopi Manove.

Kopi cannot be more than thirty-three. He says he was "so high," indicating the height of a toddler, when I was there in 1950. I recall the name and have one or two memories of his father, and it is possible I saw Kopi when he was a tiny child, but I did not know many of the Meniharove well. Though they are a segment of Nagamidzuha, they lived at that time on the floor of the valley and I spent most of my time with members of the ridge clans.

Kopi is a salaried administrator in the Department of Primary Industries. Deeply interested in economic development, he has read English texts on the subject and asked me for other references and books which are still not readily available in Goroka. Though he visits Giligilipaka frequently, he lives in a Western style house on a suburban, tree-lined street in Goroka which I remember gratefully from a brief stay at the end of my first return visit. He usually dropped by to visit me whenever he went to Giligilipaka, and on weekends took me on excursions through the valley and to Bena Bena.

Driving along the Highland Highway, with his small son Konrad sleeping in my lap, I remembered it when it had not yet been dignified by that name, when it had been simply the "government road" I described in *The High Valley* (chapter six): little more than a wide swathe of unsurfaced track cut from the soil by men, mostly prisoners from the government compounds, wielding pointed sticks and shovels under the relaxed eyes of native policemen. And I wondered if Kopi, handling the Mazda so confidently, dressed in his neat denim trousers, crisply laundered shirt and insoucient wide-brimmed hat, ever measured his own life and present interests against events in which I have a recollection of his father and at which he may have been present: a village street baked by sun, devoid of shade, and filled with the clamorous agitation of crowds of men and women gathered to watch the slaughter of squealing pigs brought forward one by one to be bludgeoned to death in the midst of an array of tossing, coruscating plumes on the concluding day of the great *idza nama*.

It had required no special gifts to see the general direction of some of the changes already in motion in 1950. Goroka was growing even then, and it was generally assumed it would become the principal center for development in the Eastern Highlands. Owing to their proximity to the township, it also seemed certain that the people of Nagamidzuha would be drawn more and more closely into the net of its activities and more or less Western ways of life; but I often wondered how the tourists whom I chanced to meet in airports reconciled what they may have read in my book (for I was told by some of them it was on their list of recommended reading) with what they saw on the Highland portion of their itineraries. Since they had come so far (and had paid so much money), and since they were keyed to experience the "exotic," I did not like to forewarn them of disappointment. A slight echo of the past would be presented to them at various "entertainments"; but from their hotels in the township or from the windows of their vehicles traveling the Highland Highway, they would see little more than underprivileged examples of things familiar to them in their own culture.

So I tried to tell them how beautiful the country was, how its light was probably clearer than anything they could imagine in their own cities; how the cloud shadows were like the voiceless sigh of infinity stroking the immemorial mountains, and the sun a benison drawing an answering embrace from the valleys of grass and the wind-borne honey of golden crotalaria. For it was impossible to tell them of the thirty-year drama leading to what they observed: the drama of human beings responding optimistically, within their means, to events that had altered the boundaries of certainty forever.

FIVE

FULL CIRCLE

On an afternoon two days before I left
Susuroka in 1982, I was sitting on the floor of
my room in the house Makis had built, my
head beginning to nod over the notebook in my
lap. Outside, the village was silent and empty.
The air was still and oppressive, feeling as
though the evening might bring a repetition of
the storms which had been occurring for
several days. The sun crackled on the iron roof.
The partially opened glass louvers of the
window threw zebra bars of light and shadow
across my legs and criss-crossed the bare walls
with throbbing patterns. Giving up to
drowsiness, I closed my notebook and lay
down on the bed Kopi Manove had lent me.

I dozed fitfully, to be awakened an hour or
so later by the rhythmic sound of an axe biting
into wood in the yard beyond the front

veranda. I listened to it for a while, then slept again. It had ceased when I woke eventually. There was no sound in the house or village. I realized it must be nearing five o'clock. The light in the room had dimmed, and there was a feeling of freshness and movement in the air. Soon, I thought, Lucy would be returning to unlock the door to her room, to fill my pressure lamp from her supply of kerosene and to bring it out to the veranda, readying it to light as darkness fell, a chore she had taken upon herself to perform each day. I rose, drew some cold water from a tin bucket, tipped it into an enamel basin, washed my face, and ran a comb through my hair. Then I left my room, crossed the kitchen area and opened the door to the veranda, and suddenly it seemed to be a different world from the one I had left on entering the house several hours earlier.

For a moment, I did not know what made the difference; then I realized that while I slept someone (I found out later it had been Lokilo Makis) had cut off all the lower branches of the casuarinas growing along the fence.

I sat down at the top of the ladder mounting from the yard to the veranda, transported back through half a lifetime to the years when I had left my thatched house each morning and entered one of the widest worlds I have ever seen, a world that was vast yet presented so intimately by the soft clarity of light that you could almost count each silhouetted tree on the distant mountains and follow each turn and twist of the paths descending to the gardens from the ridge of Susuroka. Lokilo's work with the axe rewakened a world which had gone forever. I knew I would not be back again. I would never know the eventual shape of the lives I had interrupted on three occasions. Goroka, the town sprung from the small settlement of four frame houses, would reach out farther toward the village, its arterial roads and the sound and smell of its vehicles suffocating the last breath of a way of life that had been often harsh and strident yet seldom as depressing as some of its present ingredients.

The spent flowers of bougainvillea stirred on the tomb of Makis. Light flickered on the topmost branches of the casuarinas and scattered coins on the ground and the green leaves of lilies I had planted in a different age, and momentarily a vanished world took charge of me, holding me in suspension beyond the present moment as a rising wave may lift you closer to the sky when you float beyond the breaking surf. Time is arrested. Past and present coalesce.

I suppose it was an accident that led me into anthropology, though many of the interests it enabled me to follow and express had been laid down long before I found it. Accident, however, is more often than not the case if colleagues can be persuaded to examine how and why they chose their own careers. Anthropology, after all, is not a household word or a profession as familiar, say, as becoming a doctor, lawyer, or most other varieties of "Indian chief." Personally, I had not heard of it until I took my first class in the third term of my freshman year at the University of Sydney, choosing it largely because its novelty might offer some relief from the boredom of classes in English literature. I had intended to make the latter my career, but texts I had collected and read without direction or any guiding taste seemed to be drained of life and immediacy by the cutting instruments of the particular surgery applied to them by my teachers.

I am sure this kind of experience is shared by many undergraduates during their first class in anthropology, as it happens also to some first-year graduate students whose initial expectations and enthusiasm, generated by more fortunate undergraduate experiences, are dampened if not extinguished by a variety of seemingly arcane concerns and the kind of debates Gore Vidal has characterized as "eel wriggling." On both counts, it may be fortunate that I was introduced to anthropology when it was less specialized, and even less professionalized, than it is at present. A probable majority of its senior representatives had entered it from other disciplines, and it is my opinion that this should still be welcomed and encouraged. They were also literate. Their work could be read for pleasure as well as instruction, which cannot be said for a mass of contemporary products, many of which are virtually impenetrable. Moreover, I don't think a majority of the masters would have been outraged if they had been associated with humanists. The discipline has always had, and still has, a foothold in both humanism and science, though the distance between the two has increased so much in recent decades that work which shows a clear connection with the former is often regarded with suspicion and tends to be labeled "novelistic," "popular," and "not professional."

The lines of this division existed forty years ago, but anthropology was a young discipline then, and youth has advantages as well as limitations. Its perspectives are less complex than they become later, and while they may seem brash and unsophisticated when viewed from the superior vantage point of subsequent increments to knowledge, they possessed, in their own time, a vividness and immediacy that is difficult for later generations to appreciate.

Virtually all those who taught me in anthropology were students of A. R. Radcliffe-Brown or Bronislaw Malinowski (and sometimes both). Both these men were associated with unified theories of culture (Radcliffe-Brown *was* addressing the nature of culture even though he denied it). Their holistic conceptions of the identity of each separate tile in the vast mosaic of human ways of life was largely responsible for moving anthropology out of antiquarianism and the piece-meal collection of data into systematics and the clear light of a contemporary world. Certainly there were shortcomings in their theories that are easily recognized today, and many of these were recognized in their own time as well, particularly after their students began to return from their fieldwork. Fieldwork as we know it now is also quite largely the product of their influence, though Malinowski, as far as I know, was the only one who gave his students specific instruction in field research methods.

Transmitted through and also transmuted by their students who taught me, the conceptions of these men were a revelation to me. Here, for the first time, were perspectives which included all human ways of life and, in a sense, made me part of them, something that was not fostered by the circumstances of my own privileged background whose limitations I had always felt confining, not knowing precisely why, yet feeling from a very early age that the boundaries of awareness, even self-consciousness, had to include far more than anything I had been presented with so far.

My first course in anthropology rolled back the boundaries of a parochial existence, exposing a vaster landscape which was knowable even if it was totally unfamiliar: a landscape in which each localized feature was imprinted with the stamp of something greater than itself, as each of these features, too, was greater than the sum of its parts.

When its academic embellishments are stripped away, this viewpoint is, of course, simply a rephrasing of a question that is probably as old as Homo Sapiens: How does everything fit together in the world? And this question seems to have preoccupied me for as long as I can remember, fostered, perhaps, by a minor physical disability. I am extremely light sensitive: glare and unfiltered sunlight, even its reflections from snow or water, cannot be endured for much more than a moment. During my country childhood in Australia, winter was the only season when I could raise my eyes and look into distances far beyond the circumference of shadow cast by my wide-brimmed hat. Beyond its protection, the solitary hill called Binnalong became a felt presence rather than a landmark made familiar through continual observation. It was something you knew was there: an immutable question mark advancing and retreating in the camouflage of smoky mirages and vibrating waves of heat rising from plains where clumps of gum trees created an archipelago of shadow disappearing and diminishing toward the insubstantial far horizon. It was the world within the circumference of shadow which I knew intimately, trying to establish it in my mind with the precision of a Dürer engraving, titled, I think, *A Piece of Lawn*, which I carried with me for many years both at boarding school in Sydney and, later, in England: a rendering of some grasses and meadow weeds at the margin of a pond, their leaves, stalks and flowers delicately defined, the pale filaments of roots below the surface of the water shown as faithfully as the parts which are usually all that is visible to the eye—a little world which yet contains the whole world and, possibly, the cosmos. For although that larger world revealed itself to me only in brief glimpses like a succession of photographs presented and withdrawn by an impatient hand, the memory of it lingered, imposing a demand to take account of it, to effect some kind of reconciliation between the richness of the particular and the more difficult apprehension of the general.

The anthropology I discovered as a first-year undergraduate showed me a particular perspective for dealing with this dialectic. It recognized the richness, complexity, and the integrity of the particular, that world within the close-focused, shadow circumference of the hat, and I suppose I was fortunate in having as teachers men and women who were able to present these particulars vividly. I doubt that I have ever matched them in this ability, though it has been a personal imperative in all my fieldwork, in the collection and recoding of data in situations vastly different from anything familiar to me from previous experience, and in synthesizing and presenting them later. I trust I have never lost the feel of people and the difference in their ways of life—the things that move them into action, those things beneath the surface of the pond; their motives, values and imaginative responses to a parochial cultural universe—the filaments of roots sustaining the leaves and flowers in the variable climates above the water. If any of my work does this for others, then I have justified my teachers.

But they did more than this. They opened the larger world outside the protecting circumference of shadow, parting the mirages and placing Binnalong squarely in perspective. It does not matter if that perspective has changed, and continues to change, since their time. What anthropology is today surely would not be the same without the benefit of their particular explorations, for they immeasurably enlarged its horizons. Knowledge is not based on absolute revelation but is the product of finite minds addressing areas in which one question answered opens the way to another, and another beyond that in a progression that may well be infinite. From the vantage point of a particular place in the progression, a question addressed previously may seem insignificant or commonplace, but humility in the face of what may be unknowable is the only safeguard against stultifying dogmatism. Anthropology has not provided any final answers to the questions within its domain, but it has provided different perspectives from which they may be approached. In the process of doing this, it has clarified some of the questions, added new ones, and increased our awareness of the complexity of the material studied.

There was, however, a particular perspective which neither my teachers nor those who had taught them followed. Gilbert H. Herdt, a member of a younger generation of anthropologists that has studied the people and cultures of Papua New Guinea, has indicated its focus as well as anyone I know when he says: "The mystery of the world is the relationship between the visible and the invisible."

I was not academically prepared to deal systematically with this dimension of Gahuku life, yet I met it intuitively every day. It was present whenever I walked with Makis, and on the occasions when I sat in my house at night and, unable to talk to them, watched the faces of people who had come to see me, trying to penetrate their changing expressions as they moved their heads and spoke to one another, drawn close to me by the circle of lamplight which seemed like a clearing wayfarers seek at the end of the day's journey through trackless forest. And I was even more aware of it when emotions were overwrought: during the marriage rites for Tarova, or when I was present at the secret rituals of the *nama* cult, which were enveloped in an aura of fantasies I had no way of comprehending except, perhaps, through an empathy derived from my own inwardness.

I did not consciously review these things as I sat at the top of the ladder and looked into the evening distances so suddenly revealed by Lokilo's work with his axe, but they formed a personal background for two vivid images superimposed on a moment of time: the Susuroka I had known more than thirty years ago, and the one now represented by the frame house behind me and the sound of motor vehicles traveling the road below the crest of the hill. I realized I had very different feelings about leaving these two places. Parting from Makis at the edge of a grass airstrip had been like severing a part of me, discarding a period of my life which had given me mostly joy; a time not only of self-discovery but also the discovery of others, though I suppose the two go hand in hand. There had been times, indeed, when I had felt I wanted to make the remainder of my life there, when the thought of what I would have to do with the material I had collected depressed me to the point of thinking it would be preferable simply to say I had failed, preserving for myself alone the depth and complexities of an experience which would be filtered away by the sieve of academic goals. I had felt that particular clearing in the forest offered enough for me, all the shelter I needed, and that there were no irrefutable reasons to respond to any competing claims or different opinions coming from a world I not only did not care to meet on its own terms but which had also lost some of its entitlements during my absence from it.

I did not feel the same about leaving this time. Indeed, it was almost a relief to know there were only two days left. No doubt this was partly due to increased age. Sitting on the floor was not as easy as it had been; it took time to get down there, and getting up again was an even slower process. The dirt irritated me. Cooking unpalatable meals on the single burner of a primus stove was so unrewarding that I did not bother to prepare more than one a day, having it in the evening and giving most of it away. The inconvenience of an outside toilet was a particular hardship. There hadn't been one near Makis' house when I arrived in 1981; I had to walk across the village to use one which was shared by the members of several households outside the barbed wire fence. I had dysentery for most of the first week, and during the night I had to wake Hunehune so that he could take my arm and help me down the ladder (which had no railing) from the veranda to the yard. I did not like to suggest that they might dig a hole and build a shelter over it closer to the house. I was not employing anyone or paying any rent. Almost everything I had was either given or loaned to me, and I felt I had no right to ask for more than they thought necessary and were able to provide. Hunehune, however, was aware of my difficulty. Despite the continual annoyances of his drunkenness, he showed the solicitude for my welfare which he had demonstrated during my illness in 1952 and, without consulting me, arranged for Lava Mokoru's hired help to build a latrine for me behind the house. It was an improvement, even though it had no door and its entrance was so placed that anyone passing that side of the house could see inside it.

None of these things would have mattered to me thirty years previously, but they were gnawing irritations now. Most of all, however, I was aware of an unaccustomed feeling of confinement. This was partly due to the fact that I could no longer wake in the morning to the prospect of walking through the countryside for most of the day. Certainly, I walked. My days were not spent alone in the house, but these excursions were confined mostly to two miles or so along the ridge. People were reluctant to allow me to go farther (cautionary tales of rascals were always advanced to dampen any such attempt), and even when I moved around, things were not the same as they had once been.

Walking the ridge in those different times, emerging from the shadow of casuarinas clothing Gohajaka into the clear light and uninterrupted sweep of grasslands extending to the distant mountains, it had been possible to feel and visualize the whole life of the valley welling toward me and enveloping me like an emanation of the air I breathed. Its multiple ingredients mingled in a distinctive scent no other place or part of the world possessed, a unique blending of harsh and gentle elements, bravura colors and soft monotones, of strident contrasts miraculously reconciled. This had gone. Though the mountains were still there, the grasslands had largely vanished under trees; you could no longer mark the course of the Asaro River cutting through the territories of Uheto and Notohana, enemy groups whose names had some of the connotations "Media" and "Persia" must have had in the ancient civilized world. It had taken several hours to walk to Kotuni in the mountains to the northeast. These people were linked closely to Nagamidzuha, providing the latter with a refuge in times of defeat and dispossession. Their mist-shrouded forests, with their crystal, rushing torrents, their undercover of tree ferns and glowing *impatiens*, provided the bamboo for the sacred *nama* flutes. Now there was a commercial trout farm there, a picnic area with tables, benches and barbeque facilities. Kotuni trout was listed on the menus of hotels in Lae and Port Moresby; station wagons and minibuses carried parties of tourists to the farm from the Bird of Paradise Hotel.

The web of life at Susuroka was wider than it had been, extending out to the town and coastal cities and to primary industries located in parts of the valley which used to be approached warily or avoided altogether. Children went to school. Except on weekends, I could walk the length of the ridge without seeing any of them, and though their ubiquitous presence had often irritated me, I found I missed them. The landscape had an emptiness it did not have when they used to appear suddenly from among the grasses, the long headdresses of the novice youths speaking unmistakably to a segment of the pageant of life which described a series of concentric circles around the village.

Not that the landscape was unpopulated. Indeed, the number of people of all ages had increased, but they were scattered, and those who stayed near home were fewer and mostly old. During the day the silence in the village had a different quality. Once it had been like a natural pause, no more than the naturally dictated rest of a self-contained organism; now, a good deal of the organism's life had been channeled away from its former center. The daytime silence responded to events in a pattern of life that wasn't natural and was also staled by familiarity.

I do not mean that all the elements having a recognizable origin in my own culture could be accepted at face value, that is, that they had the implications they carried in their own context. Many had undergone transformations after being implanted in new tissue, yet because of their recognizable origin it was difficult to avoid judging and rejecting them by standards I customarily applied when meeting them on their home territory. The movies screened at the theater in Goroka were mostly old B-grade westerns. I suppose I should have accepted when people asked me if I would like to join them at this kind of entertainment. My refusal is not, perhaps, a critical omission in my observations, but the lack of interest it shows applied to many other matters as well. In a sense, the nearer people approached me culturally, the less I thought their interests worthy: relativism could not be sustained.

It was not that I mourned the passing of everything associated with a former way of life and wished it could have been preserved in its entirety. No less than others who had forgotten or had never known many of the things I knew, I did not regard the past as a golden age or abstract its standards and use them to measure the faults of the present. Rather, I tended to measure a good deal of the present by many of the faults of my own culture.

This may have the ring of elitism, yet I don't think anything of this kind colored my perception of the people who flocked to the B-grade movies, patronized the taverns, or danced Western style throughout the night to a local band at a "six-to-six." I did not think the less of *them*; rather, I deplored the fact that such things seemed to be so easily transferable; that they seemed to be *representative* of my culture; that people, recognizing their origin, advanced them as an indication of how far they had come from an unsophisticated tribal past.

My rejection focused on my own culture rather than on those whose behavior and pastimes mirrored it. I deplored the fact that these superficial things seemed to be *all* it was capable of exporting, or at least were among the things which marshaled its greatest effort or represented its greatest treasures.

The motivations behind the exporting process were varied: crassly commercial in those elements which represented popular culture, political (and economic) leverage in others, and moralistic-spiritual in yet more. All, however, bore the stamp of certainty, as though they represented the final revelation of what the world should be.

Human life cannot be reduced to revealed certainties, even though conceptions of those certainties may embroil nations in wars and may lead, eventually, to a holocaust which destroys it. The labor of Sisyphus never ends, and it is hubris for anyone to think that the stone has been arrested for all time.

The imprint of an outward-reaching global uniformity had been laid on the fabric of Gahuku life, and the richness of the whole cloth had been diminished: faded and reduced to colors which, temporarily at least, obscured the original creative patterns. Even though I had not been comfortable with some elements of the original pattern, I was even less comfortable with the reduction most of the fabric had suffered since I had viewed it in its even then expiring brilliance more than three decades previously. It was best to leave and to return to the center from whence the influences came, where, paradoxically, it was not only possible to criticize them but also to elect some degree of isolation from them.

These kinds of judgments did not include the persons of the members of my Susuroka family or anyone else connected to me through my former life there. They remained individuals, some whom I liked more than others and a few whom I disliked and tried to avoid. Some of those in the first category were more fully involved in the new world than some of those who were most uncongenial. I don't think my rejection of a general direction took precedence over my appreciation of individuality, as I also trust it had not affected my previous relationships with anyone. I was enormously grateful for being accepted once again, but there was a difference: there was no one who meant as much to me as Makis. He had been the lens through which I had first begun to comprehend many of the subtleties of Gahuku life—the finer shades not visible to eyes that concentrated only on the polished and enameled surface. There had been, I think, a level of understanding in our relationship which transcended background. This is rare in the multiple encounters we have with others and is, therefore, to be grasped, incorporated, and protected more carefully. The life I observed and wrote about is in large measure a distillation of him. Certainly it is not the way in which he would have presented it, for it shows the perspectives of my own eye and that of my professional training. But his presence breathes in everything I wrote, however it may be obscured by ends of which he was unaware. For he was a microcosm of Gahuku culture: the embodiment of its pride and flashing brilliance, of its bent toward personal achievement, of its harshness and its underlying tenderness. My relationship with him was as complex as those we have with anyone we love, yet it was also as strong as any, despite the greater impediments of the worlds of difference separating us. He was my anchor in a foreign harbor, as he was also the pilot who had led me to a protected berth.

No one could take his place. His children and other younger members of his family had ready-made ties with me, but at least a generation stood between us. Makis had not been much older than me in years, though far older in his experience of the culture I had entered. He chose to assign me the status of his "younger brother," and this was appropriate because of our relative degrees of experience. But in many other ways, its quality was more like that of age-mates (*aharu*), the social relationship between men (sometimes separated by as many as seven chronological years) who had been initiated into the *nama* cult together. This was the only Gahuku relationship, not excluding that between older and younger siblings, which had no formal elements of superiority and subordination. Age-mates, ideally, were equals and companions, choosing each other's company by preference and, when fully adult, often building their houses side by side and apart from those of senior men and older brothers. I chose the company of Makis by preference, and I am sure he often did the same with me, though of course he was also involved in a multitude of other concerns in which I had no place. He built his own house next to mine, and he often sought for me along the ridge, calling out from wherever he happened to be, inquiring if anyone had seen me. There were times when I heard my name echoing back and forth across the grasslands and gardens, and later he would appear, or those who were with me would say, "Makis wants you to go to him." And he gave me his confidence (also expecting me to do the same with him), not waiting for a formal question but explaining things he thought I ought to know, even matters of a personal nature.

I did not have this kind of mutuality with anyone else, either then or when I returned. The members of my family and clan who were my own age or older recognized my place among them and did not treat me as an outsider. They were at ease with me and I with them. They also gave me confidences which they would not have shared with anyone who wasn't a member and, therefore, personally involved in their affairs and fortunes. And I think this was done freely and not tainted by any expectations that I could influence matters for them. Whatever influence they may have thought I had with the authorities of a colonial past could not be imputed to me now. Indeed, that particular shoe was on the other foot. The Ozahadzuha man said to me before I left, "If the government doesn't want to let you back, give them my name and tell them we say you belong here."

I also cannot fault the attitudes of those who were now my children. There was mutual affection there, particularly with Lucy and Lokilo Makis. In many ways, these two seemed to reflect different sides of their father's character as I knew it—Lucy the assertive and independent one, and Lokilo the quieter, more comfortable and contemplative: the one I had seen in Makis for the first time when, disturbed by something I could not understand, I had chased after him through the grasses and had come upon him alone on a hill, standing aside and watching him pierce the evening sky with his arrows. When I looked at Lokilo sitting silently on the floor of my room in his father's house, looking down at his small son sleeping in his lap, this memory often rushed to my head and filled me with an aching loss which he partially filled when, feeling my eyes upon him, he looked up and exchanged a smile with me.

Yet these younger people could not provide the center the village had once had for me. The differences in our years precluded the companionship I had found with their father. A certain formality in our relationship was imposed even by the kinship term they always used in addressing me, and their interests and activities included many of those I rejected at their origin.

A period in time had vanished. It was neither possible nor proper to try to bring it back, to try to live in the Susuroka that *is* with the image of what it *was*. Doing that amounts to no more than an endless passage through the spiral of recollections. Yet at the end the spiral turned and closed, and then released me.

On my last day in Susuroka in 1982, all the members of my extended family gave a feast for me. People had recognized my departure in the same way in 1981, but on that occasion it had been a more formal affair which had included most of the clans of Nagamidzuha. When Lucy told me of the arrangements this time, she said, "This is just for family, because we don't think you'll be coming back." She was not telling me all, however, for the Ozahadzuha man, his wife, and other close kin had helped to organize it, and he, being more wealthy than any of my own kin, contributed more than anyone else. He had been in my company far more frequently during my 1982 visit than in 1981. Having recovered completely from surgery for a stomach ulcer, he often came to see me when I was alone in the house. Since I had lost almost all the Gahuku I knew and he couldn't speak pidgin (though he understood a good deal), our conversation was limited. But I became quite comfortable with the inevitable silences, remembering him as he had been when he was one of Makis' principal supporters. And sometimes, as we sat silently together, he could hear someone passing in the village street and would call to them through the open door, telling them to come inside and act as interpreter for him.

I had liked and even admired him during my first fieldwork (and I have a real affection for his wife), and I felt for him the personal tragedy of his estrangement from the adopted son of whom he had been previously proud. But I resented what he had done after the death of Makis. It seemed like an unjust and self-serving betrayal of loyalties which he had seemed to espouse, though I forgot that even in these kinds of matters it did not do to transpose, without qualification, the ideal standards of our own culture to that of Gahuku. But in any case, I felt he had suffered enough.

When the day arrived for the family feast, I kept to the house, going through the motions of packing (though this would have taken me no more than fifteen minutes if I had applied myself to it), and arranging in separate piles the few more or less permanent things I had bought and would leave behind, apportioning them for those to whom I would give them. Some of them would remain in the house in the care of Lucy in case I should ever return and need them. Others I intended to give to various sons and daughters. It was a meager array, but I knew most of it would be returned, in deteriorated condition perhaps, if I did come back again: a few of my belongings had survived for thirty years and had been given back to me.

The feast was the Gahuku equivalent of a barbeque. Those responsible for it had gone to Goroka and had bought a quarter of a sheep, additional chops and a few beefsteaks from a freezer store. Sweet potatoes, greens, some corn and pit-pit came from their gardens. There was store-bought bread and margarine and, of course, beer.

The larger meats and vegetables were cooked in an earth oven belonging to Bihore; the others would be cooked later on a wood fire above the ground. The traditional earth oven of the Gahuku takes hours to prepare and to complete the cooking process. The hole in the ground is opened in the morning and debris from its previous use is removed; then firewood is brought, stacked and set ablaze to heat the large stones which will be placed at the bottom of the oven. Grass also has to be cut and brought in sheaves to line the sides of the hole when the heated stones have been carried to it with large wood tongs, and water must be ready to pour onto the oven after all the food is in place, has been covered with grasses drawn inward from the sides and, finally, sealed with a mound of earth. During the long wait between sealing and opening it, people move to a distance from it. They sit about in whatever shade is available, talking, sometimes sleeping or, nowadays, playing cards. They come to life again between four and five o'clock in the afternoon, when it is time to open the oven and bring out the food, which, if it is a whole pig, is seldom cooked to the point of removing all doubts about possible health hazards. Having received such warnings, founded or not, before my first fieldwork, I always carried away the portions given to me and recooked them on my own primus stove.

I did not go outside while the food was cooking. When I had packed and arranged the disposition of my other belongings, I lay down on Kopi Manove's bed, read a book, and slept. I felt I had already gone. Everything happening outside was unnecessary. It couldn't bring me back to what I had known. It was like an attempt, though kindly motivated, to keep me within the spiral of memory, whereas I knew the circle had to close, that this time there was no coming back. What they were giving me was not a release but a prolongation, one spiral more, and I would rather have gone in my own way, with departure marked by no more than a few customary farewells in the bustle of an airport when a flight number is announced and there is time for nothing more than a hurried embrace.

I waited until I could tell from the light in my room that it was late afternoon, and gathered from the rising sound of voices, the rapid-fire of instructions, the shattered wail of a child reprimanded for being in the way, and the general atmosphere of bustle in the yard, that the oven had been opened and the food carried to the place where everyone was seated on the ground. Then I went outside and joined them.

All my family were there, as well as the Ozahadzuha man and his wife, and there, too, was his estranged son. Gotome and Guma'e, widows of Makis, were also there, though they could not join the close company sharing the meal on the ground, for they were not permitted inside the enclosure containing the house and tomb of their dead husband. But they were handed their portions of food across the barbed wire fence, and later I stepped over it and held them for a while in the village street.

We ate and drank beer. I received departing gifts of arrows, and people had fun seeing if I could identify the various kinds by name. The only one I was sure of was "nagisa," the arrow used to wound brides at marriage or men convicted for adultery, and this brought gales of laughter and some off-color jokes.

Then, in the midst of laughter, the Ozahadzuha man began to sing an unaccompanied song. His head was lowered and his voice was soft at first. Some people did not hear him and kept talking. He ran through it once, then began again, lifting his head and projecting his voice more strongly. There was dead silence. Then everyone joined him. I recognized the tune as a traditional lament, having heard it most poignantly in a different age at the dawn ceremony in the house of Tarova's father on the day they gave her away to her first husband. As the first light of morning had entered the doorway, the people who had kept watch through the night ceremonially extinguished the fire which glowed on the hearth and lifted their voices again and again in the keening lament; and as the sounds reverberated within me, I felt I had been lifted beyond myself, joined to others by a universal sense of loss and protest which recognizes, however, that we have but limited means to shape events as we might wish to have them.

The song continued, growing in strength, as other people learned the words I could not understand. I knew they were singing it not only to me but to someone else as well. The Ozahadzuha man, his head still bowed, was crying. His voice faltered, interrupted by sobs, but others caught the words and sounded them clearly, and I looked at him from the distance of a few feet and felt my own chest constricting and the sting of tears in my eyes.

Lucy, seeing my distress, came and sat beside me, and I heard her through a wash of tears I could not control. "He composed it for you," she said. "It's his present." She translated the words for me. I did not write them down then or later, for the moment was enough, but I think I remember both the gist and quality of them:

"Makis, we were together when Goroha Gipo was here before. Now he is here again, and all of us are together as we used to be. This is how it is."

As the song ended, Lucy, Lokilo's wife, and some other women of my old companion's family went to the dracaena hedge surrounding his tomb. They shook the leaves of the shrubs and cried:

"Makis, you hear! Your belly can be good now. We are all together."

After this, we drank more beer, made jokes and laughed a lot. When it was dark, Lucy lit my lamp and brought it out to where we sat. I watched the faces for a while. As I looked at Lokilo, so like his father, who, with his son in his lap, lifted his head to joke with someone behind his shoulder, the lamp-light projected his features, the wide smile, high cheekbones, strong nose and deep set eyes, against the silent darkness of the village, and I recalled my sudden lightening of spirit when Makis had materialized from shadow to sit with me at the beginning.

I excused myself early, leaving the lamp outside and going to bed in darkness. I lay there, feeling it was over now. I had been released. Before I had thought there was any possibility of going back, I had written that I "kept the hope that some-day I would be able to make my own pilgrimage to the grave of Makis"; and it was there, not many feet from my bed. And the house was quiet. He wasn't disturbing it. His family and some people who may have abused his memory were drink-ing beer and laughing together not far from where both of us lay. I had come full circle, back to the beginning. There was only one thing left to say:

Ave atquae vale

INDEX

Uheto, 55, 173, 248
Urugusie, 55, 56

Vidal, Gore, 241
Village Court, 220; on
  boundary dispute, 69, 71, 72,
  73; Hunehune on, 28, 146,
  152; women use, 228, 229
Vomiting, 197, 219

Warfare, 40, 51–52, 104, 132;
  and clan membership, 154;
  v. feuding, 204; suppressed/
  ceases, 7–8, 92, 121, 123–124,
  172, 224, 233; tests manhood,
  172
Warrior, 10, 116, 117, 151, 193;
  ideal, 51–52; Makis as, 11, 56,
  123
Watson, James B., 52, 85
Weakness/softness, 52. *See also*
  Hard men
Weapons, 62 n., 72, 73, 100
Western Highlands Show, 167
Whites. *See* Europeans
Women: acculturation of, 201;
  age groups of, 120–121; in
  ceremonies, 158, 192, 193;
  and colonial government,
  227–228; controlled by men,

133, 215, 231–234; as
dangerous to masculinity,
133, 198, 199, 202–204, 206,
209, 222; education of, 189;
experience of, 209, 210, 211,
214; houses of, 122; influence
of, 190, 192–193, 214–215,
225–226, 227, 228–229, 231;
inherit, 63, 187–188;
opportunities for, 234;
pollute, 205; privileges for,
115, 192; rebel/question
authority, 40, 187–188, 190,
214, 229–230, 231–232, 233;
rituals for, 194, 197, 201;
secrets from, 115, 215; and
sorcery, 206; status of, 27–28,
192, 194, 209, 227–228, 230;
treatment of, 11, 78, 205, 206,
209, 211, 214, 229, 230,
231–232, 233; use Village
Court, 228, 229; work of, 46,
120, 192–193

Young-Whitforde, Dudley, 23,
  36; on patrol, 93, 94, 98, 99,
  102, 104, 106, 107, 108, 112,
  114

Zokozoi Hotel, 32
Zokozoi River, 31

STUDIES IN MELANESIAN ANTHROPOLOGY

General Editors

      Gilbert H. Herdt

      Fitz John Porter Poole

      Donald F. Tuzin

Michael Young, *Magicians of Manumanua: Living Myth*

      in Kalauna

Gilbert H. Herdt, ed., *Ritualized Homosexuality in Melanesia*

Bruce M. Knauft, *Good Company and Violence: Sorcery and Social*

      Action in a Lowland New Guinea Society

Kenneth E. Read, *Return to the High Valley: Coming Full Circle*

Designer:	Kitty Maryatt
Compositor:	Publisher's Typography
Printer:	Vail-Ballou Press
Binder:	Vail-Ballou Press
Text:	10/13 Palatino
Display:	Michelangelo